Andrew Dalby is a classical scholar, historian, linguist and translator most well known for his books on the history of food, in particular the Greek and Roman empires. *Siren Feasts*, Andrew Dalby's first food book, won the Runciman Award and his second, *Dangerous Tastes*, won the Guild of Food Writers Food Book of the Year in 2001. He is also the author of *The Classical Cookbook* and *Empire of Pleasures* as well as biographies of Bacchus and Venus.

Tastes of Byzantium

The Cuisine of a Legendary Empire

ANDREW DALBY

TP

TAURIS PARKE
Bloomsbury Publishing Plc
50 Bedford Square, London, WC1B 3DP, UK
29 Earlsfort Terrace, Dublin 2, Ireland

BLOOMSBURY, TAURIS PARKE and the TAURIS PARKE logo are trademarks of
Bloomsbury Publishing Plc

First published in 2003 in Great Britain as by Prospect Books
This edition published in 2010 in Great Britain by I.B.Tauris & Co. Ltd

A catalogue record for this book is available from the British Library

Library of Congress Cataloguing-in-Publication data has been applied for

ISBN: PB: 978-1-83860-036-5; eBook: 978-0-85771-731-3

4 6 8 10 9 7 5

Printed and bound in Great Britain by CPI

To find out more about our authors and books visit www.bloomsbury.com and sign up
for our newsletters

Table of Contents

Preface

There has never been a book in English about the foods and wines of the Byzantine Empire. *Flavours of Byzantium* is a beginning. It is also a reply to the readers of *Siren feasts* who were intrigued by what was said there of Byzantine food and wine and asked if any more was known.

No single source can serve as our guide. There is no recipe book like the Latin *Apicius*. There is no medieval encyclopaedia of social history that gathers the literary source materials as does Athenaeus's *Deipnosophists* for classical Greece. This book includes new translations of four short Byzantine Greek texts on aspects of diet. Throughout, other sources help to fill out the picture, supplying a social context, practical details and occasionally even recipes.

Byzantine research is a wide open field. There is much more information waiting to be gathered and used. As one example, this book draws chiefly on literary works (e.g. history, poetry, letters) and technical texts (e.g. pharmacology, dietetics), largely leaving aside documents such as those that lay down the rules of daily life for the inmates of monasteries, and, in so doing, tell us what they ate or were supposed to eat.

The phrase-book of Byzantine food, which forms chapter 8, is based directly on the texts. Many of these are translated, or referred to, in the earlier part of this book. It incorporates a fair proportion of material that had been collected by the great scholars who worked on the vocabulary of Byzantine life – giants such as du Cange, Korais and Koukoulès. There is also a lot that is gathered in this phrase-book for the first time or that was not clear till now. The few existing Greek dictionaries that focus on Byzantine terminology tend to slip out of focus when they approach a technical field such as food: they contain some serious misunderstandings. So this phrase-book is not intended for time-travellers alone: it will help all those who are interested in Byzantine history. After browsing through it, any reader will have a clearer idea of how food was talked about, classified, bought, sold, cooked and enjoyed in Constantinople.

This phrase-book, incidentally, is one of a series of three glossaries resulting from my exploration of ancient gastronomic pleasures. *Siren feasts*, published in 1996, includes a five-language glossary (classical Greek, modern Greek, Turkish, scientific Latin, English) of the sources of ancient Greek foods, arranged under classical Greek terms. *Food in the ancient world from A to Z*, published by Routledge in May 2003, is arranged under English words and includes indexes in classical Greek and Latin.

Postscript: April 2003

After completing the text of *Flavours of Byzantium* I learned of two very different recent books dealing with Byzantine food.

One is the collection of monastic *typika* published at Dumbarton Oaks (Thomas and Hero 2001 in the bibliography). *Typika* are instructions on food and other aspects of monastery life. Because these documents have until now been very difficult to collect, study and compare I have deliberately avoided dealing in detail with monastic meals in the present book: I knew I could not do them justice. Well, anyone can now buy this five-volume set – the bargain of the twenty-first century – and set to work, beginning with appendix B 'The regulation of diet in the Byzantine monastic foundation documents' on pp. 1696–1716.

The second is the self-published collection of materials on Byzantine cuisine by Henry Marks (Marks 2002). This includes translations of the Prodromic poems, of Simeon Seth *On the Properties of Foods*, and Boissonade's version of the *Dietary Calendar*. None of these is otherwise available in English; as it happens, I had chosen to translate a different version of the *Dietary Calendar* in the present book (chapter 6 text 4). Marks's translations are unreliable, but his book also includes one hundred Byzantine recipes, reworked for the modern kitchen.

My thanks to Linda Makris for seeking and finding Byzantine information in Greek libraries and bookshops; and to Tom Jaine, official publisher to a team of ancient food writers including Archestratus, Cato, Anthimus and now, at last, Hierophilus the Sophist.

Chapter 1

An Introduction to Byzantium

Those who had never seen Constantinople before were enthralled, unable to believe that such a great city could exist in the world. They gazed at its high walls, the great towers with which it was fortified all around, its great houses, its tall churches more numerous than anyone would believe who did not see them for himself; they contemplated the length and breadth of the city that is sovereign over all others. Brave as they might be, every man shivered at the sight.[1]

This vision of the great city comes from a man who was intelligent, clear-sighted, and anything but visionary. Geoffroi de Villehardouin was a major figure in the Fourth Crusade, as well as one of its most engaging historians. He was a hero of the first years of the 'Latin' Empire of Constantinople, established on the ruins of the Byzantine Empire in 1204. His nephew and namesake was destined to rule as Prince of the Morea (the mountainous peninsula known to classicists as the Peloponnese) and to establish a French dynasty there. If Geoffroi de Villehardouin says that brave crusaders shivered at their first sight of Constantinople, as they sailed along the shore of the Sea of Marmara under its walls, that is what they really did.

[1] Geoffroi de Villehardouin, *The Capture of Constantinople* 128.

Nineteen hundred years earlier, about 660 BC, a Greek colony had been established at this place, which was then known as Byzantion. Even then it already had a legendary history (and a down-to-earth history as well). The Argonauts had passed this way, in one of the best known of Greek mythological tales, on their way to the land of the Golden Fleece; they had navigated the Bosporus and dodged the *Symplegades* or 'Clashing Rocks'. The Clashing Rocks had since ceased to clash and had been renamed *Kyaneai* 'Blue Rocks'. As for the down-to-earth history, there was a settlement on the site of Byzantion, as archaeology confirms, as early as the twelfth century BC.

When we come to the colonization itself, the well known story is that the first band of Greeks to seek a site in this neighbourhood had recently settled on the opposite side of the Bosporus, named by them Kalkhedon and known now as Kadiköy. It was not a bad place, but when the Delphic Oracle was next asked by the small city of Megara (west of Athens) to advise on a site for a colony, the response was: 'found your settlement opposite the blind men'. The Megarians obeyed this ordinance and established a colony at Byzantion, a site so much better than that of Kadiköy that the earlier colonists must, indeed, have been blind to have overlooked it.[1]

So, if we adopt the terminology used by historians of classical Greece, the Megarians 'founded' Byzantion. Whether they 'founded' it by agreement with its existing inhabitants, or after expelling or enslaving them, no one knows.

Byzantion, in Greek hands, soon outshone its mother city of Megara. It was a site of spectacular beauty, unmatched in its potential for trade. This was where you began the short, though difficult, journey up the narrow Bosporus. Every ship that travelled from the

[1] Although a well-known story (Strabo, *Geography* 7.6.2; Tacitus, *Annals* 12.63), it is unlikely to be true. Herodotus (*Histories* 4.144), a much earlier source, attributes the observation to a perceptive Persian and not to any divine oracle.

Mediterranean and the Aegean to the Black Sea must sail under the walls of Byzantion. Every cargo from the Black Sea and its shores must pass this way to reach the wider world. Not only that: Byzantion was rich from its own produce too. Once a year, great shoals of tunny (more precisely, bonito) descend the Bosporus en route for the Mediterranean. The economic significance of this to Byzantion is best explained by the Roman geographer Strabo:

> The Horn, which is close to the Byzantians' city wall, is an inlet extending about 60 stadia towards the west. It resembles a stag's horn, being split into several inlets, branches as it were. Into these the young tunny stray, and are then easily caught because of their number and the force of the following current and the narrowness of the inlets; they are so tightly confined that they are even caught by hand. These creatures originate in the marshes of Maiotis [Azov], and, getting a little bigger, escape through its mouth [the Straits of Kerch] in shoals, and are swept along the Asian coast to Trapezous and Pharnakeia. That is where the tunny fishery begins, though it is not a major activity, because they have not yet reached full size. As they pass Sinope they are more ready for catching and for salting. When they have reached the Kyaneai and entered the strait, a certain white rock on the Kalkhedonian side so frightens them that they cross to the opposite side, and there the current takes them: and the geography at that point is such as to steer the current towards Byzantion and its Horn, and so they are naturally driven there, providing the Byzantians and the Roman people with a considerable income.[1]

Thus Byzantion prospered for a thousand years on its exports of tuna, mackerel and other Black Sea produce, and on its position as a hub of trade and transport. Its capture by Philip of Macedon in 340 BC, its sacking by Septimius Severus in AD 196 after Byzantion had

---

[1] Strabo, *Geography* 7.6.2.

chosen the wrong side in the Roman civil war of that year, were temporary setbacks, soon consigned to memory.

The emperors at Constantinople

Constantine I, the first Christian Emperor of Rome, was as good at choosing sites for cities as the Greek settlers who had preceded him by a thousand years. In AD 330 he selected Byzantion to be his new eastern capital, the second Rome. 'Re-founded' and renamed by him Constantinopolis, the venerable city was destined for eleven hundred years of worldwide fame as capital of the later Roman Empire – usually known nowadays as the 'Byzantine Empire', after the original name of its capital.

The table on the following pages shows the emperors who succeeded Constantine (omitting some very ephemeral figures) with the dates at which they reigned. It includes the 'Latin' emperors who ruled Constantinople between 1204 and 1261. The third column gives an approximate date to some of the important events mentioned in this book and to many of the writings that are translated and quoted here.

Byzantine historians had no consistent equivalent to the traditional Roman numerals that go with the names of monarchs. Throughout this book I have added these Roman numerals to translated extracts, or in the surrounding text, to make it easier to identify individuals in this table.

At first Constantinople was, to put it at the very highest, Rome's junior equal. The vast Roman Empire had been administratively divided into two in 286, in an arrangement first put into effect by the reforming emperor Diocletian (284–305), and Constantinople was chosen by Constantine to be the capital of the eastern half. The two halves of the Empire had very different fates. So did the two capital cities.

Rome soon gave way to Milan as western capital, and in 476 the Western Empire was finally extinguished. Rome was fated not to regain its status as capital city for 1,400 years, with the reunification of Italy in the nineteenth century, though all through that period the Popes continued to rule their spiritual realm and an extensive secular domain from the Vatican City just across the Tiber.

Meanwhile the eastern emperors maintained themselves in what was for quite long periods a stable monarchy – albeit interrupted by changes of dynasty, sometimes violent, sometimes peaceful. The emergence of one such new dynasty is thus narrated by the historian Procopius:

> When Leo I occupied the imperial throne of Byzantium, three young farmers of Illyrian origin, Zimarchus, Dityvistus, and Justin who came from Vederiana ... determined to join the army. They covered the whole distance to Byzantion on foot, carrying on their own shoulders cloaks in which on their arrival they had nothing but twice-baked bread that they had packed at home.[1]

This young farm boy Justin would eventually become the emperor Justin I, father of the lawgiver and conqueror Justinian I, who was hero of Procopius' eight books of *Wars* and villain of the same author's *Secret History*.

The second sentence of the extract just quoted above can also be found – abridged, unattributed and omitting the names – in two of the manuscript dictionaries that were compiled in Constantinople in later Byzantine times, several centuries after Procopius. They did not need to mention the names: everyone who was likely to use them would know Procopius' work and would recall this story of Justin's youth. But what was the 'twice-baked bread' that Justin and his two comrades carried in their knapsacks? Procopius, like many Byzantine authors, did his best to write strictly classical Greek. He knew very well that the everyday word he would have liked to use here was simply unacceptable: it was to be found in no classical author. So he used instead a

---

[1] Procopius, *Secret History* 6.2. Translation after G. A. Williamson.

EMPERORS, EMPRESSES	REIGN	CHRONICLE
Constantine I	324–337	330: Byzantion refounded as Constantinopolis
Constantius II	337–361	
Julian	361–363	Oribasius's *Medical Collections* is dedicated to Julian
Jovian	363–364	
Valens	364–378	
Theodosius I	379–395	
Arcadius	395–408	
Theodosius II	408–450	
Marcian	450–457	
Leo I	457–474	
Leo II	474	
Zeno	474–491	476: end of the Western Roman Empire
Basiliscus	475–476	
Anastasius I	491–518	
Justin I	518–527	
Justinian I	527–565	Procopius's *Wars* and *Secret History*
Justin II	565–578	Agathias's *History* and poems
Tiberius II	578–582	
Maurice	582–602	Menander the Guardsman's *History*; Maurice's *Stratagems*
Phocas	602–610	
Heraclius	610–641	Theophylact Simocatta's *History*
Constantine III	641	Building of the 'Triclinium of Magnaura'
Constans II	641–668	640–642: Muslim expansion: loss of Palestine and Egypt
Constantine IV the Bearded	668–685	*De Cibis* is addressed to Constantine IV
Justinian II	685–695, 705–711	

EMPERORS, EMPRESSES	REIGN	CHRONICLE
Leontius	695–698	
Tiberius III	698–705	
Philippicus Bardanes	711–713	
Anastasius II	713–715	
Theodosius III	715–717	
Leo III the Isaurian	717–741	717–718: repulse of the Arab siege of Constantinople
Constantine V	741–775	
Leo IV	775–780	
Constantine VI	780–797	
Irene	797–802	
Nicephorus I	802–811	
Michael I	811–813	
Leo V	813–820	Theophanes' *Chronicle*
Michael II	820–829	
Theophilus	829–842	
Michael III	842–867	
Basil I	867–886	
Leo VI the Wise	886–912	*c.* 895: *Book of the Eparch* 911–912: Harun ibn Yahya detained in Constantinople
Alexander	912–913	
Constantine VII Porphyrogennetus	913–959	*Book of Ceremonies* and *Geoponica* edited by the Emperor 949: Liutprand of Cremona's first visit
Romanus I Lecapenus	920–944	
Romanus II	959–963	
Nicephorus II Phocas	963–969	968–969: Liutprand of Cremona's second visit
John I Tzimisces	969–976	
Basil II the Bulgar-killer	976–1025	
Constantine VIII	1025–1028	

EMPERORS, EMPRESSES	REIGN	CHRONICLE
Romanus III Argyrus	1028–1034	
Michael IV the Paphlagonian	1034–1041	
Michael V Calaphates	1041–1042	
Zoe	1042	
Theodora	1042, 1055–1056	
Constantine IX Monomachus	1042–1055	
Michael VI Stratioticus	1056–1057	
Isaac I Comnenus	1057–1059	
Constantine X Ducas	1059–1067	Michael Psellus's *Chronographia*
Eudocia	1067, 1071	
Romanus IV Diogenes	1068–1071	
Michael VII Ducas	1071–1078	Simeon Seth's *Properties of Foods* is addressed to Michael VII
Nicephorus III Botaneiates	1078–1081	
Alexius I Comnenus	1081–1118	1095–1097: visit of Bohemond of Taranto and others of the First Crusade
John II Comnenus	1118–1143	Anna Comnena's *Alexiad*
Manuel I Comnenus	1143–1180	*Prodromic Poems? Timarion?* 1147: visit of Odo of Deuil on the Second Crusade Visits of William of Tyre and Benjamin of Tudela
Alexius II Comnenus	1180–1183	
Andronicus I Comnenus	1183–1185	
Isaac II Angelus	1185–1195, 1203–1204	
		1191: opening of Constantinople's first mosque
Alexius III Angelus	1195–1203	1200: visit of Anthony of Novgorod
Alexius IV Angelus	1203–1204	
Alexius V Murtzuphlus	1204	1204: Fourth Crusade; loss of Constantinople
Baldwin I of Flanders	1204–1205	

EMPERORS, EMPRESSES	REIGN	CHRONICLE
Henry of Flanders	1206–1216	Nicetas Choniates' *Chronicle* Geoffroi de Villehardouin's *Capture of Constantinople*
Peter of Courtenay	1216–1217	
Yolanda	1218–1219	
Robert of Courtenay	1219–1228	
John of Brienne	1228–1237	
Baldwin II	1228–1261	
Michael VIII Palaeologus	1259–1282	1261: recapture of Constantinople
Andronicus II Palaeologus	1282–1328	
Andronicus III Palaeologus	1328–1341	*c.* 1330: visit of Ibn Baṭūṭā Brocardus's *Guide to the Voyage Overseas*
Michael IX Palaeologus	1294–1320	
John V Palaeologus	1341–1391	Nicephorus Gregoras's *Roman History*
John VI Cantacuzenus	1347–1355	1349: visit of Stephen of Novgorod
Manuel II Palaeologus	1391–1425	1389–1392: visit of Ignatius of Smolensk and the Russian 'Anonymous Traveller' 1419: visit of Zosima the Deacon
John VIII Palaeologus	1425–1448	visits of Bertrandon de la Broquière and (in 1437) Pero Tafur
Constantine XI Palaeologus	1449–1453	1453: sack of Constantinople by Mehmet the Conqueror

respectable paraphrase, 'twice-baked bread'. Zonaras, one of those two later lexicographers, kindly gives us a hint as to Procopius' meaning. 'Twice-baked bread is what the Romans call *paxamas*', writes Zonaras[1] ('Romans' means the people of the Byzantine Empire). And Zonaras is right. At this crucial moment – the long walk of Justin I – the *paximadi* emerges into the bright light of history; a thick slice of barley bread, baked till bone-dry and almost bone-hard, that still offers the basis of many a simple Greek meal.

We know a good deal about the wars that Byzantine emperors fought. We know too much about the sectarian controversies in which they engaged with greater or less enthusiasm. We know rather little about what these emperors were like, individually, in everyday life. Byzantine history is fairly well covered by a series of narrative histories written by contemporaries, but these histories seldom strike the personal note. There are just a few texts that seem to give us palace life as it really was. Procopius' fiercely critical, indeed scurrilous, *Secret History* is one of them. A few centuries later we can turn to the dry and observant court memoirs of the scholar Michael Psellus, entitled *Chronographia*. This is how Psellus introduces one of the thirteen emperors under whom he lived:

> Constantine VIII was very big in stature, over eight feet tall, and had a fairly strong physique. His stomach was strong, too, and his constitution was well able to deal with whatever he ate. He was a highly skilled mixer of sauces, seasoning his dishes with colours and flavours so as to arouse the appetite of all types of eaters. He was ruled by food and sex. His self-indulgence had brought on a disease of the joints. Both feet, in particular, were so bad that he could not walk, and ever since he became emperor no one knew

[1] Zonaras, *Lexicon* s.v. *dipyros artos*. This, with other similar definitions, will be found in the phrase-book (chapter 8) s.v. *paxamas*.

him to choose to go about on foot; firm in his saddle, he would ride everywhere.[1]

Constantine VIII was, so far as we now know, the only amateur chef in the whole list of Byzantine emperors (later we shall encounter an empress who was an amateur blender of perfumes). Not long afterwards, with the successful revolt in 1081 by the brothers Alexius and Isaac Comnenus, we are reminded that food can serve as a potent metaphor. The source is Alexius' daughter Anna, who wrote her father's life. The first secret moves toward revolution, she tells us, were reported in a coded message sent to a trusted sympathizer: '"We have prepared an excellent dish, well sauced. If you would like to share the festivity, come as soon as you can to join our meal".'[2]

The last of the great insider narratives of palace life is the *History* of Nicetas Choniates. This powerful work, written after the fall of Constantinople to the Crusaders in 1204, is at the same time a private history of the doomed court, a public history of the fall of Empire and a lament over what had been lost. It happens to show us, in the portrait of Alexius's grandson, Manuel I Comnenus, that this populist emperor used the food metaphor in a completely different way.

> On another occasion Manuel had spent the day at the Palace at Blachernae. Returning from there late in the evening he passed the saleswomen who had street food – 'snacks', in everyday speech – out on display. He suddenly felt like drinking the hot soup and taking a bite of cabbage. One of his servants, called Anzas, said that they had better wait and control their hunger: there would be plenty of proper food when they got home. Giving him a sharp glance Manuel said rather crossly that he would do exactly what he pleased. He went straight up to the bowl that the market woman was holding, full of the soup that he fancied. He leaned over, drank it down

[1] Psellus, *Chronographia* 2.7.
[2] Anna Comnena, *Alexiad* 2.6.5.

greedily and had several mouthfuls of greens on the side. Then he took out a bronze *stater* and handed it to one of his people. 'Change this for me,' he said. 'Give the lady her two *oboloi*, and make sure you give me back the other two!'[1]

In a sense, Manuel I was the very last Byzantine emperor: he was the last who exercised real and durable power over an extensive realm. Until his time, Byzantine history is a history of long and slow shrinkage, balanced to some degree by the extension of Byzantine cultural influence far beyond the borders of the Byzantine state. After Manuel's death the decline becomes a collapse from which there is no recovery. The rulers that follow him have neither the time nor the skill to govern. The great city at the sight of which Geoffroi de Villehardouin and his fellow-crusaders shiver in 1203 – only twenty-three years after Manuel's death – will be a great city no longer when they have done their work. The Empire re-established by Michael Palaeologus in 1261 is a small, weak, almost bankrupt realm, an Empire only by courtesy. Soon it is a mere city-state, tributary to the Turkish Empire, to which it will fall in 1453. Whereupon the Turkish court, most recently established at Adrianople, was immediately moved to Constantinople, which now entered upon its new role as capital of the Ottoman Empire.

And so – to look ahead beyond the time-frame of this book – Byzantion and Constantinopolis were reborn under a third name. This name – the one that the great city still bears – betrays its timeless status as metropolis. What is the origin of *Istanbul*? It is the medieval Greek peasant's answer to the typical question posed by a stranger anywhere near Constantinople. 'Where does this road go? Where can I buy food and wine? Where will I find lodging tonight?' The answer was *is tin boli*, 'to the City, at the City'. This was, without rival, 'the City'.

[1] Nicetas Choniates, *Chronicle* p. 57 van Dieten. The *stater* and *obolos* are ancient Greek terms, adopted by Nicetas here to keep up the tone of his narrative.

Peoples, languages and 'ethnic foods' of Constantinople

It is easily forgotten to what extent the Byzantine Empire was a multi-cultural and multilingual state.

In its origin it was the Greek-speaking half of an Empire founded by Latin speakers. Its founding marks the moment when Christianity became the state religion of the Roman Empire. Constantine's mother Helena was Christian and he himself was baptized on his deathbed. All his successors were Christian with the single exception of Julian. Constantinople was thus the capital of a great Christian empire with a magnificent inheritance of pagan literature, art and philosophy.

After the division in 286, Latin, though the mother tongue of only a small proportion of the Eastern Empire's subjects, remained for some hundreds of years an official language of administration in the East. Latin, or rather the Romance speech of the Balkans, was still the language of command in the Byzantine army. So we are not surprised to find names of foods that seem to have Latin roots. There is *boukellaton* (Latin *bucellatum*), the ring-shaped dry loaf typical of the rations for which the auxiliary armies depended on their commanders. There is *phouska* (Latin *posca*), the watery, vinegary wine that was typical of soldiers' drinking in early Byzantine times. There is *konditon* (Latin *conditum*), the famous spiced wine aperitif of late Rome and Constantinople. Then there are *rodakina*, peaches, whose Greek name seems to describe these fruits as 'rosy' (Greek *rodos* 'rose') but actually derives from the old Latin variety name *duracina* 'clingstone'.

All the peoples of the Empire were naturally represented in the population of Constantinople. Some of its inhabitants had come from much further afield, as observed in about 1096 by a participant in the First Crusade: 'In this city are Greeks, Bulgarians, Alans, Comans, Pigmaticans, Italians, Venetians, Romanians, Dacians, English,

Amalfitans, even Turks; many heathen peoples, Jews and proselytes, Cretans and Arabs and people of all nations come together there.'[1]

Russians were naturally well-represented, for Constantinople was the source of their Christian culture. So Ignatius of Smolensk, member of a party of Russian pilgrims, was able to find homely food and familiar company at the monastery of St John the Baptist: 'On the first of July we went to the Monastery of St John Prodromus, which means "the Forerunner", and worshipped. The Russians who live there entertained us splendidly.'[2] North Europeans, including English, were also at home in the city, some of them as mercenary troops enrolled in the famous Varangian Guard, others as traders. It was these, we must suppose, who introduced the novel delicacy of *rengai* 'herrings' to late medieval Constantinople. Arabs and other Muslims had a settled community in Constantinople and achieved freedom of worship by treaty in the course of the twelfth century. Arab historians tell of the day on which Islamic worship was first practised publicly in the city.

> The ship brought a preacher, a pulpit, several *muezzin* and Koran reciters. Their entrance into Constantinople was a day noteworthy in the history of the religion ... The preacher mounted the pulpit and pronounced the liturgical prayer in honour of the Abbasid Caliphate, in presence of all the faithful and of the resident merchants.[3]

[1] Bartolf of Nangis, *History of the Franks who stormed Jerusalem*. Crete had been Arab territory from 823 to 961; that is why Cretans and Arabs are listed together. 'Greeks' means particularly those of the city, while 'Romanians' means the peoples subject to Constantinople, including Greece and including Greek speakers. 'Dacians' means the inhabitants of what is now Romania. 'Bulgarians, Alans, Comans' were independent and partly nomadic peoples generally to be found north and east of the Black Sea. Venetians and Amalfitans both had special relationships with the Empire, which is why they are distinguished from the 'Italians', the remaining peoples of Italy. The Pigmaticans are unknown, at least to me. If you want to know why the English were there, read on.
[2] Ignatius of Smolensk, *Pilgrimage*.
[3] Abu Shama, *Book of the Two Gardens* [*RCHO* vol. 4 pp. 470–2].

The delicacies that came 'from the city of Mosul' were brought by Arab merchants (actually, they came from far to the east of Mosul, but it was at Mosul that they emerged into Byzantine knowledge); they included 'the best kind of cinnamon' according to the eleventh-century dietician Simeon Seth. This may be the earliest reference to the cinnamon of Sri Lanka.[1]

How much blending of local traditions went into the Byzantine culinary melting-pot? There is plenty of evidence that the blending took place. We shall encounter some fine flavours inherited from early Greece, notably the fish (*kephalos* 'grey mullet', *labrax* 'bass' and many others) that were just as important to the gourmets of Constantinople as they had been to those of Athens. We shall find tastes introduced long ago from the early Greek colonies: *garos*, for example, the fermented fish sauce first encountered as a product of the northern Black Sea coast, later to become ubiquitous in the food repertoire of the Romans, by whom it was more often called *liquamen*. Some favourite foods indicate by their names that the Romans of the early Empire had brought them into fashion: *laktenta* 'sucking pigs'; *konditon* 'spiced wine'. A new focus on Asia Minor, natural consequence of the establishment of Constantinople as Imperial capital, leads to important gastronomic discoveries, such as the gazelle, the 'deer commonly called *gazelia*' noted by Simeon Seth (*On the Properties of Foods* p. 33). For the same reason the Black Sea and its great rivers became the sources of new fish specialities with strange northern names, including the sturgeons *mourzoulin* and *berzitikon* and their caviar *khabiarin*.

The end result was a massive amount of cultural exchange. The *paximadia* in Justin I's knapsack were a standby that was well known Empire-wide, to judge by later derivatives of the name: these extend from Venetian *pasimata*, Croatian *peksimet* and Romanian *pesmet* to Turkish *beksemad* and Arabic *bashmat, baqsimat*. The *lucanica* sausages

[1] Simeon Seth, *On the Properties of Foods* p. 55.

that early Roman soldiers learnt to appreciate while on campaign in Lucania (southern Italy), in due course inherited by Byzantium from the Roman army, were transmitted in their turn to Bulgaria (*lukanka*), Greece and Cyprus (*loukanika*), Spain (*longaniza*) and eventually even Brazil (*linguiça*).[1] Several important foods were introduced from the east after Egypt and Syria became Muslim lands, and these new foods naturally have Arabic names: *mazizania* 'aubergines', *nerantzia* 'oranges', *spanaki* 'spinach'. As Arab power expanded, much of Byzantium's eastern trade came under Arab control; hence the Arabic names of foods, especially spices, became well known in later Constantinople, sometimes supplanting the native name, as did *nanakhoua* for older *ammi* 'ajowan'. Eastern spices and aromatics that were wholly unknown in the earlier Mediterranean include *iasmion* 'jasmine' and *koubebe* 'cubebs'.

Greeks and others: some travellers to Byzantium

We will never quite know how ancient Greek cuisine tasted to those to whom it was unfamiliar: all we know of these ancestral flavours is what ancient consumers happen to say about them. We have very little idea how the banquets of the Roman Empire tasted to outsiders, since no Indian or Persian adventurer has left us a record of the grandeur and decline of Rome.

Constantinople marks a new stage in our ability to recreate the past. The Western Roman Empire had collapsed, but its culture still thrived, ever more distinct from that of the east. Egypt and the Levant passed from Byzantine into Arab sway. From both of these regions, culturally independent of and sometimes opposed to the Byzantine Empire, traders, ambassadors and warriors crossed the frontier and visited the city. That is why we know how Constantinople seemed from the outside.

[1] Mathiesen 1993.

We can draw on several such observations. Among the most lively and opinionated are those of Liutprand, bishop of Cremona, who visited Constantinople, acting as ambassador of Berengarius, regent of Lombardy, in 949. Liutprand returned, this time as emissary of the Holy Roman Emperor Otto I, in 968–9. His two reports are very different in tone. In 949 he was a young man, not at all a practised diplomat, and he had been deliberately starved of funds by his own monarch. It is clear that he was favourably impressed by the real friendship shown to him by the Emperor Constantine VII *Porphyrogennetos*.[1] Here Liutprand describes one of the entertainments at Christmas dinner at the Palace in 949 (we shall hear more of the same dinner later).[2]

A man came in carrying on his head, without using his hands, a wooden pole twenty-four feet or more long, which, a foot and a half from the top, had a cross piece three feet wide. Then two boys appeared, naked except for loincloths around their middles, who went up the pole, did various tricks on it, and then came down head first, keeping the pole all the time as steady as though it were rooted in the earth. When one had come down, the other remained on the pole and performed by himself: that filled me with even greater astonishment and admiration. While they were both performing, their feat seemed barely possible; for, wonderful as it was, the evenness of their weights kept the pole up which they climbed balanced. But when one remained at the top and kept his balance so accurately that he could both do his tricks and come down again without mishap, I was so bewildered that the Emperor

[1] The honorific title was given to those fortunate princes and princesses who chanced to have been 'born in the Purple Chamber', the empress's apartments at the Palace. If you were to have a reasonable chance of achieving this, your father had to be Emperor at the time, and your mother had to be a stay-at-home, not one of the more energetic empresses who travelled and campaigned with her husband.

[2] Liutprand, *Antapodosis* 6.9. Translation by F. A. Wright. Liutprand, reporting home in Latin, likes to drop into his text a few apposite words of Greek that he heard or spoke.

himself noticed my astonishment. He therefore called an interpreter, and asked me which seemed the more amazing, the boy who had moved so carefully that the pole remained firm, or the man who had so deftly balanced it on his head that neither the boys' weight nor their performance had disturbed it in the least. I replied that I did not know which I thought *thaumastoteron*, more amazing; and he burst into a loud laugh and said he was in the same case, he did not know either.

On his second embassy, twenty years later, a maturer and more cynical Liutprand was faced with Nicephorus II Phocas, who had no liking for Liutprand or Otto I, no interest in their aims and no time left for diplomacy. Nicephorus may be forgiven if he was feeling insecure: he was actually about to be butchered by his wife's lover, who then supplanted him to become John I Tzimisces.

This time, for whatever combination of reasons, Liutprand was treated with mistrust. His report is always critical, often caustic, sometimes bitter, whether he is speaking of Constantinople itself or of a far-off province:

On the sixth of December we came to Leucas, where, as by all the other bishops, we were most unkindly received and treated by the bishop, who is a eunuch. In all Greece – I speak the truth and do not lie – I found no hospitable bishops. They are both poor and rich: rich in gold coins wherewith they gamble recklessly; poor in servants and utensils. They sit by themselves at a bare little table, with a *paximacium* in front of them, and drink their own bath water, or, rather, they sip it from a tiny glass. They do their own buying and selling; they close and open their front doors themselves; they are their own stewards, their own donkey-men, their own *capones* – I meant to say *caupones*, 'innkeepers', but I have written *capones*, 'eunuchs', which is all too true and against canon law. And the other is against canon law too. True it is of them:

Of old a lettuce ended the repast:
Today it is the first course and the last.[1]

Ambassadors were not supposed to allow themselves to be overawed by Constantinople. Others, generally, found the city impressive, and this is not surprising. With at least half a million inhabitants it was the biggest city they would ever see. More than that, they found it magical and fearsome. Stephen of Novgorod, one of the numerous Russian pilgrims who passed through Constantinople, may be allowed to speak for many of them: 'The entrance to Constantinople is as if you were in a vast forest, and you cannot find your way without a good guide. If you try to find your way cheaply or stingily, you will not be able to see or kiss a single saint, except, perhaps, that you can do so if it is that saint's feast day.'[2] The young Liutprand on his first visit allowed himself to give Constantinople a couple of generous superlatives – 'its inhabitants, as they surpass other peoples in wealth, also surpass them in wisdom' – but another Western visitor, Odo of Deuil, who passed through Constantinople on the Second Crusade in 1147, gives a pejorative twist to the same observation.[3] 'Constantinople is a city of extremes. She surpasses other cities in wealth, and she surpasses them in vice.'

Not only can we see how Constantinople and its food appeared to outsiders. Occasionally we are told how outsiders and their food appeared to those of the City. The adventurers of the Fourth Crusade, though overawed by their first view of Constantinople as Geoffroi de Villehardouin described it, succeeded in seizing the city and its empire in 1204. This is how the Byzantine historian Nicetas Choniates

---

[1] Liutprand, *Embassy* 63. Translation after F.A. Wright. The classical couplet that Liutprand quotes is taken (not quite accurately) from a Latin epigram by Martial (13.14). The *paximacium* is the same barley biscuit packed by Justin I in his knapsack.
[2] Stephen of Novgorod, *The Wanderer*. Translation after G. Majeska.
[3] Liutprand, *Antapodosis* 1.11; Odo of Deuil, *Expedition of Louis VII*.

describes them. 'They revelled and drank strong wine all day long. Some favoured luxury foods; others recreated their own native dishes, such as an ox rib apiece, or slices of salt pork cooked with beans, and sauces made with garlic or with a combination of other bitter flavours.' To this meticulous author, filled with bitter hatred for the destroyers of the world he had known, we owe a first precious record of that favourite dish of the wild warriors of southern France, cassoulet.

Chapter 2

Tastes and Smells of the City

Constantinople and its environs

The 'New Rome' was set in a landscape of unrivalled beauty. It lay at the meeting place of two continents, as we are reminded in reading an early Byzantine poet's appreciation of a palace on the shores of the Bosporus, just north of the city:

> Where the land is cut in two by the winding channel whose shores open the way to the sea, our divine emperor erected this palace for his most illustrious consort Sophia. O far-ruling Rome, thou lookest from Europe on a prospect in Asia the beauty of which is worthy of thee.[1]

There were many nearby beauty spots to delight those who lived in Constantinople. Liutprand, on his second mission, was summoned to a meeting with the emperor Nicephorus *eis Pegas* 'at the Springs', half a mile west of the city, where there was a monastery, a palace and a royal park running down to the shore of the Sea of Marmara. For Liutprand it was an uncomfortable occasion (he had a headache and hadn't wanted to go) but most visitors found this a beautiful place. Russian pilgrims, in 1390 and after, made special excursions to these

---

[1] Marianus, 'The Palace of Sophianae' [*Anthologia Palatina* 9.657]. Translation by W.R. Paton.

famous springs, which were sacred to the Virgin. They were told of the miraculous little fish that swam in those healing waters,[1] fish that also figure in later legends – according to which, they had been intended for a monk's lunch: he dropped them into the pool in shock when told of the capture of Constantinople, and their descendants lived there ever since.

Fishermen brought their produce ashore daily to many small harbours near the City; the harbour of Region or Rygin, where you could buy grey mullet, was only a stone's throw from the 'Springs'. The enthusiasm for fish at Constantinople fully matched that at classical Athens, as we are reminded by an amusing exchange in the satirical squib *Timarion*. The hero, unexpectedly visiting Hades, is accosted by a resident:

> 'Welcome, newly-dead!' he said. 'Tell us the news among the living. How many mackerel do you get for an obol? Bonitoes? Tunnies? Picarels? What's the price of oil? Wine? Wheat, and all the rest of it? And I forgot the most important thing: how's the whitebait catch? I used to enjoy shopping for whitebait when I was alive – I liked it better than sea bass.'[2]

One of the royal gardens near Constantinople is allowed to speak for itself in a poem by Arabius: 'I am rich in waters, gardens, groves, vineyards, and the generous gifts of the neighbouring sea. Both fisherman and farmer offer me pleasing presents, from sea and land. Those who rest in me are soothed either by the song of birds or the sweet call of the ferryman.'[3] The poet allowed himself a smile as he thus

---

[1] Liutprand, *Embassy* 25–29; 'Anonymous Traveller' (see Majeska 1984 p. 326). On Ascension Day the emperor came here, apparently by boat, returning on horseback in the evening (Constantine Porphyrogennetus, *Book of Ceremonies* 1.8 with Vogt's commentary).
[2] *Timarion* 21. The author of *Timarion* is possibly the twelfth-century writer Nicholas Callicles (so Romano 1974 pp. 25–31).
[3] Arabius, 'An Estate Near the City' [*Anthologia Palatina* 9.667]. Translation after W.R. Paton.

characterized 'the sweet call of the ferryman', but he knew that he was only slightly embellishing the truth. The waters around Constantinople were criss-crossed by ferry services, an everyday essential for the suburbs and satellite cities of the great capital.

In its last years, Christian Constantinople is frequently said to have been a rather empty city, and for this reason more fruitful than the big cities of Western Europe. 'This city of Constantinople is made up of villages; there is much more open space than buildings,' reported Bertrandon de la Broquière. Bertrandon, a Burgundian noble, travelled East for political reasons in 1432.[1] His observation parallels that of Brocardus, titular Latin Archbishop of Smyrna, who wrote a manual for prospective Crusaders about a century earlier. Brocardus has to admit that Constantinople is a very big city (his readers would, after all, be familiar with earlier and impressive descriptions such as that of Geoffroi de Villehardouin) but he skilfully plays down the dangers.

> Although the city is large, only a modest number of people live there in relation to its size. Barely a third of the city is inhabited. The rest is made up of gardens or fields or vineyards or waste land. The population consists of fishermen, merchants, artisans and cultivators. The nobles are few in number: they are as weak as women and as fearful as Jews.[2]

The circuit of its great walls was so extensive that it is possible Constantinople always gave this impression to the open-minded traveller. Those walls may always have enclosed a fair proportion of market gardens and vineyards among the buildings. Earlier descriptions, however, suggest the opposite; the impression we get from them is of an overcrowded city.

[1] Bertrandon de la Broquière, *Voyage d'Outremer*.
[2] Brocardus, *Guide to the Voyage Overseas*. Why did he write his book? A side effect of a successful Crusade might well have been Brocardus's restoration to his diocese of Smyrna, which had just been captured by the Turks.

Constantinople itself is squalid and fetid and in many places afflicted by permanent darkness, for the wealthy overshadow the streets with buildings and leave these dirty, dark places to the poor and to travellers. There murders and robberies and other crimes of the night are committed. People live untouched by the law in this city, for all its rich men are bullies and many of its poor men are thieves. A criminal knows neither fear nor shame, for crime is not punished by law and never comes entirely to light.[1]

Odo's view of the street crime of Constantinople was not universally shared. Liutprand of Cremona, in his early *Antapodosis*, tells a lively (though unlikely) story of how the Emperor Leo VI the Wise had been caught out by his own excellent night watch arrangements and, as a result, had spent a night in prison. Liutprand himself, on the later visit reported in his *Embassy*, had cause to regret the efficiency of Constantinople's state security.

Guards were placed to prevent myself and my people from leaving my house. Any poor people of Latin speech who came asking charity were seized and killed or imprisoned. My Greek interpreter was not allowed to go out, even to buy food. We had to send the cook, who did not know Greek and could only speak to the shopkeeper with signs or nods: he paid four *nummi* for supplies that the interpreter had bought for one. If any friends sent spices, loaves of bread, wine, or fruit, the guards smashed the gifts on to the ground and drove the messengers away with their fists.[2]

The aromas of the city

'The feast of St Marcianus's church is on Good Friday. At the other churches, even St Sophia, no service takes place on Good Friday. On that day the churches are washed, and violet leaves are spread on the

[1] Odo of Deuil, *Expedition of Louis VII*.
[2] Liutprand, *Antapodosis* I.11, *Embassy* 46.

ground,' so we are told by the pilgrim Anthony of Novgorod.[1] Everyone knows of the nasty smells bred in crowded medieval cities.[2] This Russian traveller, who saw Constantinople in 1200 just before it fell to the Crusaders, reminds us that medieval cities were also aromatic in the best sense. There are similar reminders in the *Book of Ceremonies* compiled by Constantine Porphyrogennetus.[3] Rosemary, though seldom if ever used in cookery in early medieval times, was among the aromas ('chips of pine and wreaths of ivy, bay, myrtle and rosemary') that were used to improve the streets of Constantinople in preparation for an imperial progress; rosemary, myrtle and ivy are similarly prescribed for the decorations of an imperial dining room. On the feast of the Ascension crosses are woven of roses, then in flower, and one of them is presented to the emperor. On Palm Sunday palm leaves, marjoram and other seasonal aromatic plants are made into wreaths for presentation by the emperor to the members of the Senate in the church of St Demetrius.

The spice market is now a familiar feature of Istanbul. Long before the city had this name it was already a focus of long distance trade, and in those days spices and aromatics were among the most important and the most costly trading commodities. Just before 900 the Emperor Leo VI (known to later generations as 'the Wise') issued a book of

---

[1] Anthony of Novgorod, *Pilgrim Book* p. 61 Ehrhard.

[2] But here is a reminder, an epigram inscribed '*On a public convenience in the suburbs of Smyrna*. All the extravagance of mortals and their expensive dishes, by the time they are excreted here, have lost their charm. The pheasants and fishes, the spice and herb mixtures pounded in the mortar, and all such fancy preparations, here turn into dung. The belly rids itself of all that the ravenous throat took in, and a man sees at last that in the pride of his foolish heart he spent all that gold on nothing but dirt' (Agathias [*Anthologia Palatina* 9.642]). The poet and historian Agathias, according to another poem in the same anthology, was honorary 'father of the city' of Smyrna and paid for the rebuilding of these public toilets himself: he wrote a total of four epigrams on them – one for each wall, perhaps.

[3] Constantine Porphyrogennetus, *On Ceremonies* 1.1 [pp. 4, 18 Vogt], 1.27 [p. 103 Vogt], 1.40 [p. 158 Vogt].

regulations for Constantinople's guilds of retail traders, regulations that were to be enforced by a local magistrate, the City Eparch. Naturally the trade in aromatics figures prominently in the *Book of the Eparch*, most obviously in the chapter dealing with *myrepsoi* 'perfumiers'. These tradesmen dealt not only in perfumes and dyes but also in the spices that were used in food, drink, medicines and incenses.

Every perfumier shall have his own shop, and not invade another's. Members of the guild are to keep watch on one another to prevent the sale of adulterated products. They are not to stock poor quality goods in their shops: a sweet smell and a bad smell do not go together. They are to sell pepper, spikenard, cinnamon, aloeswood, ambergris, musk, frankincense, myrrh, balsam, indigo, dyers' herbs, lapis lazuli, fustic, storax, and in short any article used for perfumery and dyeing. Their stalls shall be placed in a row between the Milestone and the revered icon of Christ that stands above the Bronze Arcade, so that the aroma may waft upwards to the icon and at the same time fill the vestibule of the Royal Palace ... When the cargoes come in from Chaldaea, Trebizond or elsewhere, they shall buy from the importers on the days appointed by the regulations ... Importers shall not live in the City for more than three months; they shall sell their goods expeditiously and then return home ... No member of the guild may purchase grocery goods or those sold by steelyard. Perfumiers shall only buy goods that are sold by weight on scales ... Any perfumier who currently trades also as a grocer shall be allowed to choose one or other of these trades, and shall be forbidden henceforth to carry on the trade that he does not choose.[1]

This translation is based on the standard one by E.H. Freshfield, but it has needed several corrections in the list of aromatics – a sign of the

[1] *Book of the Eparch* 10.

difficulties that can be caused by the special vocabulary of Byzantine trade.[1]

Already by the 890s, the date of this important text, Byzantine trade with southern Asia – by way of 'Chaldaea' or Iraq – had been under Arab control for more than two centuries. Hence there are several Arabic loanwords in the text, *barzen* 'balsam', *loulakhi* 'indigo' and *lazouren* 'lapis lazuli'. Byzantine control of Trebizond, a possible terminus of the Silk Road at the eastern end of the Black Sea, did not prevent an Arab monopoly over the trade in eastern exotics: the Silk Road passed through Iran, which was itself under Arab rule.

Some of the demand for spices and aromatics came from religion. To assist their customers and increase their profits, dealers set up stalls in the precinct of St Sophia, and apparently sometimes right inside the great church. 'One must not establish a shop within the sacred precincts or display foodstuffs or conduct other sales,' instructed the *Canons of the Council at Trullo* (section 76), safe evidence that some people did exactly this. They continued to do so in spite of the *Canons*: the later commentary by Zonaras and Theodore Balsamon draws attention to the problem. 'Note that this Canon relates to those who trade in the perfume shops and barbers' shops around the most holy Great Church, and even more so inside it. These deserve severe punishment,' the lawyers impotently insist.[2]

The perfumiers' shops even find their way into literature. For reasons that will become evident, Constantinople was fascinated by

[1] Freshfield supposes that there are green herbs in the second half of the list, which in fact consists of dyeing products: instead of lapis lazuli he writes 'mint', while for Greek *zygaia* his wild guess is 'capers'. This word was a mystery to me too, until I came across the narrative of the Russian pilgrim Daniel, who describes the harvesting of storax resin in southern Asia Minor and uses this same term for it (Daniel, *Pilgrimage* 4). The interpretation of *lazouren* as 'lapis lazuli' seems unproblematic and is confirmed by other texts (see Kriaras 1968–). In addition to these misunderstandings Freshfield carelessly translates Greek *ambar* by 'amber': the word always means 'ambergris', a very different thing.

[2] Translation after S. Vryonis.

41

spices and aromatics – some of its inhabitants even more than others. The Empress Zoe, joint ruler of the Empire in 1042 and a power behind the throne for a rather longer period, took a very special interest in the subject, as Michael Psellus makes clear.

> [Zoe] was an enthusiast for all the most exotic [*Indikotata*, literally 'the most Indian'] of substances, and particularly for aromatic woods that had not yet lost their natural juices, and for special very small olives, and for very white bay berries ... Her only occupation, to which she devoted all her efforts, was to blend perfumes and to make aromas, to invent or replicate or improve them. Her private apartment was no more royal than a workshop off the market-place complete with perfumers and distillers: she had braziers set up all round it, and her maids were all employed in weighing, blending and other such work.[1]

The courtier Psellus evidently had occasion (on Palace business of course) to invade Zoe's apartment, to inhale its charged atmosphere and to observe her maids toiling over their unfamiliar tasks. He is no doubt right that Zoe's private hobby was an unusual one for an empress. But the scent of spices and aromatics was a normal one in the Imperial apartments. The *Book of Ceremonies*, which will not be suspected of lying on such matters, lists a whole range of them that must be stocked in the Emperor's cabinet, 'ointments, various incenses, fumigations: mastic, frankincense, sugar, saffron, musk, ambergris, aloes and dry aloeswood, true cinnamon of first and second grades, cassia [*xylokinnamomon*] and other aromatics'.[2] The list begins to show us how many uses such products had, with those initial words 'ointments, incenses, fumigations', to which one might add 'medicines, flavourings for foods and drinks'.

[1] Psellus, *Chronographia* 6.62–64.
[2] Constantine Porphyrogennetus, *Book of Ceremonies* p. 468 Reiske.

Spices and perfumes were necessities across the whole Mediterranean and Near Eastern world. Here Constantinople was not at odds with its neighbours. The importance of exotic aromatics is signalled afresh by a curious story of military standoff in the sixth century, at the period when the nomadic Avars were threatening the Empire's northern frontier.

> Meanwhile the Avar Khagan gathered his forces and advanced through Moesia, suddenly appearing at the gates of Tomis. Priscus heard of this and made for the threatened city. Romans and enemy both encamped in the neighbourhood of Tomis and did not break camp when winter came on.
>
> As spring approached, the Roman troops faced famine, which became acute just before the great Feast of the Passion and Resurrection [30 March 598]. The Khagan miraculously made an offer to the Romans to relieve their famine. Priscus was puzzled and suspicious at this unusual offer, but after guarantees from both sides a five-day truce was agreed: fears were allayed, and the Khagan sent wagons laden with food to the starving Romans. This instance of enemy compassion is still counted as a miracle.
>
> Three days later, while the Romans were enjoying this unexpected windfall, the Khagan sent Priscus a request for some Indian spices. The general, in response, sent pepper, tejpat, cassia and putchuk, and the enemy leader took great pleasure in these exotic aromas. During the subsequent cease-fire, which lasted until the Romans had celebrated their great public festival, the two forces mingled with no fear on either side.[1]

Some Byzantine spices

Saffron was grown in several Mediterranean localities, though its historic origin was said to be the limestone depression of Corycus near

[1] Theophylact Simocatta, *Histories* 7.13.1–7.

the coast of Cilicia (south-eastern Turkey). The expansion of Islam eventually brought into Muslim control not only Cilicia but also the historic plantations of saffron in Iran and in Kashmir; the Byzantine Empire, however, continued to demand saffron, which was henceforth imported. The reader will learn in chapter 6 that saffron 'is cold and dry, is bad for the stomach, causes pain and heaviness in the head, is soporific, and cheers the heart' (text 2 section vii). With such a range of powers it will not be in everyone's daily diet but must be available to the careful physician to prescribe whenever a heart might need cheering.

Mastic, frequently used in baking bread and cakes in Constantinople, is produced in only one location in the world, the island of 'Chios, where the Saint and Martyr Isidore is buried. This island produces mastic, good wine and all kinds of fruits,' asserts the Russian traveller Daniel.[1] Chios no doubt continued to manufacture and export medicinal mastic oil and mastic wine, as it had done in Roman times; but a large proportion of the annual production of mastic was probably exported from Chios in pure form, to be used in cookery and to be chewed, for mastic is the original, natural and health-giving chewing-gum of the Mediterranean world. Chios fell to Genoa in the fourteenth century, and mastic then became a staple of the Genoese economy. One of the impulses for Christopher Columbus's exploration was the hope of discovering a new source of mastic, a hope that was fated to be disappointed. Nowadays mastic ouzo and liqueur, successors to the old medicinal products, are still produced on the island and remain a favourite with discriminating drinkers in Greece. Some Greeks still like the flavour of mastic in toothpaste and chewing gum, but peppermint and spearmint, heavily sweetened, have tended to supplant it – a bad thing for dental health.

[1] Daniel, *Pilgrimage* 2.

A third typically Byzantine aroma is that of storax, recommended by Hierophilus the Sophist (it must be the *best* storax, of course) in a 'dry soup' required for reasons of humoral theory to be taken in January.[1] The pilgrim Daniel was told of the storax harvest in south-western Asia Minor and describes it with some admixture of fantasy.[2]

> From Samos to Rhodes it is 200 versts, and from Rhodes to Macrie 60. This last town, and the country round as far as Myra, produces black incense [some MSS. red] and benzoin. This is how it comes: it runs from a tree like a sort of pith, and is collected with an iron blade. The tree is called *zygia* and resembles alder. Another small tree, resembling the aspen and called *raka* [some MSS. *stourika*, *stiouriaka*, i.e. storax] is gnawed under the bark by a fat worm, a sort of big caterpillar. What it has gnawed, resembling wheat bran, falls from the tree and collects on the ground like the resin of cherry trees. It is collected, mixed with the product of the first tree, and cooked together in a cauldron. That is how they prepare the benzoin incense, which is sold to merchants in skins.

Like these three, balsam of Mecca, the resin of *Commiphora Opobalsamum*, was also produced within Byzantine frontiers – but only down to the time of the earliest Islamic conquests, in the seventh century. This is because, although it is native to southern Arabia, there had been plantations of the precious tree in Egypt and in Palestine, the latter very ancient and associated in legend with the Queen of Sheba's visit to Solomon. Palestine, in fact, became the main economic source of balsam of Mecca to the Roman Empire. Pierre Belon, the last recorded observer of the manufacture of fish sauce in Constantinople,

[1] Text 4 section i. A 'dry soup' is one flavoured with ingedients such as pepper and cinnamon that are 'dry' in terms of humoral theory.
[2] Daniel, *Pilgrimage* 4. The Russian verst is roughly a kilometre. The term 'benzoin' is incorrectly used: it belongs to an Indonesian aromatic. Storax, which does indeed come from Lycia in south-western Turkey, is the product of one tree only (*Liquidambar orientalis*).

was also the last person who saw balsam growing at 'Materea' (al-Matariyah) near Cairo. Merchants told him that this was transplanted and maintained at Cairo at great cost and trouble, and that the ordinary trade balsam all came from Arabia[1] – which is evidence that by his time the balsam groves of Palestine were a thing of the past. Perhaps they were finally ruined by the Crusades. However that may be, balsam of Mecca came to Constantinople from Muslim territory after the seventh century, which explains why the *Book of the Eparch*, around 895, refers to balsam under its Arabic name *barzen*, which was evidently by then the normal trade term, instead of the classical Greek *balsamon*. The latter word certainly remained familiar, because of its use in the Bible, but eventually ceased to have a specific everyday meaning.

Sugar, ginger and sandalwood came to the Byzantine Empire from India, though their original habitats were much further east. Spikenard, apparently a very popular aromatic in Constantinople, also came from India, aloeswood from south-east Asia. Nutmeg, mace and cloves came from the far-off Spice Islands of eastern Indonesia, where no Byzantine – so far as we know – ever went. Cinnamon came from Sri Lanka or southern China: most likely, at least by the ninth century, supplies of cinnamon came from both places, since the *Book of Ceremonies* and Simeon Seth, both quoted above, recognize more than one quality. Nowadays the cinnamon of Sri Lanka, the inner bark of *Cinnamomum zeylanicum*, is universally recognized as the best.[2]

Whatever may be said of the effect of possible monopolies, it remains the fact that all such spices as these were inevitably very rare and extremely costly. The slowness and the real and reputed dangers of

---

[1] Belon, *Observations* book 2 chapter 39, cf. Clusius 1605 pp. 110–111.
[2] Simeon Seth, *On the Properties of Foods* p. 55; Constantine Porphyrogennetus, *Book of Ceremonies* p. 468 Reiske. There is doubt among historians as to when the cinnamon trees of Sri Lanka began to be exploited. See Dalby 2000 pp. 36–9.

travel, whether by land or by sea, ensured their extremely high price. They were commodities quite as valuable in their way as gold, silver and precious stones. It is not surprising that when Byzantine troops invaded Persia, in 626, spices had an important place among the booty that was taken.

> In the palace at Dastagerd the Roman soldiers found ... goods which had been left behind: aloes and aloeswood of seventy or eighty pounds; silk; so many linen shirts as to be beyond counting; sugar, ginger, and many other goods ... In these palaces they also found countless numbers of ostriches, antelopes, wild asses, peacocks and pheasants. Huge lions and tigers lived in Chosroes' hunting grounds.[1]

But prices are fixed by the interplay of supply and demand. Supply difficulties ensured that, if they were wanted at all, the price would be high. But why were they wanted? Why, for example, was it thought necessary to use cinnamon, pepper and sugar in cookery?

Humoral theory and the need for spices

The system of nutrition spelt out by Galen, in his second-century manual *On the Properties of Foods*, has been among the most influential of all scientific theories. It has two branches.

The first branch is 'humoral theory'. The human body has four humours, blood, phlegm, yellow bile and black bile. Ideally these humours should be in balance, but in practice they are not. According as each one of them rules a particular individual's constitution, he or she may be described as sanguine (ruled by blood), phlegmatic (ruled by phlegm), choleric (ruled by yellow bile) or melancholy (ruled by black bile). We still remember the words, even if we forget the theory that lay behind them. According to the thory, an unbalanced constitution causes one to be subject to ill health. The aim of the physician-

[1] Theophanes, *Chronicle* AM 6118 [p. 322 de Boor]. Translation after H. Turtledove.

dietician, or of the self-prescriber, is to balance the humours and to keep them balanced, which will ensure good health. To do this one must correctly identify the individual's temperament, and one must know the dietary properties of foods.

That brings us to the second branch: the 'powers of foods'. Each dietary ingredient can be located on several scales, and the two most practically important are these: What humours does it assist in producing or assist in eliminating? How easily and quickly does it act at each stage in its passage through the digestive system? Once the 'power' of each foodstuff is known, an appropriate range of foods and drinks can be prescribed in a daily regimen whose purpose is both to give sufficient nourishment and to establish the ideal balance of humours.

That is the general purpose of the texts translated in chapter 6. Specifically, text 2 is arranged under '*Categories of Foods*'; text 3 is arranged by humoral and dietary effects; text 4 is arranged as a monthly calendar. The fact that these little handbooks use the technical language of Greek humoral and dietary theory does not mean that they were intended for physicians alone. On the contrary, the manuscript compilation known as *De cibis* (the basis of text 3) is addressed to a seventh-century emperor, presumably by a court physician. Inconclusive as it is, the evidence suggests that numerous Byzantines – among those who had any choice of food at all – were more or less conscious of their 'constitution' and 'temperament' and gave attention to the good and bad effects of foods and drinks on these. They took advice from private physicians and dieticians, just as modern sporting and media personalities do, or they read books about diet, just as many of the rest of us do. Their reading might consist of short texts like those translated in full in chapter 6; or they might go further and study the longer works (by Simeon Seth and others) from which occasional extracts are quoted in this book. However, the really extensive textbooks on diet, such as those of Galen or the one embedded in the

Medical Collections gathered in the fourth century by Oribasius, were quite evidently written for physicians and were probably read by them almost exclusively.

We should notice the special place of spices and other powerful flavours and aromas in this system. They had greater 'powers' than ordinary foodstuffs, as might be guessed from their strong taste and aroma. Therefore they were used, by anyone who could afford them, to make rapid and perhaps radical adjustments to the diet. Such adjustments were needed partly in response to the climate and the seasons, but also for more irregular reasons – either to treat a sudden illness or digestive problem, or to counteract the effect of inappropriate foods, or to compensate for a sudden change in life style or regimen. Travellers, for example, need greater-than-usual stamina and may not be able to eat the same foods, or at the same times, as usual. Athletes in training, or facing a major competition, equally must make adjustments to their diet.

Those who still live by a version of humoral theory – as do many millions of people in southern and eastern Asia – still make such adjustments to their diet, and they make much use of spices in particular in doing so. But even in modern Europe and North America, where humoral theory no longer rules, it is fashionable, under newer theories of nutrition, to make similar quick and radical adjustments to the diet with what are now called 'health foods' and 'dietary supplements'. Oddly enough, one or two of them are actually identical with herbs and spices used in medieval Constantinople.

In chapter 6 there is a handy summary (text 2 *'Categories of Foods'*, sections vi–vii) of the dietary powers of some major aromatics – including some so powerful that we would call them 'drugs' rather than 'foods', and some that were not eaten at all but contributed, as wreaths, to the atmosphere of the dining room. Aromas as well as flavours were a part of dining. Medicinally, aromas were significant in their own right. Already in classical Greece manuals had been compiled detailing the health effects of aromatics – both spices and fresh plants – with special attention to their presence at banquets. When the Roman emperor Elagabalus strewed the floor of his dining room with roses, or arranged for a rain of violets to fall upon the diners, he intended the effect to be both pleasurable and health-giving.[1] Incidentally, both roses and violets, which come first among the 'medicinal plants' in the list in text 2, were also taken internally as constituents of flavoured wines.[2] They are accompanied in text 2 by jasmine, an aromatic plant that had by now spread both east and west from its original habitat in south-western Asia. Basil and marjoram are also there; both are nowadays often regarded as food herbs, but they were probably not used in food or wine in medieval Constantinople.

Of the true spices listed in text 2, three – saffron, cloves and nutmeg – are relatively familiar in modern Europe as food spices. All the rest have sometimes been used in food or drink: musk, ambergris, camphor and attar of roses more frequently; sandalwood and aloeswood much more rarely. It will be seen that though the majority of spices are 'hot and dry', camphor and attar of roses have exactly the opposite power, and the list as a whole allows the user to select spices with any desired combination of effects.

Because of the different circumstances in which dietary adjustments were needed, there were several ways of making them. Everybody needed to adjust to the seasons – see next section – so, as far as that was concerned, suitable choices of ingredients could be made when dishes and spiced wines were prepared for a whole household. But some people, depending on their 'constitutions', might have more need for certain spices than others: for these, sauces could be offered in the form

[1] It is said that he overdid it: some diners were suffocated under the violets. *Historia Augusta* ['*Lives of the Later Caesars*'], *Heliogabalus* 19.7, 21.5.
[2] Recipes are given for both, and also for chamomile wine, in chapter 7.

of dips, giving each person the choice of how much to take. An individual who was ill, or had very particular dietary needs, might require a special dish, a specially formulated digestive to take after dinner, or a special flavoured salt to add to food. A traveller might carry a mixed spice powder to stir into whatever wine was available, or a supply of spices to improve the nutritional qualities of food cooked at inns. Rose sugar, a popular medieval confection, may well have originated in Byzantium as an easy way of harnessing the cold, moist, headache-preventing power of roses to the heat of sugar. Spoon sweets, now so typical of traditional Greece, were already known (as *glykismata me tas apalareas*) in the twelfth century and played a similar dietary role.[1] Aromatic soft drinks (required on fast days) and aromatic wines were perennially popular, or, at least, continually prescribed: the ones flavoured with mastic, aniseed, rose and absinthe were especially well known. In the specimen recipes given in chapter 7, from manuscripts of the fourth-century *Medical Collections* of the Imperial physician Oribasius, three favourite Byzantine aromatics – saffron, mastic and storax – figure prominently. Storax boasts its own unique 'storax wine', unknown to civilizations before or after the Byzantine. Saffron and mastic are both included in the 'anise wine', if that heady concoction is truly a single recipe (some editors believe that at least two recipes have been conflated under this heading).

There is a real connection between – on the one hand – medieval anise wine, mastic wine and other versions of *conditum*, and – on the other hand – modern vermouth, absinthe, ouzo and other spiced wines and spirits. And it is still widely accepted in 2003 that, when taken at a certain time of day as part of a daily regimen, such drinks contribute to health. Yet the connection is not easy to trace in the historical record – because beliefs of this kind have not, for quite some time now, corresponded with current scientific opinion. They have been driven

[1] *Prodromic Poems* 3.321.

underground. For a different reason, as shown by the following quotation, the drinking of aromatic spirits had already become an underground affair in the Ottoman centuries that followed the fall of Constantinople.

> The art [of fermenting date wine] is still remembered in Anatolia, though less commonly and rather secretively practised because it contravenes Islamic rule. It was specifically forbidden by the lawgiver Jāfar, who listed wine among the 'ten pollutions'. Although outlawed, spirits are often distilled, being described as medicine to cure indigestion and colic. To improve their medicinal qualities the richer people have China root, ambergris and spices added before distillation; the common people, licorice root and the herb *afsinthīn* or Persian wormwood, a plant that differs somewhat from the wormwood known in Europe (to whichever of them the name *absinthium* truly belongs). I have seen others add the root of *nagīr* or *ischir*, *schoenanthus verus*, a plant native to Persia.[1]

The calendar and the Byzantine diet

Among the translations in chapter 6, text 4 '*A Dietary Calendar*', attributed to a certain Hierophilus the Sophist (otherwise unknown), is a very practical piece of work.[2] For each month of the year, January to December, the reader is informed of the ruling or dominant humour and is then advised on the choice of foods and wines, often beginning with a modest intake of spiced wine to start the day. January, the coldest month, requires three doses of aromatic wine; the appropriate meals consist of roast meats or game birds or fried fish, all served hot, and all of them sauced with the hottest spices (pepper, spikenard, cinnamon). Mustard is also recommended.

---

[1] Kaempfer 1712 pp. 750–751.
[2] See the survey and discussion of this text by Jeanselme 1924. Koder (1992 p. 16) suggests that it was compiled in the 7th century.

Other aspects of regimen are not forgotten in this calendar. The recommended number of visits to the baths varies little through the year, but different soaps and lotions are specified. Lovemaking is authorized relatively frequently in winter: it is proscribed totally in June (and by implication also in July and August).[1]

These recommendations did not exist in a vacuum. Two other imperatives had to be considered by any user of this little handbook, in addition to the health issue to which the author explicitly gives all his attention.

Firstly, fresh foods were not available unchangingly through the year. Quite the opposite: almost all foods were in some way seasonal. It's not surprising that the vegetables Hierophilus prescribes in January are the cabbage, turnips and carrots that have been stored for winter alongside the leeks and wild asparagus that are currently available; not surprising that the list of January fruits consists of dried fruits and nuts, alongside pomegranates (because they store well) and pears (since some varieties do not ripen till early winter); not surprising that the broad beans recommended in March are dried, and therefore have to be soaked and boiled well before being 'tossed in salt and the best green olive oil'. It's quite natural that the reader is enjoined to look out for 'green olives in brine' in March, because early olives cured over the winter will now be ready for eating. It is quite natural that the scent of aromatic flowers is to be inhaled in April. Fruit-growers will work together with Hierophilus to ensure that red cherries are eaten in June, plums and melons in July, sweet apples, peaches and walnuts in September.

---

[1] 'Eight baths', as most often recommended by Hierophilus, is a larger number than luxury-lovers usually bothered with, if we can believe the author of the third of the *Prodromic Poems* on this point: 'He goes to the baths four times a month; you don't see a bath from one Easter to the next. He's always off to market for sea bass and gurnard, you wouldn't even buy caviar from the dregs in the barrel' (*Prodromic Poems* 3.80–83). I know of no similar statistics regarding the frequency of lovemaking among inhabitants of medieval Constantinople.

Secondly, the religious calendar enjoined certain observances – some fasts, and also some important feasts – and Christian practice was so universal in Constantinople that we should expect practically everybody's diet to be adjusted to it. We have already heard, from a tenth-century Christian observer, of the Christmas dinner enjoyed at the Palace. The bolder of historians may combine these reports with the instructions given for December by Hierophilus the Sophist, or perhaps with the December verse of a doggerel dietary poem by Theodore Prodromus:

> December: I hunt hares, festival food from the wild; I fill my dishes with tasty partridges, and I celebrate the Feast of the Nativity, the greatest feast of the Word of God. Take generously of all foods, I say, and reject the melancholy cabbage.[1]

On the subject of cabbage in December, Theodore Prodromus and Hierophilus the Sophist are in perfect agreement. It will help us to picture the Byzantine midwinter diet if we paint in, as a backdrop, the description of the hard winter of AD 763–4. We have an eyewitness report of it from Theophanes the chronicler, who was a boy at the time.

> It was bitterly cold after the beginning of October, not only in our country, but even more so to the east, west and north. Because of the cold the north shore of the Black Sea froze to a depth of thirty cubits a hundred miles out ... Since the ice and snow kept on falling its depth increased another twenty cubits, so that the sea became dry land. It was travelled by wild men and tame beasts from Khazaria, Bulgaria and the lands of other adjacent peoples. By divine command, during February ... the ice divided into a great number of mountainous floes. The force of the wind brought them down to Daphnousia and Hieron, so that they came through the Bosporus

[1] Theodore Prodromus, *Verses on dietary rules* [Ideler 1841–2 vol. 1 pp. 418–420].

to the city and all the way to Propontis, Abydos and the islands, filling every shore. I myself was an eyewitness and, with thirty companions, went out on to one of them and played on it. The icebergs had many dead animals, both wild and tame, on them. Anyone who wanted to could travel unhindered on dry land from Sophianae to the city and from Chrysopolis to St Mamas or Galata. One of these icebergs was dashed against the harbour of the acropolis and shattered it. Another mammoth one smashed against the wall and badly shook it, so that the houses inside trembled along with it. It broke into three pieces, which girdled the city from Magnaura to the Bosporus and were taller than the walls. All the city's men, women and children could not stop staring at the icebergs; finally they went home lamenting and in tears, at a loss as to what to say about this phenomenon.[1]

The other great Christian festival, that of Easter, was preceded by the long fast of Lent, during which meat and animal products were forbidden. The date of Easter varied (it was on this very point that the Eastern and Western churches had finally split) but was most often in early April. Lent therefore normally accounted for the month of March, and that is why Hierophilus the Sophist makes no recommendations for meat in March: his readers would seldom have been able to take advantage of them. Lent itself was preceded in Constantinople by *e tyrine* or *e tyrophagos*, 'the cheese week', during which you were still allowed to eat milk, butter and cheese, but already not meat. That week began with the Sunday known in the West as Sexagesima, in Constantinople as *tes apokreos*, the Sunday 'of no more meat'. The end of Lent – in dietary terms – came on 'Great Thursday', the Thursday of Easter week. It was on this day, explains the princess Anna Comnena, 'that we both sacrifice and partake of the mystical Paschal

---

[1] Theophanes, *Chronicle* AM 6255. Translation after H. Turtledove. Khazaria was, roughly, the lower Don valley; Great Bulgaria was an adjacent region on the middle Volga.

lamb,' known in Greek as *Paskha*.[1] Anna borrows her phraseology from the gospels of Mark and Matthew. This domestic feast was followed, on Easter Sunday, by a public festival, in which the Emperor went in procession from the Palace to St Sophia. On this day, so the Muslim hostage Harun Ibn Yahya reported, not water but spiced wine flowed from the fountain that lay on the route of the procession.

> On the festival day this tank is filled with ten thousand jars of wine and a thousand jars of white honey, and the whole is spiced with a camel's load of nard, cloves and cinnamon. The tank is covered so that no one can see inside. When the Emperor leaves the Palace and enters the church, he sees the statues and the spiced wine that flows from their mouths and their ears, gathering in the basin below until it is full. And each person in his procession, as they go towards the festival, gets a brimming cup of this wine.[2]

[1] Anna Comnena, *Alexiad* 2.4.9, 2.10.4, 8.1.1.
[2] Ahmad Ibn Rustih, *Kitab al-a'lah al-nafisa*.

Chapter 3

Foods and Markets
of Constantinople

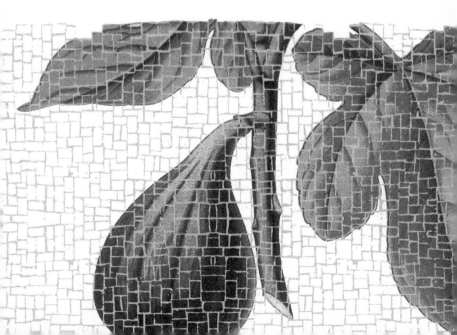

The markets of Constantinople

Although less extensive than the old Roman Empire, for many centuries the territories of the New Rome continued to form the largest political unit in the Mediterranean world. The trade and tribute of this great and varied empire still made its way to Constantinople, as observed by Bartolf of Nangis, a participant in the First Crusade: 'The citizens are continually supplied with all their needs by busy seaborne trade. Cyprus, Rhodes, Mytilene, Corinth and many islands minister to the city; Achaea, Bulgaria and Greece labour to satisfy it, and send it all their finest produce. The cities of Romania, in Asia and Europe and Africa, never cease to send it their gifts'.[1] Much external trade also came this way. The produce of the Black Sea, the Sea of Azov and the great Russian rivers flowed to Constantinople, including such delicacies as salt or smoked sturgeon and – first mentioned in late medieval sources – caviar. Along eastern trade routes, making contact with the Byzantine world by way of Trebizond, Mosul, Edessa and Alexandria, rare spices and aromatics reached Constantinople, and these included several exotic oriental aromas that had been unknown or very little known in the Mediterranean world before Byzantine times. One such is *moskhos* 'musk', which Simeon

[1] Bartolf of Nangis, *History of the Franks who stormed Jerusalem.*

Seth with fair accuracy says came from 'a city called Toupat some way east of Khwarezm': in other words, it came from Tibet. Others are *maker* 'mace', *moskhokaryon* 'nutmeg', *santalon* 'sandalwood', *xylaloe* 'aloeswood'.

Not surprisingly in view of its strategic position on the trade routes, Byzantion had been notable for its markets for many centuries before it was refounded as Constantinople. Xenophon, returning with the 'Ten Thousand' to Greece by way of the Black Sea coast, is the first observer to mention the market place of Byzantion. A little later the historian Theopompus, whose theme was the rise of Philip of Macedon, emphasized the unique character of this city.

> The Byzantians had long been democratic; their city was a port of call; its people all spent their time at the market and the harbour, and were dissipated and accustomed to meeting and drinking in taverns. The Kalkhedonians used not to be a part of that democracy, and in those days devoted themselves to employments and the better life; once they tasted the Byzantine democracy they were ruined by luxury. Previously very sensible and moderate in their daily life, they now became drunkards and spendthrifts.[1]

Whatever we make of the prejudices that underlie Theopompus's argument,[2] his view of Byzantion as principally a trading centre is accurate, and it was a character that Constantinople retained. By the time of Justinian we know that the *Mese*, the 'Middle Street' that ran through the city from east to west, was a busy daily market – and that 'more than 500 prostitutes' conducted their business there according to Procopius.[3] The *Book of the Eparch* has already been mentioned: this

[1] Theopompus, *Philippic History* 115F62 [Athenaeus 526d].
[2] In his time, the fourth century BC, most prosperous Greeks drank in one another's homes, not in taverns. The relative merits of democracy and oligarchy were much debated: Theopompus favoured the latter and was himself a member of the local aristocracy that intermittently ruled his native Chios.
[3] Procopius, *Secret History* 17.5.

decree of Leo the Wise, compiled about 895, regulated the trading guilds of Constantinople and thus provides a good deal of information about retail trade there.

> Grocers may keep their shops anywhere in the City, in the broad streets and in the city blocks, so that the necessities of life may be easily procurable. They shall sell meat, salt fish, gut, cheese, honey, oil, legumes of all kinds, butter, solid and liquid pitch, cedar oil, hemp, linseed, gypsum, crockery, storage jars, nails, and in short every article which can be sold by steelyard and not by scales. They shall not sell any article which belongs to the trade of perfumers, soap-merchants, drapers, taverners or butchers ...[1]

The 'broad streets' of Contantinople, mentioned in the regulation just quoted, are a feature that it shared with medieval cities elsewhere. In Greek they are *plateiai*, a classical Greek name that was adopted into Latin very early[2] and is linked with Italian *piazza*, French *place* and Spanish *plaza*, though in the West these words soon came to denote a square rather than a wide colonnaded street. The importance of these market streets in the everyday trade of Constantinople is specially noticed by two diplomatic travellers, an Arabic-speaking North African who arrived in 1332 and a Spanish diplomat who passed through the city in 1437. The former, Ibn Baṭūṭā, fulfilled a lifelong ambition to visit the historic metropolis when he succeeded in being chosen as one of the party that accompanied a Greek princess returning to her homeland from Central Asia. He writes thus:

> It is one of the customs among them that anyone who wears the king's robe of honour and rides on his horse is paraded through the city bazaars with trumpets, fifes and drums, so that the people may see him. This is most commonly done with the Turks who come

[1] Leo the Wise, *Book of the Eparch* 13.
[2] Liddell and Scott 1925–40 note the first Greek use of the name at Miletus in the fifth century BC. In Latin it occurs in Plautus's plays in the second century BC.

from the territories of the sultan Uzbak, so that they may not be molested. In this way they paraded me through the bazaars.

As becomes clearer from the following details of Ibn Baṭūṭā's narrative, these 'bazaars' are not yet the vast covered markets familiar from modern Istanbul, including the spice bazaar: they are open spaces, the *plateiai* or colonnaded streets of the early medieval city.

One of the two parts of the city is called Astanbul: it is on the eastern bank of the river and includes the places of residence of the Sultan, his officers of state, and the rest of the population. Its bazaars and streets are spacious and paved with flagstones, and the members of each craft have a separate place, no others sharing it with them. Each bazaar has gates which are closed upon it at night, and the majority of the artisans and salespeople in them are women.[1]

Incidentally, it is because the Golden Horn turns north-eastwards at its mouth – and because, as it happens, Ibn Baṭūṭā approached the city from the north – that he places Istanbul 'on the eastern bank' of this inlet. The other part of the city as he describes it consists of Galata and Pera, on the 'western', or rather northern, shore of the Golden Horn.

A hundred years later came the visit of the Spanish emissary Pero Tafur. Outside the church of St Sophia, he observed, 'are big markets with shops where they are accustomed to sell wine and bread and fish, and more shellfish than anything else, since the Greeks are accustomed to this food ... Here they have big stone tables where both rulers and common people eat in public'[2] and the last detail suggests that the hot street food so much enjoyed by Manuel I remained a special feature of Constantinople four centuries later.

'Fat milk-stuffed suckling kids are rich and nourishing above all other foods,' wrote Constantine Manasses (*Moral Poem* [9.62.638

[1] Ibn Baṭūṭā, *Travels*.
[2] Pero Tafur, *Travels and Voyages*.

Miller]). To those who cared for a varied diet, the range of meat available for purchase in the markets of Constantinople was very varied indeed. Among favoured game were gazelles of inland Anatolia, '*dorkades* commonly called *gazelia*', recommended above all other game by Simeon Seth. There were also the wild asses, of which herds were maintained in imperial parks. They were – says Liutprand – the emperor's pride and joy, though he himself considered them in no way different from the domestic asses of Cremona, and felt sure that any predatory wolf would agree with him. Moreover it was in Byzantine times that dried meat first became a delicacy in the region – a forerunner of the *pastirma* of modern Turkey.

At this period, and for many years before and after, the central cattle and sheep market of Constantinople was *en to Strategio* 'at the Commandery'.

> Butchers must not wait at Nicomedia or other cities for the foreign dealers who come to sell flocks of sheep: they must go to meet them beyond the river Sangarios, so that they will get the meat cheaper. [Local] people who keep sheep are to sell their animals to the appointed butchers and deal through them alone. They are not to hinder country people from coming to town to sell sheep.[1]

The swine market, oddly enough, was *en to Tauro* 'at the Bull'. This meeting-place played an extra part as the centre of sales of spring lamb, a favourite luxury, between Easter and Whitsunday – and was, as it were, prepared for its special spring role by way of a ceremony in which the Emperor was welcomed to 'the Bull' with songs of praise on the Feast of the Apostles on the Tuesday after Easter.[2]

> All those who buy, slaughter and sell swine must do their business *en to Tauro* 'at the Bull'. Any tradesman who goes outside the City

[1] Leo the Wise, *Book of the Eparch* 15.
[2] Constantine Porphyrogennetus, *Book of Ceremonies* 1.5 [p. 44 Vogt].

to meet the swineherds and buys from them there, and any who brings swine secretly into the City districts, and any who sells pork at an inflated price, is to be flogged, shaved, and expelled from the guild of pork butchers. Any who takes swine to a nobleman's house and sells them there privately is to be liable to the same punishment. The masters of the guild are to record the names of all swineherds who bring their animals into the city, so that they cannot sell pork to unofficial dealers. All sales must take place publicly *en to Tauro*.[1]

From 'the Bull' the emperor processed, on that same Feast of the Apostles, to the 'arch of the Bakers', *en to phourniko ton artopolon*. The same route is followed on other occasions; the two landmarks were close together.[2] These bakers of Caonstantinople are the subject of quite special regulations in the *Book of the Eparch* compiled under Leo VI. The municipal regulations specify with great precision the price to be charged for bread, and also exempt the human and animal staff of bakeries from being commandeered for public service.

Bakers shall sell bread by weight fixed from time to time according to the price of wheat, as ordered by the Eparch. They are to buy wheat in the Assistant's warehouse, in units corresponding to the amount on which a tax of one gold nomisma is payable. After grinding, proving and baking, they shall calculate the price by adding one keration and two miliaresia per gold nomisma: the keration being their profit, and the two miliaresia the cost of employing the men and the animals who do the milling, and also the cost of fires and lighting. Bakers are never liable to be called for any public service, neither themselves nor their animals, to prevent any interruption of the baking of bread. They must not have their ovens under any dwelling-house ...[3]

[1] Leo the Wise, *Book of the Eparch* 16.
[2] Constantine Porphyrogennetus, *Book of Ceremonies* 1.5, 1.8 [pp. 44, 51 Vogt].
[3] Leo the Wise, *Book of the Eparch* 18.

The 1600 fishing boats of Byzantium (the statistic comes from the work of a historian of the fourth Crusade, Gunther of Pairis)[1] were officially enjoined to bring in their daily catch each morning to piers and sea beaches within the city walls. The fishmongers were to buy them directly from the boats at anchor, to sell them to the public in one of several market streets through the city. Local fish was only to be sold fresh: salting for export was specifically forbidden, and the selling of offcuts was the regulation way to dispose of any surplus. Wholesale and retail prices were regulated on a daily basis depending on the size of the daily catch; the market inspectors as well as the state took their share. Two measures were supposed to keep the system working and remunerative. The masters of the fishmongers' guild were to go to the Eparch daily at daybreak to report the quantity of white fish brought in; and sale direct to the public from the fishing boats was forbidden.[2] But we know that in practice there was an alternative source – a black market, perhaps. The *Prodromic Poems*, which may be legitimately taken as slices of Constantinopolitan life (albeit highly coloured) tell of a *kephalos tripithamos augatos ek to Rygin*, 'a grey mullet of three hands' breadths, with its roe, from Rygin'.[3] Now this 'Rygin' is certainly Region, the first harbour west of Constantinople, just outside the city walls along the north coast of the Sea of Marmara.[4] As confirmation of its status as an extramural (and presumably less-regulated) market for Constantinople we have the observations of Pierre Belon, who visited the city about a hundred years after the Turkish capture and reported that he found *melca*, *caimac* and *oxygala* – in other words, curds,

---

[1] Gunther of Pairis p. 78 Riant.

[2] *Book of the Eparch* 17.

[3] *Prodromic Poems* 3.153 Hesseling and Pernot.

[4] There was a bridge across the inlet, which Mehmet II repaired (Agathias, *History* 5.3; Critobulus of Imbros 2.10.1). Korais suggests that the city gate named *pyle tou Resiou*, commemorated in *Anthologia Palatina* 9.691, was at Region, but this is unlikely because the gate that led to Region was the Golden Gate.

clotted cream and yoghourt – on sale at this same place, 'the last harbour where Constantinople meets Thrace'.[1] The word *oxygala* survives, slightly altered, in modern Greek *xinogalo*, which nowadays usually means 'buttermilk' but is also still used (I quote Diane Kochilas) as the name of 'a primitive, deliciously sour, yogurtlike cheese, made by placing raw buttermilk inside a sheepskin and agitating it over several days'.[2] This kind of cheese, made from buttermilk, is specifically favoured by one of the Byzantine dietary authors (text 2 section x) – other cheeses, he states sweepingly, are 'all bad'.

So the roofed bazaars of modern Istanbul, including the famous spice bazaar, do not trace their history directly to the medieval city. It was the Turkish conqueror, Mehmet II, in the course of his replanning and rebuilding of Constantinople in the mid fifteenth century, who 'ordered the building of a very large and fine market-place not far from the Palace, surrounded by strong walls, and arranged with beautiful and spacious arcades inside and a ceiling of ceramic tiles and translucent stone'. The same monarch, according to his eulogist, 'erected fine houses, inns, markets throughout the city'.[3]

Fish and fish sauce

This sketch of the medieval markets of Constantinople serves to introduce a quick survey of Byzantine foodstuffs.

Early Byzantion had been a fine place for fish, and so is modern Istanbul. Imperial Constantinople was no different. Empty nets in the Hellespont in the tunny season were rare indeed – and were considered the work of the Devil.[4] In addition to all the seafood delicacies known to classical Greece, the Byzantines appreciated salted grey

---

[1] Belon, *Observations* bk. 3 chap. 27. He equated Turkish *kaymak* with ancient *aphrogala*.
[2] Kochilas 2001 p. 140.
[3] Critobulus of Imbros, *History of Mehmet the Conqueror* 2.10.2, 2.22.1.
[4] *Life of St Parthenius* [Migne, *PG* vol. 114 col. 1357].

mullet roe, *ootarikhon* (literally 'egg pickle': the Greek word is the source of Coptic *outarakhon* and thus of Arabic *butarkhah* and of the modern term 'botargo');[1] by the twelfth century they had tasted caviar, *kabiari*, the new fish delicacy of the Black Sea. Still later they imported kippered herrings, *rengai*, from distant Britain.

In surveying the fish (and other foods) detailed in the texts in chapter 6, one keeps in mind that dieticians do not write about foods that nobody eats. They advise, wisely or unwisely, those who have the power of choice. One author thought that 'grey mullet is rather unhealthy' and that 'oily fish...are poor eating and produce bad humours' and that tuna is 'to be eaten pickled or salted'; we conclude that grey mullet, oily fish (such as mackerel) and (in season) fresh tuna were certainly on the Byzantine menu. Also on the menu were red mullet, as highly favoured as ever it had been in classical times;[2] sea bass, still one of the pleasures of Istanbul; skate, monkfish and also sting-ray and electric ray, the last two less favoured nowadays. Crabs,[3] lobsters and crayfish were sought after; so were octopuses, curled octopuses, squids and cuttlefish. The range of shellfish included oysters, mussels, scallops, cockles and winkles.

The fish sauce of Constantinople is very circumstantially mentioned by Liutprand of Cremona. He expresses drily his distaste at being sent a portion of a fat kid of which the Emperor had himself partaken, 'proudly stuffed with garlic, onion, leeks, swimming in fish sauce'.[4]

---

[1] Modern etymological dictionaries trace the word back as far as Coptic but not beyond. The link with Greek is demonstrated in Georgacas 1978.

[2] The two Mediterranean species were perhaps distinguished: see phrase-book (chapter 8) s.vv. *triglai*, *triglai megalai*.

[3] Crabs have two names in classical and Byzantine Greek, but it seems impossible to identify them with different species or genera: see phrase-book (chapter 8) s.vv. *karkinoi*, *pagouroi*.

[4] Liutprand, *Embassy* 20.

This was not his first encounter with the product. He had been invited to dine at the Palace shortly after his arrival:

> That day he summoned me to dine with him. But he would not place me above any of his own great men, so I sat fifteen places from him and without a tablecloth. Not only did no one of my suite sit with me: they did not even set eyes upon the building where I was entertained. This dinner was quite nasty and unspeakable, drunkenly awash with oil and drenched with another very unpleasant liquid made from fish.[1]

To judge from the way Liutprand puts it, fish sauce (*garum* or *liquamen* in Latin), once a familiar flavour across the whole Roman Empire, had clearly been forgotten in the West by the tenth century, for better or for worse. He and his expected readership knew little of it. But Constantinople, as he discovered, retained its liking for *garos*. In fact it continued to do so until the early years of Turkish rule and the visit of Pierre Belon in the sixteenth century:

> There was a liquor called *garum* which was once as widely used at Rome as vinegar is now. We found it as popular in Turkey as it ever was. There is not a fishmonger's shop in Constantinople that has not some for sale ... The *garum*-makers of Constantinople are mostly in Pera. They prepare fresh fish daily, sell it fried, and make use of the entrails and roe, steeping them in brine to turn them into *garum*.[2]

Fermented fish sauce gives a strong and unmistakable aroma to any food, but, just as with soy sauce, its chief nutritional effect is to add salt. Fish sauce had been an ingredient in hundreds of the Roman recipes of *Apicius* (salt *per se* was called for in only three of them). Similarly, salt is seldom mentioned in the Byzantine texts translated in this book, while fish sauce occurs in them frequently.

[1] Liutprand, *Embassy* 11.
[2] Belon, *Observations* book 1 chapter 75.

The recipes for *garos* in chapter 7 are probably of Roman date, like most of the texts incorporated in the Byzantine farming manual *Geoponica*, which, incidentally, was compiled in Liutprand's own life-time. The bishop, when dining at the Palace, may be supposed to have smelt and tasted the result of just such processes as these. The traditional method for making fish sauce as a cottage industry in modern south-east Asia is entirely similar.

Meat, eggs, milk and cheese

Once I trod the Roman road in hunger and thirst. On that road a smell of roast meat assailed my nostrils, stirred up my entrails, reawoke my hunger. I followed the smell and landed in a butcher's shop, and found roast meat turning on a big spit. I began to sweet-talk the shop-woman:

'Mistress, lady, *madame la charcutière*, honoured helpmeet of the master-butcher, give me a little offal, a tiny bit of udder, a slice of your generous spitted meat, a goaty slice from the tough side, the skinny side, the lean side ...'

I saw the lovely woman, I saw the lovely meat; I did not know that my attempt was doomed and my arts fruitless; I did not know that she was planning treachery. She took me by the hand, she fetched me a stool, she laid a table for me and said,

'Sit down, *effendi*,[1] sit down, bachelor of law, sit down, doctor of philosophy ...'

She laid the table for me, she gave me a napkin, she set me a plate laden with sliced meat. I sent down the first mouthful, and the second, and the third, and I was just bending my head to cut a fourth piece when suddenly (where could she have hidden the smelly, shitty missile?) she threw a sausage at my head and said,

[1] Greek *authentes* is an honorific form of address to a scholar or professional man; Turkish *effendi*, borrowed from this Greek word, has the same meaning and is familiar enough in English to be used in the translation.

'Eat that, handsome master, bachelor of law, master of philosophy, sluicer of offal and entrails! Why don't you drink your own
ink rather than eat our humble meat?'[1]

We have seen the anxiety expressed in the *Book of the Eparch* that
the butchers of Constantinople should get fresh meat at the best price.
We shall see the variety of domesticated animals that came to be sold,
some of them from great distances, at the annual fairs at Constantinople and Thessalonica. The author of the fourth *Prodromic Poem*
gives us the consumer's perspective, and tells us that the hot meat
shops of the city already offered slices of meat roasting on a spit –
something not far different from souvlaki – to those who could face
the shopkeeper's biting wit.

The dietary texts show that ox, buffalo, goat, sheep and pig all
provided meat for Constantinopolitans to eat. They show also that finer
distinctions were normally made – veal is distinguished from beef; male
and female goat are distinguished from one another (female is nearly
always preferred, and male was often considered too rank to eat) and
from kid. In one text, the best mutton or lamb is said to come from
one-year-old castrated males. By contrast, the dietary texts say rather
little about everyday things like sausages, which seem to belong to less
serious literature such as popular verse and saints' lives. We have to
learn the Greek for a 'string of sausages', *seira salsikion*, from the *Life of
St Simeon Salos*: in one of the more engaging anecdotes of this lively life,
the saint is seen 'taking a string of sausages around his neck, and
holding mustard in his left hand, and so dipping them and eating
them'.[2] Yes, the dietary texts do confirm that mustard went well with
pork. This meat 'produces an excess of moisture and phlegm in the
body, but its moisture is neutralized' if eaten with mustard. Another

[1] *Prodromic Poems* 4.227–257 Hesseling.
[2] Leontius of Naples, *Life of St Simeon Salos* p. 160 Rydén: see phrase-book (chapter 8) s.v.
salsikia.

meat preparation that was familiar in Constantinople, yet seldom occurs in the texts, is *apokti*, cured dried meat. This happens to be mentioned in the meticulous *Book of Ceremonies* of Constantine Porphyrogennetus.[1] Offal is catalogued assiduously by the dietary authors; head, brain, bone marrow, lung, liver and heart are all evaluated and are in general classed as nourishing, especially liver. Brain, however, is 'emetic' (some modern readers might agree) and should therefore be eaten with pepper or mustard. Even spleen is listed, though not favoured.

Game animals eaten at Constantinople included the deer of Europe and the gazelles of Asia Minor; wild goats, wild boars and even bears from the Greek and Balkan mountains; and, perhaps most commonly, hare. Rabbit, however, was at this date still unfamiliar east of Italy. There were also wild asses, the *onagroi* of Asia Minor and the Levant, though the ungrateful bishop Liutprand was not impressed by 'what they claim to be wild asses'[2] – indeed, the donkey meat proudly served at the Palace came from a herd long maintained in an imperial hunting park and therefore, in the truest sense, not wild at all.

Chickens were the commonest of the birds that Byzantines ate. This is the best and lightest of all meats, according to one of the dietary writers, and 'chicken soup cures coldness in the intestines' (for dietary opinions on meat see especially text 2 section viii). Also familiar were duck, goose, quail, pigeon, partridge, peafowl, crane, thrush and many other smaller birds. The eggs of hens, ducks, geese, partridges, peahens and those of small birds are separately evaluated from a dietary point of view. Eggs were the basis of a recipe for a soufflé or mousse, incorporating minced chicken and sometimes scallops, which seems to have been in use for several centuries.[3]

---

[1] Constantine Porphyrogennetus, *On Ceremonies* p. 464 Reiske. For a modern recipe from Santorini see chapter 7.

[2] Liutprand, *Embassy* 38.

[3] See phrase-book (chapter 8) s.v. *oa* 'eggs'. For a soufflé recipe see chapter 7.

Neither milk nor butter had been favoured foods in the classical world. In fact both were commonly seen as typical of wild northern barbarians; civilized Greeks and Romans had turned their milk into cheese. Byzantines were just as enthusiastic about cheese, which some already called *prosphagion*, the relish *par excellence*.[1] Breaking with tradition, however, Byzantine dieticians are prepared to look afresh at milk. Milk is the first food dealt with, under the heading 'Foods that produce good humours', in the handbook *'Humoral and Dietary Qualities of Foods'* translated in chapter 6:

> Of all foods the one that is most productive of good humours is best quality milk, particularly from healthy animals, and if drunk immediately after milking. It should be taken before any food or drink, and nothing else should be eaten until it has been digested and passed through. If even a little of anything else is mixed with it, it goes to decay and so does the milk. A good way is to drink it early in the morning, freshly milked, to eat nothing with it, and to walk quietly about. Initially it moves the bowels, but then gives nourishment; it is not itself excreted but settles the digestion (text 3 section i).

Milk also has an important place, alongside butter and (of course) cheese, in the handbook *'Categories of Foods'*. Milk is 'cold and moist'; butter is moist and 'suited to those with a rather hot temperament ... Young cheese without salt is nourishing and good to eat ... other cheeses are all bad, except those made of buttermilk' (text 2 section x). Bad they may have been, but they were eaten. The following quick survey of cheesemaking techniques is attributed to the late Roman author Berytius. Evidently abridged from the now-lost original, it forms part of the compilation on farming, *Geoponica*, which was put together at the orders of the emperor Constantine Porphyrogennetus

---

[1] See the quotation from Michael Choniates on page 72.

in tenth-century Constantinople – and was probably chosen as being still relevant to contemporary practice.

> Most people curdle cheese using what some call juice and others rennet; the best is from kids. Roast salt also curdles milk, and the fig tree's sap and green shoots and leaves, and the hairy inedible parts of globe artichokes, and pepper, and the rough lining of the stomach of the domestic hen, found in its droppings ... Milk keeps for 3 days if, the day before you transport it, you pour it into a jar, boil it, and transfer it into another, stirring it with a fennel stalk or reed while it cools. If you sprinkle a little salt into the cheese it stays 'fresh' for longer, dipped in warm honey, or warm water with safflower seed. Cheese keeps if washed in drinking water and dried in the sun and put up in earthenware with savory or thyme, the cheeses kept apart from one another so far as possible, then sweet vinegar or *oxymeli* poured over until the liquid fills the gaps and covers them. Some keep cheeses in sea water. Cheese keeps white in brine. Harder and sharper-tasting if smoked. All cheese seems to last longer if kept in [dried] pulse, especially grass-pea or pea. If it is harsh or bitter from age it is to be soaked in raw barley meal (i.e. milled from unparched barley) and water, and the scum removed.[1]

Athotyro, a type of cheese, is mentioned but not described in the third *Prodromic Poem.* Adamantios Korais, whose commentary on the *Prodromic Poems* was published in 1828, says that in his time *athotyro* was a speciality of Paros and Antiparos. The name denotes a whey cheese, and probably it always did. In some parts of Greece *a(n)thotyro* is made to be eaten fresh; elsewhere, for example on Lesbos and at Iraklio, it is a hard, dried, blue-rind cheese. The way they do it on Lesbos is reported by Diane Kochilas:

> *Anthotyro Lesvou:* These are the hard or semihard, blue-rind, fez-shaped, aged whey cheeses made from sheep's milk and traditionally

---

[1] *Geoponica* 18.19.

used for grating ... Local custom dictates that the cheese, once air-dried, be dried even further in a low oven. The cheese ages for anywhere from two months to a year. When it is just a few months old, it is still soft enough to be eaten as a table cheese, and although this is not generally the tradition, it is delicious and buttery.[1]

Fruits and vegetables

The long and careful list of fruits in the dietary texts (see especially text 2 section iv) is a sign of the range of cultivated fruits in the Byzantine diet and of the importance accorded to them. To the wealthy, who had their own orchards in or near Constantinople, fresh fruit was an everyday luxury. A Russian traveller wrote:

> In the precinct of St Sophia there are wells, and the Patriarch's garden, and many chapels. All kinds of fruit for the Patriarch: melons, apples and pears, are kept there in a well: they are placed in a basket on the end of a long rope, and when the Patriarch is to eat they pull them out, quite chilled. The Emperor eats in this way too.[2]

Almost unknown to the classical menu, the lemon became an important fruit in the Byzantine period. It is called *kitron* in classicizing texts: this was the classical name for the citron, at first applied to the lemon as well. It has a new name, *lemoni*, in the colloquial, and it was already used for making a conserve or 'spoon sweet' with honey and spices, *to dia kitrou*, a luxury food with excellent dietary qualities. 'It warms the stomach and aids digestion,' says Simeon Seth, 'but is not so good to eat without the spices.' Meanwhile new varieties of fruits were arriving from the East, such as the 'so-called Saracen melon' and the large jujubes that were called 'Edessan', named after an ancient city and religious centre which for many centuries had marked a

---

[1] Kochilas 2001 p. 271; cf. p. 393 for the *anthotyro* of Crete.
[2] Anthony of Novgorod pp. 58–9 Ehrhard.

frontier between Roman and Persian spheres of influence. Even newer fruits were the aubergine, *mazizani* or *melitzana*, and the orange, *nerantzi*. Both these names are of Eastern origin, though etymologists see them as having reached Greek by way of the medieval Italian of Venice, Genoa or other trading cities. Simeon Seth, casting about for a classical term for aubergine, identifies it with the *strykhnos kepeutos* or 'garden nightshade' of Galen – not a bad attempt, since both belong to the same genus. Galen's garden nightshade is still used as a fruit in Crete, though elsewhere in modern Greece it has gained the reputation of being poisonous and is avoided.[1]

Meanwhile new ways with old Mediterranean fruits were being discovered. The history of modern Greek spoon sweets has not been traced, but somewhere in their prehistory lie the *kydonata* 'quince conserve or marmalade' and the *karydaton* 'walnut conserve' of the Byzantine Empire. Quince marmalade is now known all over southern Europe, but the old-fashioned French name for it, *cotignac*, was borrowed, by way of Provençal, from the Greek.

The dietary qualities of fruits were worked out in great detail. The recommendation (text 3 section vi) to eat capers before the meal with honey vinegar or oil and vinegar corresponds precisely with one of the favourite ways to use capers, the so-called 'rose of summer', in modern Greece. Aphrodisiac properties were attributed to several fruits, nuts and seeds. Apart from the guidance given in text 3, we may note that pine kernels, taken with honey or with raisins, were 'good for the semen'; so were poppy seeds with honey, but on the other hand poppy seed could cause headache.[2]

Among fruits we must deal with table olives, an essential element of the Byzantine diet. It was observed that olives could not be grown

---

[1] Simeon Seth pp. 53, 70. Information from Myrsini Lambraki. Garden nightshade or black nightshade is *Solanum nigrum*.
[2] Simeon Seth pp. 51, 68.

more than thirty-eight miles inland, and the consequent difficulty in obtaining olives suffered by any who lived further away from the sea than that was regarded as a serious misfortune.[1] There were many recipes for olives. The phrase-book lists under *elaiai* several kinds of table olives called for by dieticians: *elaiai thlastai*, young olives bruised and cured in salt; *elaiai di' oxous syntithemenai*, olives conserved in vinegar; *kolymbades*, green olives conserved in brine, a famous and ancient recipe; *elaiai oxomelitai*, green olives in honey vinegar, especially recommended for the month of March. Recipes for *elaiai thlastai*, for *kolymbades* and for olives in honey vinegar are given in the *Geoponica*, the farming manual compiled from classical sources under Constantine Porphyrogennetus (see chapter 7 for these recipes).

The dietary effects of vegetables are carefully described in the dietary texts. Simeon Seth adds the well-known facts that lettuce was soporific and antaphrodisiac: those wishing to become parents should avoid lettuce. Celery was useful, he continues, because it made women more uninhibited in their sexual behaviour, but it was to be avoided by women who were nursing as it reduced the quantity of milk that they produced.[2] It was also well known that rocket 'is very heating. It produces semen and awakens the appetite for sex. It causes headache' (bad luck).

The dietary authors offer no advice on mushrooms. Such advice is given briefly in the household manual of the Byzantine author 'Cecaumenus', who simply instructs his son: 'Never eat raw mushrooms! They have killed off many a large family.'[3] Various fungi (including the valuable truffle) were certainly eaten, but no author gives a detailed description of the favoured kinds, the poisonous kinds and their names.

[1] Simeon Seth p. 39.
[2] Simeon Seth pp. 46, 64, 97.
[3] Cecaumenus, *Strategicon* 110.

The wild greens that are said (text 2 section v) to produce 'bad humours' will have included borage, purslane, poppy leaves, sow-thistle and star of Bethlehem, among many others; but mallow, with its mucilaginous texture and taste and its additional uses as a food wrapper, generally counts as a garden vegetable rather than one of the wild greens. Wild fruits are also listed in the manuals – some of them not easy to identify. The distinction between wild fruits and someone else's orchard fruits – the difference between foraging and scrumping – was observed by some more punctiliously than others, as indicated by a guilty reminiscence of a Byzantine hermit:

> 'When I was a little boy, out with the other children, I used to eat rowan-berries and they used to go off and steal figs. Once they ran away and dropped one of the figs, and I picked it up and ate it. Every time I remember this, I sit down and cry.'[1]

Bread, grains and legumes

The dietary qualities of bread depended on four variables (so Simeon Seth carefully explains): the kind of grain, the making of the dough, the form of oven and the baking process. He later adds a fifth, the length of time between baking and eating: different qualities are allowed to bread which is still warm, to today's bread which is cold, and to bread one or two days old: after that, it is not good to eat.

One can tell the superior power of wheat, Simeon Seth continues, from the fact that the raw grain can scarcely be broken by the teeth. By contrast with bread made from fine wheat, emmer bread (*artos olyrites*) was a makeshift when there was no other bread to be found; for example, the people of Thessalonica, almost starving in the course of the siege and sack of the city by the Normans in 1185, managed to keep

---

[1] *Apophthegmata Patrum* ['Sayings of the Desert Fathers', alphabetical collection], *Macarius* 37.

going on emmer bread and on bran bread baked under the ashes.[1] Again, it was possible to make bread from oats. But oats were 'food for cattle, not people, except when extreme famine dictates that bread be baked from them ... Such bread has an altogether unpleasant flavour' (Simeon Seth, *On the Properties of Foods* p. 137).

One almost-poetic evocation of good bread is due to the enthusiastic compiler of the dietary text *De Cibis* (see text 2 section i). He calls for white bread 'with a moderate use of yeast and salt, the dough kneaded midway between dryness and rawness', but that is only the beginning. There should be 'a little anise, fennel seed and mastic', additions still favoured by many Aegean bread-makers. Those same aromatics also contribute their flavour to the favourite spirits of modern Greece, *ouzo* and *mastikha*, and this is no coincidence: their health-giving qualities are widely recognized. Readers 'with a hot constitution' will not be averse to including sesame, as further instructed; bread sprinkled with sesame seeds, poppy seeds or linseed was familiar in Greece from the very earliest records and was evidently commonplace in the Byzantine Empire.[2] The idea of kneading in a little almond oil – a very good idea – seems to be unique to *De Cibis*.

Bread was the staple food of Byzantium. That evaluation is strongly suggested by the fact that grain comes first in '*Categories of Foods*' (text 2) and wheat comes first among grains. Bread likewise comes first in Simeon Seth's *On the Properties of Foods* – admittedly it is helped to do so by a roughly alphabetical arrangement: the classical Greek word for 'bread' begins with alpha, *artos*. *Epithymo to psomin kai kytalon kai psikhan*, 'I love bread, both crust and crumb', wrote a hedonistic and hungry author in one version of the fourth *Prodromic Poem*.[3] The

[1] Nicetas Choniates, *Chronicle* Andronicus 1.9; Eustathius, *Capture of Thessalonica* 96; Simeon Seth pp. 18–20, 137.
[2] Simeon Seth pp. 135, 138.
[3] *Prodromic Poems* 4.17, manuscript g.

phrase-book (chapter 8), under classical *artos* and the colloquial medieval Greek word *psomin*, lists all the usual types of Byzantine bread. Each had its devotees; each had its moral and dietetic qualities. 'I won't eat the bread they call "white foam", but the not-so-white bread they call wholemeal. This is the kind that grammarians and versifiers like,' to quote once more the fourth *Prodromic Poem*;[1] and the grammarians and poets knew, from reading dietary handbooks, that this wholemeal bread was much better for the digestion than any imaginable bread called 'white foam'.

Close substitutes for freshly-baked bread, for those unable to get this prized commodity, were the ring-shaped loaf *boukellaton* and the thickly sliced barley bread *paximadi*, both of them to be discussed when we come to army food. Pasta in some form was known, under the classical name *itria*,[2] but it was not a major part of the diet. The cereal grains of the Byzantine diet were often eaten in the form of soups and porridges. These were the usual ways to eat *pistos* or *kenkhros*, millet, names that were synonymous, for the princess Anna Comnena, with unsatisfactory food. *Zeia* or *olyra*, emmer, was eaten in similar ways. Perhaps the most frequently encountered among such products was *grouta*, emmer gruel, the same as what is called *kourkouti* in late Byzantine Greek and essentially the same as *korkota* in dialectal modern Greek. There was also *alix*, emmer groats, eaten 'well boiled and rather watery, seasoned with honey, spikenard and cinnamon'. There was the rustic standby now called trakhanas – emmer dried and formed into balls with milk or yoghourt, later to be reconstituted as a sourish gruel. Trakhanas was already well known in Byzantium under the names *tragana*, *traganos*, *tragos*, and the oldest recipe for it, from

[1] *Prodromic Poems* 4.80–82.
[2] Defined thus by Galen: 'There are two kinds of *itria*, the better kind called *ryemata* ['flowed out'] and the poorer called *lagana* [usually translated 'wafer']' (Galen, *On the Properties of Foods* 1.4.1). See Perry 1981.

the *Geoponica*, is quoted in chapter 7.[1] Slightly less of an acquired taste was frumenty, *katastaton*,[2] which with the addition of ground almonds and sugar became a luxury dessert, quite aside from the virtue (attributed to it in text 2 section i) of 'relieving dysentery'. Rice, *orizin*, still a relatively rare commodity, was customarily eaten in the form of a dessert – cooked with milk (as Simeon Seth helpfully specifies) and sweetened with honey or with sugar.[3]

The use of pulses, too, reached a high level of sophistication. Like the bread so much enjoyed by the scribe of *De Cibis*, these staple foods were carefully spiced, full of astonishing flavours. The phrase-book (chapter 8) gives some brief sketches of suitable recipes: see under *aukhos* '*Lathyrus Ochrus*', *erebinthos* 'chickpea', *lathyris* 'grass pea', *phaba* 'broad bean', *phasioulia* 'black-eyed pea', *telis* 'fenugreek seed'. The '*Dietary Calendar*' (chapter 6 text 4) shows how the spicing was to vary depending on the seasons, in order to keep the human constitution properly in balance. Simeon Seth recommends a soup of 'black chickpeas',[4] turnips and celery, seasoned with almond oil, for anyone afflicted with renal and urinary problems. Of grass pea and *L. Ochrus* we read that they 'can be seasoned with olive oil and ground cumin'; broad beans might be boiled then 'tossed in salt and the best green olive oil'; black-eyed peas were boiled with pepper or mustard or oregano or caraway, and served with olive oil and vinegar or with honey vinegar. Fenugreek seed or *telis*, not much eaten by humans these days, was recommended by Byzantine dieticians in at least three

---

[1] Charles Perry, who has studied the history and etymology of this traditional dish, doubts that these Byzantine terms are connected with the modern Greek and Near Eastern *trakhanas* (Perry 1997 with references).
[2] *Katastaton* and its classical equivalent *amylos* mean both 'starch' and 'frumenty'.
[3] Simeon Seth p. 75.
[4] Presumably black gram or urd, *Vigna Mungo*. Simeon Seth p. 38.

forms – as soup;[1] as a dried bean 'steeped, sweetened, and sprouted, eaten as a starter' with a variety of dressings; or 'well boiled, cold, flavoured with honey, spikenard and cinnamon', and in this form fenugreek was ideal as a component of the March menu.

---

[1] *Apozema tes teleos* 'fenugreek water, fenugreek soup' was misunderstood (by Koukoules 1947–55) as 'lime (linden) tea'. Other occurrences of the word *tele, telis* in Byzantine texts prove that a legume is meant: thus the word is to be connected with classical Greek *telis* 'fenugreek', not with modern Greek *tilio* 'lime (linden) tea', a word that derives by way of Italian *tiglio* from Latin *tilia* 'linden tree'.

Chapter 4

Water and Wine, Monks and Travellers

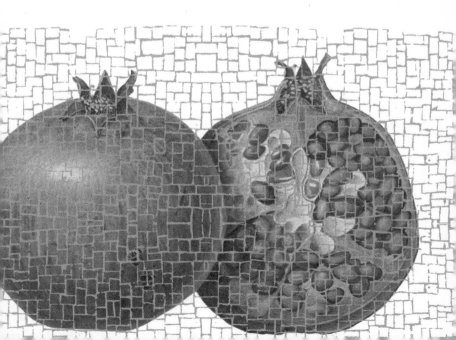

Water and wine

In the monastery of St John Prodromus, said an anonymous Russian traveller of the late fourteenth century, there was a fountain of water that flowed miraculously from the Danube, hundreds of miles and many mountain ranges away. As we have seen, this monastery was one of those with a community of Russian monks, though whether these two northern connections are supposed to explain one another is not clear.

Setting aside such miraculous beliefs, the water supply really did come from far to the north. Most major Roman cities had their aqueducts and Byzantium/Constantinople was no exception. 'In Constantinople there is an aqueduct that brings water from the country called Bulgaria,' explained the Arab hostage Harun Ibn Yahya – and he is writing not long after the Bulgars had established themselves in what used to be northern Thrace and given their name to the region, which we still call Bulgaria. 'This water flows for a distance equal to twenty days' journey. When it reaches the city, it is divided into three channels, one to the Royal Palace, one to the prison in which the Muslims were, and a third to the baths of the nobility; the population of the city also drinks from this water, which has a slightly salty taste'.[1] And water was commonly drunk in Constantinople.

[1] Ahmad Ibn Rustih, *Kitab al-a'lah al-nafisa*. On this aqueduct see Vogt 1935–9 vol. 1 part ii p. 88.

According to a dietary author (text 2 section ii), 'it is suitable for those with hot and dry temperaments, and is ideal in the hottest weather and in summer. Light, sweet water is the best of all waters, particularly if it has no bad smell. There are five kinds: spring water, well water, river water, rain water, lake water. Spring water that is pure and sweet is hot in winter, cold in summer, and is the best of all waters.'

Curiously, the statement quoted above that Constantinople's water was 'slightly salty' is supported by another, almost contemporary observer, Liutprand of Cremona. The bishop regards it as self-explanatory that his people were ill during their stay in the capital, because, instead of good wine, they had only Constantinople's salty water (*salsugo*) to drink![1]

There was plenty of wine, of course, even if Liutprand did not deign to consider it 'good'. The handbook '*Categories of Foods*' is interesting not least for its summary (text 2 section iii) of the good and bad effects of wine. If 'wine drunk in moderation restores the constitution and nourishes the body, in all age groups,' it is equally true that 'drinking wine to repletion, and continual drunkenness, harm certain parts of the body such as the liver, the brain and the nerves. They produce a tremor of the whole body and cause ... heartburn, regurgitation, weakening of the eyes, general paralysis'. As an outline this can hardly be faulted. As with similar surveys in classical texts, the author describes all the most obvious symptoms of chronic drunkenness, to the point where it becomes life-threatening, without ever discussing the psychological side: addiction, or what would now be called alcoholism, is not described.

The 'heat' that the same text attributes especially to raisin wine and to strong dry white wine is closely related to what we would identify as its alcohol content. It is in this light that we can understand the statement that 'wine made from ripened, fully sweet grapes is hot and

[1] Liutprand, *Embassy* 13.

wine made from unripe and not fully sweet grapes has less heat.' Wine had not been distilled. Alcohol as a constituent of wine had not been identified. Thus the effect of alcohol, the element that made grape juice differ from light wine and light wine differ from strong wine, could only be attributed to the inherent 'heat' of the beverage.

Byzantium was an empire of *Wīnburga*, 'cities of wine', to Anglo-Saxon tradition in the seventh century. In the mysterious poem *Widsith* a well-travelled bard is made to claim: 'I have been with the Saracens and with the Seringas. I have been with the Greeks and with the Finns; with Caesar who held sway over cities of wine, over riches and desirable things and over the empire of the Romans.'[1]

The great capital of this empire must have enjoyed a varied range of wines, transported from Thrace and western Asia Minor, the Aegean, the Black Sea shores, and sometimes even further afield, yet no medieval text gives us a survey of them: Byzantine authors are in fact wilfully misleading, often slipping the names of classical Greek wines, such as Pramnian and Maronean, into what appear to be contemporary contexts.

Western travellers offer a useful corrective. William of Rubruck, looking for worthwhile presents to take from Constantinople to Khazaria, chose 'fruit, muscat wine and fine biscuit' (*Report* 9). There were two grape varieties that provided the favourite sweet wines of the medieval Aegean. One, yielding the *vinum muscatos* to which William referred, is still widely grown in many Mediterranean countries. Its name is borrowed by most modern languages from Byzantine Greek, in which *moskhatos* meant 'musk-flavoured'. The vineyards of Samos and Lemnos today produce muscat wine very much of the style that William might have selected. The other variety was the *monembasiós*,

---

[1] *Widsith* 76–8. Translation after S.A.J. Bradley. Caesar is evidently the Byzantine Emperor, ruler of the Greeks but not the Finns. The 'Seringas' are the Chinese: a long journey for an Anglo-Saxon.

French *malvoisie*, English 'malmsey', the typical sweet grape of Crete. Its product, in later Byzantine times, was beginning to be exported to western and northern Europe through Monemvasia, hence its name.[1] This grape is now less widespread in Greece, but was in due course found to be ideally suited to the volcanic slopes of Madeira.

Here are a few of the wine-producing districts favoured by Byzantine authors. Chian and Lesbian, the most honoured of all Greek wines in the Classical world, were still appreciated by travellers in Byzantine times and even under the Ottoman Empire. Writing in the sixth century AD, before the Muslim expansion, the medical writer Alexander of Tralles lists the 'heating' wines of Asia, 'Isaurian, Ascalonian, Mysian, Teruine, Gazan'. In one of the *Prodromic Poems* Cretan, Samian and Ganitic – from Mount Ganos in Thrace – are listed as good; Varniote, from the Black Sea port of Varna, is not so good. In other texts Euboean and Rhodian wines seem to be classed as not too far below Chian. In later Byzantine times Monembasiote appears for the first time – not a variety name, but rather the name for wines exported from Monembasia. From the mainland of Asia Minor there are Bithynian wines called Triglian and Nicaean: this is the Nicaea that served as Byzantine capital during the half-century (1204–1261) when the Latin warriors ruled Constantinople. There is also wine from Cuzinas in the Thracesian theme in western Asia Minor. In the fourteenth century the Florentine merchant Francesco Pegolotti, in his trading manual *Pratica della Mercatura*, listed Triglian, Monembasiote, Cretan and Theban wines.[2]

Resinated wine – retsina, in other words – was already popular. This was a flavour familiar in wine since very early times, for three

---

[1] Lambert-Gócs 1990; references in Koukoulès 1947–55 vol. 5 p. 125 notes 7, 11.
[2] Alexander of Tralles, *On the Eyes* p. 172 Puschmann; *Prodromic Poems* 3.285–313; Isaac Chumnus, *Letters* 216, 218; Michael Choniates, *Letters* 50; further references in Kazhdan 1991 s.v. 'Wine production' and in Koukoulès 1947–55 vol. 5 pp. 124–7.

reasons: because pine resin was used to waterproof the big earthenware vats in which wine was matured, and the earthenware amphorae in which it was stored; because an admixture of resin helped to stabilize wine and prevent spoilage; and because people had come to like it. But not everybody; not all foreigners and not all Byzantines liked retsina. Greek wine was 'owing to its mixing with pitch, resin and gypsum, undrinkable by us' said the supercilious Liutprand in the tenth century.[1]

Classical Greeks had believed that the only civilized way to drink wine was to mix it with water. Their usual practice was to drink it at less than half strength. Romans of the Empire had come to perceive some virtue in neat wine; but their doctors were Greek, and continued to recommend mixed wine *à la grecque* to all who paid attention to medical advice. There are signs in the middle Byzantine period, at last, that the attractions of neat wine are beginning to assert themselves even to the dieticians: they permit their Byzantine readers up to three doses of neat wine on a cold winter morning (text 4 section i), and in general they seem to recommend rather stronger than half-and-half mixtures.[2] This must be the sign of a more widespread change in behaviour. In the sixteenth century, Pierre Belon, on a visit to Venetian-governed Crete, found that ancient and Byzantine customs were no longer followed.

> [The Greeks] all consider it bad to put water in their wine. Their present practice is to drink equally and by turns, especially the Cretans ... with frequent little sips of their strong malmsey ... It must be understood that the Greeks' tables are usually very low, and their custom is to drink as they sit, by turns, never getting out of sequence. If anyone asked for wine out of turn he would be

[1] Liutprand, *Embassy* 1.
[2] *De diaeta* 1 [Ideler 1841–1842 vol. 2 p. 194].

considered rude. The quickest at pouring has the wine-jug and pours for all the company. The custom is to drink from a small glass without a stem, and to drink all that is poured out, not leaving a drop ... They always have the water urn at hand and drink water as well, in big mouthfuls, to restore themselves. Women never take part in their banquets, and are not present when they drink and eat in company.[1]

Wine – product of the fermentation of grapes – was by far the most important of the alcoholic drinks available to Byzantine drinkers. There is a good reason for this: in regions where grapes grow to full ripeness, they produce a stronger and better-tasting alcoholic drink, more quickly and with less expenditure of human effort, than any rival raw material. For all that, wine was not the only alcoholic drink known in Constantinople. Mead, which is made by fermenting diluted honey and was a beverage of high status in contemporary northern Europe, was familiar. 'Mead has more heat and dryness than any wine,' according to a dietary text. 'It is suited to those with cold and moist temperaments and constitutions, and in cold weather and in cold climates ... Some people mix in hot spices when making mead' (see text 2 section 3). Beer, too, was well known in northern Europe, and barley and millet beer had certainly been produced in the southern Balkans, not far from ancient Byzantium, in Classical times. Was beer ever familiar in Constantinople? The answer is not clear; it depends on whether the Greek word written *phouska* and occasionally *phoukas* might mean beer. What it certainly meant originally, like Latin *posca*, was vinegar-and-water, the regular beverage of the classical Roman army on bad days. Thus Aetius gives, and Paul of Aegina repeats, a recipe for a 'palatable and laxative *phouska*' which includes cumin, fennel seed, pennyroyal, celery seed, anise, thyme, scammony and salt to be added to the basic liquid, which is explicitly called

[1] Belon, *Observations* book 1 chapter 4.

oxykraton 'vinegar diluted with water'.[1] So far, so unambiguous. But the Roman army had taken to drinking beer in such provinces of the barbarian north as Pannonia, Germany and Britain, and it seems possible that the word *phouska/phoukas* was eventually used as a collective term for all low-grade wine substitutes. This would explain why Simeon Seth says of *phoukas* that 'simply made it is cold and wet, but with spices it becomes hot and dry'; *phoukas*, to him, cannot be vinegar, because vinegar was not cold and wet in ancient humoral theory. He adds that ivory is more workable after steeping in beer.[2] *Phoukas* is listed among foods that hurt the head in *De Alimentis* 31.

For all who could afford it, wine remained an everyday necessity as well as a luxury. Byzantine diplomats, when travelling in the savage north, immediately notice its absence. Those on a sixth-century embassy to the Turks of the Altai mountains reported that 'they drank wine, but not a wine pressed from the grape as ours is, because the grape vine is not native to that country and will not grow there. Some different, barbarous juice was served to them instead' (Menander Protector, *History* 10.3 Blockley), and it was probably *kumiss*, fermented mare's milk.[3]

Whatever range of drinks the term *phouska* included, these drinks were for sale at Constantinople at drinking shops called *phouskaria* and were prepared and dispensed by barmen called *phouskarioi*. But in the Byzantine Empire, as in Imperial Rome and its provinces, few inns can

[1] Aetius, *Medicine* 3.81; Paul of Aegina, *Medical Epitome* 7.5.10.
[2] Simeon Seth p. 118. See also glossary *s.v. khoumele.*
[3] Other possibilities are mead (but this, as we have seen, was known in the Byzantine Empire; neither the finished product nor the raw material, diluted honey, could well be described as barbarous) and rice wine. *Gleukos*, translated 'juice' in the text, is misunderstood as 'sweet wine' by Blockley: in fact it means the raw juice from which alcoholic drink is fermented. The meaning may be extended, as it is by Menander here, to the product of the fermentation, with the implication that it is still on the raw side. A juice destined for fermentation will always be somewhat sweet (which is why its Greek name is derived from *glykys* 'sweet') but the product will normally not be so.

claim a respectable position in literature. For Constantinople we have an epigram of the fifth century with a convincing picture of the City's amusements: 'the Zeuxippus', mentioned here, was a gymnasium and bath, or, in modern jargon, a sports centre.

> *On a hostelry between the Zeuxippus and the Hippodrome.* On the one side I have close by me the Zeuxippus, a pleasant bath, and on the other the race-course. After seeing the races at the latter and taking a bath in the former, come and rest at my hospitable table. Then in the afternoon you will be in plenty of time for the other races, reaching the course from your room quite near at hand.[1]

It is not by chance that the poet celebrates the attractions of his chosen tavern at midday, at siesta time. In the late evening, if the ninth-century rule already applied, that tavern would have been closed.

> Innkeepers must not open their taverns or sell wine or foodstuffs before 8 o'clock on the mornings of great feasts or Sundays. They must close them by 8 p.m. and put out every fire, because, if the customers of these inns had the right of access to them at night as well as through the day, the result might be that under the influence of drink they would be able to indulge in violence and rioting with impunity.[2]

The same regulation tells us that the price of wine at taverns was fixed centrally by reference to the current market price of wine; also that wine must be served in standard measures, officially stamped. The *phouskaria* were certainly separate businesses, as they were also in Ottoman times; it is not clear whether they were bound by this regulation.

Aegean wines were exported westwards in some quantity in the Middle Ages. Cretan malmsey, like earlier Greek wines intended for

---

[1] Leontius [*Anthologia Palatina* 9.650]. Translation by W. R. Paton.
[2] *Book of the Eparch* 19.

long-distance export, was specially treated. Belon's description of this practice shows that the *solera* method of blending sherry, and the 'cooking' undergone by French fortified wines such as Banyuls and Maury, may both be traceable to medieval Greece.

> The wine we call malmsey is only made in Crete, and we are able to assert that what travels furthest, to Germany, France and England, has first been cooked, for the ships that come to Crete to carry it abroad insist on loading that of Rethymo. This is well known to keep its quality for a long time, and the more it travels the better it is. In the town of Rethymo there are big cauldrons all along the harbour side, which they use to boil their wines each vintage. We do not say that all malmseys are boiled. Those of the town and district of Candia, which are only exported as far as Italy and are not expected to turn sour, are not boiled. But, refreshing their wines annually, they correct the old with the new and reinforce the new with the old ... Crete also produces very good muscat ... There is muscat and malmsey of two kinds, one sweet, one not sweet ... but the latter is not exported, because it is not cooked as the sweet is, and does not keep so long.[1]

Monasteries, monks and their food

Throughout its long history Byzantium was a staunchly Christian Empire. The feasts and fasts of the Church were built into its calendar, and these fasts, in their full form, were frequent and austere. In explaining why shellfish were so much seen in the markets of Constantinople, the fifteenth-century traveller Pero Tafur correctly appealed to this religious calendar: 'In certain times of fasting during the year they do not merely confine themselves to fish, but to fish without blood, that is, shellfish' (Pero Tafur, *Travels and Voyages*). The author of the third *Prodromic Poem*, apparently of the twelfth century,

[1] Belon, *Observations* book 1 chapter 19.

speaks in the voice of a lowly monk and makes play with the fish and shellfish rules in satirizing the epicurean luxuries that abbots and bishops generously allowed themselves.

> On Wednesdays and Fridays they keep a strict fast: they don't even eat any fish on those days, my lord, but only a bit of bread, and lobsters and nice crabs and stewed crayfish, pan-fried prawns and a few greens and lentils with their oysters and mussels, and clams and razor-shells, your worship, along with the rest: nice broad beans, rice with honey, sprouted black-eyed peas, olives and caviar, and botargo in season to keep them from starvation, sweet little apples and dates, dried figs and green walnuts, and Chios raisins, and some lemon conserve. Of course, they complete their fast-day meal with sweet Ganitic wine, and Cretan, and Samian, to throw off the evil humours with a drink of sweet wine.
>
> Meanwhile they put before us well-soaked dry beans, and quench our thirst with cumin-water, obedient to the Rule and the precepts of the Fathers. What we eat is nothing but 'holy soup'; notice the clever name. The cooks take a two-handled cauldron, about four gallons, and fill it up with water, and light a good fire underneath, and toss in about twenty onions ... The chef gives it three splashes of oil and tosses in some twigs of savory for flavouring, and pours this soup over our pieces of bread, and gives it to us to eat, and it's called 'holy soup'.[1]

The 'holy soup', as it would be called in English, might well be taken as a joke-name, since (even if it wasn't quite as thin as is described here) it was largely made of holes. *Agiozoumin* 'holy soup' is a joke-name in Greek too, or so the Prodromic poet wants us to understand: in his third mention of the name he shortens it to the almost-homonymous *iozoumin* 'poison soup'.

---

[1] *Prodromic Poems* 3.273–301.

We already knew that bishops had their choice of rich food: we are assured of the fact when we read the reflections with which the earnest bishop of Alexandria, known to later history as St John the Almsgiver, tortured himself. 'How many would like to be filled with the outer leaves of the vegetables which are thrown away from my kitchen? How many would like to dip their bit of bread into the cooking liquor which my cooks throw away? How many would like even to have a sniff at the wine which is poured out in my wine-cellar?'[1] And although we may think the apparently heartfelt complaints of the Prodromic poet slightly exaggerated, the average monk's diet was really exiguous. Not only were meat, fish and shellfish conspicuous by their rarity: the principal constituents of this diet were cereals and pulses and thin, meatless soups. This is clear from several different categories of sources, all the way from monastery documents and rules[2] to saints' lives,[3] memoirs and historical anecdotes. Just read the *Life of St Sabas* for a view of the charming asceticism that characterized *some* Byzantine monastery catering.

> It happened that this Jacob was put in charge of the refectory at the Great Lavra, and had to cook food for the hermits when they gathered there for a meeting. He boiled up a large quantity of dried peas. They served for one day, they served for the next, and after that he threw the remainder out of the back door into the ditch. Old Sabas saw this as he looked out of his own hermit tower, and he went down quietly and gathered up the peas, very carefully and cleanly, and dried them out again. In due course he invited Jacob, on his own, to share a meal with him. For the occasion Sabas boiled these same peas, cooking them and seasoning them with all his skill.

---

[1] Leontius of Naples, *Life of St John the Almsgiver* 2.21.

[2] A corpus of Byzantine *typika*, monastic rules, has now been published in English translation: see Thomas and Hero 2001. Note the studies of Dembinska 1986 and Tapkova-Zaimova 1989.

[3] See Patlagean 1968; Kislinger 1986; Harlow and Smith 2001.

'Forgive me, Brother. I'm afraid I have no skill at cooking,' he said to Jacob. 'You aren't enjoying your meal.'

'On the contrary, Father,' said Jacob, 'it's very good. It's a long time since I enjoyed a meal so much.'

'Believe me, Brother,' said Sabas, 'those are the very peas that you threw out of the kitchen into the ditch. One who cannot manage a jar of pulses, the food of his own people, without waste, will certainly not manage a synod. As the Apostle said, *If a person cannot manage his own house, will he take good care of the assemblies of God?*' Jacob returned to his own cell, much enlightened.[1]

This was no city monastery but an almost-hermit community in a desert region. The life chosen by true hermits, of which there were many, was if possible even more ascetic. Many were strict vegetarians, as this anecdote shows:

Theophilus the archbishop summoned some Fathers to Alexandria on one occasion, to pray and to destroy the heathen temples there. As they were eating with him, they were brought some veal for food and they ate it without realizing what it was. The bishop, taking a piece of meat, offered it to the old man beside him, saying, 'Here is a nice piece of meat, abba, eat it.' But he replied, 'Till this moment, we believed we were eating vegetables. If it is meat, we do not eat it.' None of them would taste any more of the meat which was brought.[2]

Even ex-emperors, it would appear, were subject to the same disciplines. The emperor Romanus Lecapenus, on being deposed by his sons Stephanus and Constantine, was forced to take the tonsure and retire to a monastery. Shortly afterwards, exactly the same fate befell these sons: they themselves were exiled to the same monastery. They were greeted by their amused father, so the story went, and congra-

[1] Cyril of Scythopolis, *Life of St Sabas* pp. 130–131 Schwartz.
[2] *Apophthegmata Patrum* ['Sayings of the Desert Fathers', alphabetical collection], *Theophilus* 4. Translation after Benedicta Ward.

tulated on the gourmet food they were soon to enjoy. 'Here is boiled water for you, colder than Gothic snows; here are sweet broad beans, greens and fresh leeks. It is not luxury seafood that will make you ill, but our regime of frequent fasts!'[1] Can we believe this legend, repeated for us by a Western visitor? At any rate there is nothing unlikely in it. In the following century – in 1081 – the emperor Nicephorus Botaneiates was also forced to become a monk. It was afterwards said in the royal family that 'when asked by one of his fellow monks if he found the change easy to bear, he said, "I hate not eating meat. Nothing else troubles me very much" ' (Anna Comnena, *Alexiad* 3.1.1). Once more, our fullest information about the monastery menu comes from the *Prodromic Poems* – and once more the contrast is drawn between the abbots' diet and that of the humble monks.

> They munch angler-fish, we have our Lent Soup. They drink their Chian till they can take no more, we have Varna wine cut with water. They have their sweet wine after their jugfuls, we have some nice water after our one-course meal. They have white bread, we have bran bread. They have a mousse after their sesame sweetmeat; we have wheat gruel with the wheat filtered out. They have second helpings of fritters with honey … They have spoon sweets, we get castor oil seeds … They have the bass and the shining grey mullet, we have the smoky-smelling Lent Soup. They have the bluefish, the catfish, the brill; we have another go at our What do you call it?[2]

Food for travellers and soldiers

The pattern of Byzantine eating meant that one looked for little food during the day, expecting a single big meal in the evening. Hence the drinking shops in the cities, if closed by mid-evening, had no reason to develop into restaurants.

[1] Liutprand, *Antapodosis* 5.23.
[2] *Prodromic Poems* 3.311–322.

Travellers, for their part, would carry a midday snack with them or rely on chance. We hear of a party of Anglo-Saxon pilgrims, visiting the holy places of Asia Minor, who 'got some bread and went to a spring in the middle of the town and sat on the bank and dipped their bread in the water and ate it'.[1] Even royalty, when out for a day's hunting, ate black bread with cheese and cress. Hoping possibly for some meat or fish, Bishop Michael Choniates, on his arrival at the island of Ceos, asked those at the harbour side: ' "Do you have any *prosphagion* 'relish', children?" They at once offered me cheese, because these islanders use the general word *prosphagion* in the special sense of "cheese".'[2]

Those who were lucky enough to be able to stay with friends while travelling found that this was much the most pleasant way to get an evening meal and a comfortable bed. 'There was always someone to meet us,' said Timarion, speaking of the nightly stages of his journey to Hell via Thessalonica. In remote districts the ancient obligation of hospitality still impinged on all householders, and was still observed punctiliously.[3] And for those with no other invitations, monasteries, country inns and travellers' hostels existed at intervals along the main roads. Of a monastery at Pera we are told by a Russian pilgrim that, in accordance with the will of the founding abbot, 'nowadays they offer bread, soup and a cup of wine to all. Every Christian on his way to and from Jerusalem is fed there for several days; the Greeks, also, are fed there, and thanks to the prayers of the Mother of God this monastery never becomes impoverished'.[4] An epigram tells us that the poet Macedonius built an inn at Cibyra, while the philanthropic Mehmet II,

[1] *Pilgrimage of St Willibald* [p. 256 Tobler and Molinier]. The travellers are St Willibald, his brother Wunebald, his sister Walpurga and their father Richard. They travelled c. 723/726.
[2] Michael Choniates, *Letters* [vol. 2 p. 194 Lampros].
[3] See for example *Apophthegmata Patrum* [alphabetical collection], *Eucharistus* 1.
[4] Anthony of Novgorod, pp. 63–4 Ehrhard.

the Empire's Turkish conqueror, in due course gave attention to the restoration of inns and *hans* on the roads that led to Constantinople. In general such establishments offered little more than shelter and security; yet one of them, at least, had once become famous for its cooking, so we learn from the *Life of St Theodore of Syceon*. Theodore himself was born at the inn in the sixth century: his mother, his grand-mother and his aunt had begun their career as prostitutes but came to rely on the quality of their food to attract customers. Their employee, 'a God-fearing man called Stephanus,' is the first restaurant chef anywhere in the world whose name is known.[1]

There were two useful substitutes for freshly-baked bread, for those who were out of reach of this prized commodity. They were the ring-shaped loaf *boukellaton* and the thickly sliced toasted barley bread *paximadi*. Both were typical food for the Byzantine army.[2]

In fact the book on *Stratagems* attributed to the emperor Maurice names three alternative basic army rations: the troops were to be supplied with *boukellaton* (ready made), or millet meal, or wheatmeal. On campaign, so Maurice instructs, a soldier should carry in his saddlebag water and one or two pounds of *boukellaton* or meal. *Boukellaton* was such a necessity that the commander of certain auxiliary troops comes to be called *boukellarios*, a name explained as 'the one who looks after the bread so that soldiers do not need to'. One of the inland provinces of northern Asia Minor came to be called *Boukellarion* after this military title.[3]

Instead of *boukellaton* other sources, such as Constantine Porphyro-gennetus *On Ceremonies*, tend to list *paximadia*.[4] Both of these can

---

[1] *Timarion* 2; Macedonius [*Anthologia Palatina* 9.648, cf. 9.649]; Critobulus of Imbros 2.10.2; *Life of St Theodore of Syceon* 3, 6.

[2] For more on army food see Kolias 1984.

[3] Constantine Porphyrogennetus, *Themes* Asia 6.12.

[4] Maurice, *Stratagems*, 5.4.2, 7.17a.13; Constantine Porphyrogennetus, *Book of Ceremonies* p. 658 Reiske.

fairly be included under the classical name *dipyros artos* 'twice-baked bread'. Their common feature is that they were baked to dryness: in fact they were practically inedible without moistening. 'The bread that soldiers are to eat in camp has to go into the oven twice and be so thoroughly baked that it will last as long as possible and not quickly spoil. Bread so baked is much lighter in weight,' explains the military historian Procopius.[1] Unenticing? Yet *boukellaton* or *paximadia* in some fancy form (*biscoctum delicatum*, 'fine biscuit' in William of Rubruck's Latin) were attractive enough and typical enough for William to take along with him to the Crimea as a present from Constantinople.

Fairs of the Byzantine Empire

Among major focuses of trade in the ancient Mediterranean were the regular festivals – usually annual, biennial or quadrennial – held in honour of the ancient gods. Centred on the great temples and sacred sites, these festivals were religious, artistic and also commercial. In the late Roman and Byzantine periods, although the worship of the ancient gods was dying, it has been demonstrated (notably in the work of Speros Vryonis) that the festivals did not die. Sometimes, but not always, individual locations were abandoned; sometimes, but not always, the calendar must have changed; but festivals continued, and even multiplied, and they were now dedicated to the saints of the new religion.

An annual festival and fair coinciding with St Demetrius's day took place both at Constantinople and at Thessalonica, the second city of the later Byzantine Empire.

The fields surrounding Thessalonica made a splendid and wealthy setting; vines on the hillsides and fish in the lagoons provided plentiful

[1] Procopius, *Wars* 3.13.15.

supplies, not to mention the deer that came down from the hills to find water. In this countryside vineyards, gardens and parks extended inland towards Berroia. The villages around here were of varied population, some of them Greek, some inhabited by old-established Balkan peoples, and an increasing number Slavonic-speaking. It would be easier (said the enthusiastic John Cameniates) to count the sand on the shore than to count the people, both local and foreign, who gather in Thessalonica to trade, whether in gold and silver, in precious stones, or in silk and wool.[1] The actual fair began six days before the saint's day and ran for a week. The excitement of the *Demetria* at Thessalonica shines through one of the most classical of Byzantine texts, the anonymous sketch of a trip to Hell and back entitled *Timarion.*

> The *Demetria* was a festival like the *Panathenaia* in Athens and the *Panionia* among the Milesians. It is the greatest of the Macedonian fairs. Vast crowds flood into it, not only locals born and bred, but all sorts from all over: Greeks from everywhere, all the neighbouring peoples of the Balkans as far north as the Danube and Scythia, Campanians, Italians, Iberians, Portuguese, Transalpine Celts – to put it briefly, the shores of the Ocean send suppliants and spectators to our Martyr, so great is his pan-European fame...
>
> The arrangement was like this: traders' stalls, row facing row, set up in parallel lines. These rows continued for a great distance, and they opened into a transverse passage, a broad street [*plateia*] that linked them all and provided relief for the pressure of the crowd...
>
> I saw every kind of woollens and linens for men and women, everything that merchant ships bring from Boeotia and the Peloponnese and everything that they bring from Italy to Greece; Phoenicia and Egypt, too, contribute much, as do Spain and the

---

[1] John Cameniates, *Siege of Constantinople* 5–6, 9.

Pillars of Heracles, weaving the most beautiful of draperies. All these the merchants bring from their own countries direct to old Macedonia and to Thessalonica. The Black Sea, though it sends its produce to Byzantion, still manages to stock the fair, because a great number of horses and mules carry the goods on to Thessalonica. All this I was to see when I had come down the hill; but even while I was still on the hilltop I had been amazed by the many kinds of animals, the numbers of them, and the confusion of their cries assailing my ears: horses neighing, cows mooing, sheep bleating, pigs grunting and dogs barking. The dogs come along as well, you see, to fight for their masters against wolves and robbers.[1]

The speaker goes on to describe the formal and religious part of the festival, the impressive procession, the hymns and acts of worship, in all of which the archbishop and the duke of Thessalonica took their part. But we should notice that the commercial fair comes first, both in the actual timetable and in the literary description. Had the fair got under way only *after* the saint's day, attendance at the religious ceremonies might have been noticeably smaller. Under the Roman Empire early Christians had repeatedly been reproached by their spiritual leaders for daring to attend pagan festivals at all; the consensus was that Christians should not take part in any way, except when necessary purchases could be made nowhere else than at the accompanying fairs. Christian saints gradually took over the pagan festivals in the century of Constantine I, and after that a new set of reproaches was addressed to those who attended them – this time for paying too little attention to the remembrance of the saints and too much to 'the rabble of *mammon* and the ceaseless activity of the sellers of goods'.[2]

---

[1] *Timarion* 4. For translations and discussion of this description of the *Demetria*, see Romano 1974 esp. p. 126 ff.; Vryonis 1981 pp. 202–4; Alexiou 1983; Baldwin 1984 pp. 43–4 with pp. 15–17 and notes 38–40.
[2] Asterius of Amaseia, *Homilies* 3.1.2. See De Ligt 1993; Vryonis 1981.

In the last two Byzantine centuries a new ethnic group was often to be seen at fairs and festivals, the Gypsies. Their arrival and their acrobatic shows are described observantly and sympathetically by Nicephorus Gregoras in his *Roman History*; he mentions, but does not give details of, their dance and music. Like his contemporary, the anonymous Bourgeois de Paris, Nicephorus traces their origin to Egypt; uniquely, he is able to record their passage through Persia, Armenia and other Near Eastern regions on their way to Constantinople, observing that they had reached Spain not very long afterwards.[1]

Far more than at any imaginable market or fair in the old Roman Empire, those of Byzantium had the capability of attracting an international clientele, simply because there were by now more states (in the world, and in the Mediterranean world in particular) that were active in long distance trade. Already in the fourth century we hear of markets and fairs held just on or just over the Imperial frontier.

> There is a town called Batne in [upper Mesopotamia] not far from the Euphrates, founded by the ancient Macedonians, inhabited by wealthy merchants. Here, in an annual festival about the beginning of September, a great multitude of all sorts of people gather for a fair, in which they deal in the goods exported by Indians, Chinese and other peoples who engage in overseas trade.[2]

As the Byzantine Empire contracted the proportion of such frontier fairs increased. They were not always peaceful. Michael Choniates, brother of the historian Nicetas and metropolitan of their home city of Chonae, tells of a dangerous skirmish at the annual fair at Chonae between the local 'Romans' and the 'Turks' who crossed the border

---

[1] Nicephorus Gregoras, *Roman History* 8.10.1–5 [1.348–351 Bonn ed.]. Cf. *Journal d'un Bourgeois de Paris* 464–8. The Gypsies arrived in Paris on 29 August 1427, about a century after they were first seen in Constantinople. The anonymous *Bourgeois* gives most attention to their fortune-telling.

[2] Ammianus Marcellinus 14.3.3.

from the Sultanate of Iconium. In ancestry the opposing gangs might have been indistinguishable, but they now belonged to different states observing different religions, and the dispute was only settled at the personal intervention of Michael himself.[1]

'The place called Scutari, on the opposite shore of the sea' – just across the Bosporus, that is – had never been regarded as part of the city of Constantinople. By the last century of the Byzantine Empire it was no longer Imperial territory – although it was the nearest town to Constantinople itself. Thus at last Scutari became one more international market like so many others: 'The Turks travel there, and the Greeks and Franks cross from this side, and they trade with each other,' wrote the Russian pilgrim Zosima the Deacon in the travel narrative that he called *Xenos* 'The Stranger'.

[1] Michael Choniates, *Letters* [Lambros 1879 vol. 1 p. 56], summarized by Vryonis 1981 p. 216.

Chapter 5

Rulers of the World

Legend and reality

Odo of Deuil, quoted in chapter one, alludes to street crime in the dark alleys of the vast city of Constantinople. His Crusader companions had every reason to be fearful during their stay outside the walls and their occasional visits inside – and not simply because the city they were visiting was far bigger than any other known to them. The time they spent within the frontiers of the Empire had in any case been punctuated by misunderstanding, open distrust, famine, vandalism and military skirmishes. Rather few of them survived to return to the West. The bitter memories of those who did so lived on in memoirs like Odo's. They were of such compelling interest to others that they were fictionalized in legend and poetry.

Most of this book is an attempt to recreate the food culture of medieval Constantinople, as it was really experienced by those who inhabited or visited the city: it is based on what they themselves wrote about it. But there is another history, the history of how Constantinople seemed to those who never went there. It was one of the three most famous cities of the medieval West, rivalling Rome and Jerusalem in the frequency with which it cropped up in epics, verse romances and prose fantasy. The original audience for the histories and memoirs quoted elsewhere in this book overlapped with the audience for romances and fantasies. An untravelled medieval Western reader's mental picture of Constantinople was a composite of real memoirs and imaginary narratives. If we ignore these, we will not realize the true magic of medieval Byzantium – a city more than half way to the edge of the world:

> They steered their galley before the Isle of Bogie, where no man goes, and there are none but apes. They passed the land of Persie, and that of Femenie; they left Coine to their left, and the land of Babiloine; they saw the tower of Marroc, where King Rabaot was, and the land of Jerusalem, and they navigated the River Jordan. They coasted Costantinoble and left behind them the land of the Griffins, and sailed on till they saw nothing but sea and sky.[1]

There are many such journeys in medieval romance. Some unexpectedly realistic narratives of land journeys in arid landscapes are closely based on the real discomfort, hunger and danger faced by the ordinary 'people' who were marching eastwards in great numbers on the Second Crusade in 1147. The author of the *Roman de Thèbes*, a French romance of the late twelfth century (supposedly retelling tales from Greek mythology), had either travelled through the Balkans himself on this recent ill-fated expedition or had heard tales from those who had:

> The people were numerous: they stripped the land bare, and had to go far for their food; they could not find food within three long days' march. The poor people were in great distress, the rich were in distress: they could not beg, they could not steal, and there was precious little food for ready money ...
>
> Far off, said [the Bulgars], near Russia, along the bank of the Danube, there is a fertile country, but there is a high mountain in our way. Beyond its summit is a wide plain, well worked, farmed,

[1] *Blancandin et l'Orgueilleuse d'Amour* 2785–2800. Coine is modern Konya, medieval Iconium, capital of a Turkish sultanate when this romance was composed – but the geography of the passage is wholly fantastic.

levelled. There is strong *Theleis* wine, good meadow grain, strong big grain, and there are wide fields of vines, and orchards enough that we might all live off fruit. There are wide ploughlands and big herds of swine: pigs, sheep, fat deer in the woods, deer and stags, goats and wild boar, and plenty of cattle in the fields ...

There was terrible famine in the army, a dearth of flour. Bread was sold for pure gold, a chunk of bread for a *marabotin*. They lived in agony, some had lost their colour: the poor, in their hunger, were sick, sallow and pale.[1]

But the traveller's troubles and fears were destined to be forgotten if he reached the Imperial Palace. Its wonders were themselves the stuff of legend, recalled and embroidered repeatedly in the *chansons de geste*, the epic poetry of medieval France. The *Voyage de Charlemagne* tells of the famous monarch's wholly fictional crusading expedition to Constantinople and Jerusalem, neither of which he ever visited. There was no Emperor Hugh to welcome him to Constantinople, and no palace that turned when the wind blew.

Charlemagne saw the palace lightly turning: the French covered their faces, they dared not look. The Emperor Hugh the Brave came and said to the French:

'Don't be afraid.'

'Sire,' said Charlemagne, 'will it never stand still?'

Hugh the Brave said: 'Wait a little longer.'

Evening approached; the storm subsided, and the French got to their feet. Supper was ready. Charlemagne sat at table, his brave nobles sat, and Emperor Hugh the Brave and his wife at his side, and his blonde daughter, her face beautiful and pale, her skin as white as a summer flower. Oliver looked at her and fell in love:

'May the glorious heavenly king grant me to take her to France or to the fortress of Dun, where I could do all I wished with her!'

[1] *Roman de Thèbes* 7885–92, 7908–25, 8231–8.

He said it between his teeth, so that no one could hear.

Nothing that they wanted was denied them: they had plenty of game, venison and boar, cranes and wild geese and peppered peacocks. Wine and *clarez* was served liberally, and the *jongleurs* sang and played their viols and their *rotes*, and the French had a fine time.[1]

There were several marriages between Byzantine and European royalty. These must have caught the imagination of the poets of epic and romance, to judge by the fact that East-West marriages are part of the plot of at least six fictional narratives of the twelfth to fifteenth centuries.[2] The *Chanson de Girart de Roussillon*, composed around 1150, tells of embassies and of an eventual alliance between East and West that was cemented by a dynastic marriage.

In the quarter of St Sophia, near the cathedral, [the Emperor] lodged each [French prince] in a noble house. There you would have seen new silk strewn underfoot, and scented many a spice, for he had balsam burning everywhere: no other king matched his wealth.

He gave them all they wished at night, and next day sat them in his palace, and they began to talk of their business. But he showed them his strange games, and had his necromancers make a storm of rain and create powerful illusions. When he had fed them with fear, he set up more magic tricks and pleasant games, enjoyable to watch, so that they were distracted until the evening of the next day ...

Then they wanted to cross the Arm of St George, but he loaded

---

[1] *Voyage de Charlemagne* 392–414. See Polak 1982.
[2] The hero of *Peredur* travels to Constantinople, takes part in a tournament, attracts the Empress, marries her and rules there 14 years. *Guillaume de Palerne* describes a Constantinopolitan wedding, as does *Lion de Bourges*. In *La Belle Hélène de Constantinople* a Byzantine princess flees westwards and marries King Henry of England. In the prose *Lancelot* the offspring of Bohort's one-night stand with the daughter of King Brangoire is 'Helyam the White, who was afterwards Emperor of Coustantinoble'. And in *Le livre de Baudouin de Flandre* Emperor Henry of Constantinople marries the French King's daughter Beatrice.

them with costly spices and mandrake. And when he had shown them the grandchildren of God, he took them to his vaulted chamber, its floor strewn with many-coloured gems. He said to each:

'Take all you want.'

He wrapped black sable pelts around their necks, he gave them rings, brooches and cups, new silk and purple and samite, and vases full of theriac and balsam.[1]

We now turn to the imperial reality. Does it match the magic and luxury of the poets' imaginations?

The emperors at dinner

In Constantinople, beside the sea and facing east, is an imperial residence known as the Constantinian Palace. Its entrance, remarkable and impressive, is from the sea. There are marble steps that run right to the edge of the sea, guarded by marble lions and marble pillars of regal grandeur ...[2]

This view of the Great Palace is the preface to the narrative of a diplomatic visit to Constantinople in 1171. The Latin king of Jerusalem, Amalric, was leader of the party. His aim was to gather military and financial support for his shaky Crusader kingdom. To the kings of the West he had sent an ambassador: to the Byzantine emperor, far richer than any of them, geographically closer, and already linked with the Crusader kingdom by ties of marriage, he applied in person. As a crowned monarch he was accorded the rare privilege of approaching the palace direct from the sea, by the marble steps of Bucoleon.

[1] *Chanson de Girart de Roussillon* 203–218, 279–288. The 'grandchildren of God' means the numerous relics of the Apostles that were then to be seen in Constantinople. Thirty years after this epic was composed, many of the relics were looted by the Crusaders and deposited in churches in the West.

[2] William of Tyre, *Historia Transmarina* 20.25.

Curtains of costly material and no less costly workmanship screened the throne room. Certain great princes welcomed the lord King at this point and led him within. I am told that this was done to maintain imperial majesty while the two made their acquaintance: I am told that among his peers, when only noblemen were present, the lord Emperor greeted the lord King with affable smiles, which, had he done so in open court, would have detracted from his dignity. After the lord King had entered the throne room, the curtains were drawn back in a moment, and we who had been left outside suddenly saw the lord Emperor, seated on a golden throne, clothed in imperial panoply. Beside him was the lord King, seated on a noble throne, though a humbler one.[1]

The narrator is William, archbishop of Tyre and historian of *Outremer*, of the Crusader states. He has visited Constantinople at least once before and will come here at least once more before he dies. On that last occasion (in 1180) it will be his privilege to attend two imperial weddings, those of the son and daughter of the old emperor Manuel. In spite of his expressions of conventional distrust for 'the Greeks' and their Byzantine diplomacy, expressions several times repeated in the course of his *Historia Transmarina*, William (unlike, say, Liutprand of Cremona) is prepared to be impressed by the wealth and the pageantry of the imperial capital.

He repeatedly honoured both the lord King himself and the members of our party with gifts of truly imperial munificence, and showed his concern for our health and welfare by frequent enquiries. The inner regions of the Palace that were closed to all but his personal staff, the altars of his private life, his sacred places never entered by ordinary people, his treasuries and ancestral repositories of everything that is desirable, these he commanded to be thrown open as if for his own household. Relics of the religion, the most

[1] William of Tyre, *Historia Transmarina* 20.25.

precious proofs of the dispensation of our lord Jesus Christ – the Cross, the fetters, the spear, the sponge, the reed, the crown of thorns, the shroud, the sandals – all these he instructed to be shown to us. Every historic and numinous object handed down from the times of the blessed and august Constantine, Theodosius and Justinian, and stored in the treasure chests in his private apartments, was liberally displayed to us. And on holidays he several times invited the lord King, and the whole party, to noble games and entertainments. Among these were presented to us concerts with various musical instruments, and with songs of wonderful sweetness remarkable for their clever harmony; there was also singing by girls' choirs, and some admirable performances by players, not overstepping the bounds of propriety.[1]

In all its visitors Constantinople encouraged the same powerful impression of ancient, legendary, timeless grandeur. It was true. The Great Palace had been there ever since Constantine refounded the city, on the rocky northeastern promontory of the peninsula (the site of the old *akropolis* or citadel of Byzantion). Yet things did change. In fact, by the time Manuel was emperor and Amalric paid this visit, the Great Palace was no longer the regular imperial residence, though it was still used on big state occasions such as this. For much of the time the Emperors lived at the smaller palace of Blachernae, close to the inland city wall, less exposed to the elements and to the busy seaway of the Bosporus, less hemmed in by the noisy Hippodrome and the great big city itself. Manuel himself had just erected a new hall at Blachernae on whose walls were narrative pictures of the wars of Byzantium.[2]

In the thirteenth and fourteenth centuries, after the catastrophe of the Latin conquest, the Great Palace crumbled, and it was left to the Turkish conqueror Mehmet II to restore it.

[1] William of Tyre, *Historia Transmarina* 20.25.
[2] Benjamin of Tudela, *Itinerary.*

Around the palace he laid out a circle of large and beautiful gardens, burgeoning with various fine plants, bringing forth fruits in season, flowing with abundant streams, cold, clear, and good to drink, studded with beautiful groves and meadows, resounding and chattering with flocks of singing birds that were also good to eat, pasturing herds of animals both domesticated and wild.[1]

Mehmet was a notable patron of architects and of landscape gardeners. This quotation from the very last historian of medieval Byzantium makes the link between the old Great Palace and what we know now as Topkapı Saray, its direct successor. The park and gardens of Mehmet II, studded as they are with the buildings of Topkapı Saray, were a recreation of the gardens that had given pleasure to the first emperors of Constantinople.

Among the many Latin loanwords in Byzantine palace jargon was the term for a dining room, Latin *triclinium*, literally 'three-couch room'. It was so called because, in earlier Roman times, dining rooms had almost universally been laid out with three large couches, arranged on three sides of a square, giving room for about nine diners to recline – and in those times it was always correct to recline to eat. Although the typical arrangement of a dining room had long since changed, Palace custom at Constantinople retained the name *triklinon* for a dining room, and for several centuries retained the custom of reclining.[2] The *Okeanos* 'Ocean' dining hall at the palace of Blachernae was sometimes used for great entertainments; and there were three famous dining halls among the buildings of the old Great Palace. One was the Triclinium of *Magnaura*: 'this building was diligently completed by two emperors on whom the Cross bestowed the power to achieve good – Heraclius and his son Constantine', so we are told in a verse couplet once inscribed at its entrance and enshrined for ever in

---

[1] Critobulus of Imbros, *History of Mehmet the Conqueror* 5.9.3.
[2] Brehier 1949-1950 vol. 3 p. 52.

the great anthology of Greek epigrams.[1] A second was the *Trikonkhos*, where there was an ever-flowing fountain. In this hall the emperor dined in state when the wind blew: perhaps it was less draughty than the other two?[2]

The third dining hall was the House of the Nineteen Couches, as is here explained by Liutprand: 'There is a hall near the Hippodrome looking northwards, wonderfully lofty and beautiful, which is called *Decanneacubita*, the House of the Nineteen Couches. The reason for its name is obvious: *deca* is Greek for "ten", *ennea* for "nine", and *cubita* are couches with curved ends'.[3] We are assisted in picturing this banqueting hall by a Muslim hostage, Harun Ibn Yahya, who was detained at Constantinople in 911.

> If you lift the curtain and enter the Palace, you will see a vast courtyard, four hundred paces square, paved with green marble. Its walls are decorated with various mosaics and paintings ... To the left of the entrance is a room two hundred paces long and fifty wide. In this room are a wooden table, an ivory table, and, facing the door, a gold table. After the festivals, when the Emperor leaves the church, he enters this room and sits at the gold table.[4]

This was, as Harun suggests, the banqueting hall that was used on great festival days. On the ninth day of Christmas, for example, the Emperor would be entertained at dinner in the House of the Nineteen Couches with traditional 'Gothic' songs and dances, which are all carefully set out with accompanying translations in the *Book of Ceremonies* compiled under the direction of the Emperor Constantine VII Porphyrogennetus.[5]

[1] *Anthologia Palatina* 9.655. Translation after W. R. Paton.
[2] Constantine Porphyrogennetus, *Book of Ceremonies* 1.75 [vol. 2 pp. 105-109 Vogt].
[3] Liutprand, *Antapodosis* 6.8.
[4] Ahmad Ibn Rustih, *Kitab al-a'lah al-nafisa*.
[5] Constantine Porphyrogennetus, *Book of Ceremonies* 1.92 [vol. 2 pp. 182-6 Vogt].

In these various dining halls, and (on appropriate occasions) at dining halls of guilds and associations in the city, the emperors ate. They took *krama* or lunch, with friends or with the whole senate; they accepted the homage of a *deximon*, a dinner on return from a journey; they invited the great and good of government, church and city to a grand *kletorion* or reception.[1] For how many years were the prescriptions in the *Book of Ceremonies* followed faithfully, as their compiler, Constantine Porphyrogennetus, surely intended? We have no idea. For the great occasions of the Palace year (and there were many great occasions), every dignitary who deserves an invitation is listed. Every loyal chorus is specified. Exchanges of convivial politeness are laid down to be spoken in half-forgotten Latin, as they must already have been spoken for hundreds of years – and the Latin is spelt out in Greek letters so that the master of ceremonies can read it, even if he will not understand it.[2]

Christmas at the Palace

Byzantine festivity, as we have seen elsewhere in this book, was generous in scale. At the marriage of the emperor Maurice, in 582, 'the city celebrated for seven days and was garlanded with silverware: deep platters, basins, goblets, bowls, plates and baskets. Roman wealth was spent; a luxury of golden display, secrets of the Household, formed a theatre for all who wished to feast upon visions. Flutes, pipes and lyres sounded, at once carefree and seductive. Many conjurors, all day long, presented their different acts to eager audiences. The actors who abuse whomever they wish presented their satirical plays with rivalry as keen as if engaged in something serious. Chariot-races were performed. The

[1] Constantine Porphyrogennetus, *Book of Ceremonies* 1.1, 1.9, 1.23-24, 1.26, 1.36, 1.37, 1.70, 1.74 [vol. 1 pp. 13, 20, 61, 84-89, 96-97, 141, 148, vol. 2 pp. 86, 102-104 Vogt].
[2] Constantine Porphyrogennetus, *Book of Ceremonies* 1.76, 1.84 [vol. 2 pp. 110-111, 171-172 Vogt].

Emperor entertained men of rank in the Palace,' so the historian
Theophylact Simocatta (*History* 1.10.10–11)[1] summarizes the occasion.

There are no fewer than four descriptions, extending chronologi-
cally over three centuries, of how the Emperor and his guests dined in
the House of the Nineteen Couches on Christmas Day itself. The first
description is a theoretical one: it forms part of the *Book of Ceremonies*,
whose compiler was Liutprand's host on the occasion to be described
below. Here we are told of the procession in which the Emperor was
conducted from St Sophia to the Palace; we are told with what fulsome
acclaim the monarch was greeted on this special day by those who
attended him at dinner, and we find confirmation that his guests
would include people from beyond the Empire, including *Phrangoi* or
Franks like Liutprand, and *Agarenoi* or Arabs like Harun.[2] But we are
not told what went on in the dining hall.

The second description comes from Liutprand, on the first of his
visits, in 949, when Constantinople still had power to impress him. By
that time, so he tells us, the practice of reclining at dinner had become
exceptional even at the Palace.

> On the day when our Lord Jesus Christ was born in the flesh,
> nineteen covers are always laid here at the table. The emperor and
> his guests on this occasion do not sit at table, as they usually do,
> but recline on couches: and everything is served in vessels, not of
> silver, but of gold. After the solid food fruit is brought on in three
> golden bowls, which are too heavy for men to lift and come in on
> carriers covered over with purple cloth. Two of them are put on the
> table in the following way. Through openings in the ceiling hang
> three ropes covered with gilded leather and furnished with golden
> rings. These rings are attached to the handles projecting from the

---

[1] Translation after M. and M. Whitby.
[2] Constantine Porphyrogennetus, *Book of Ceremonies* pp. 741-759 Reiske, cf. 1.2 [vol. 1 pp. 32-34 Vogt].

bowls, and with four or five men helping from below, they are swung on to the table by means of a movable device in the ceiling and removed again in the same fashion.[1]

Slightly earlier than this is the narrative of the Syrian hostage Harun Ibn Yahya. The description is made to sound generalized: in fact it is of the one Christmas dinner at which Harun was present, in 911.

This is what happens at Christmas. He sends for the Muslim captives and they are seated at these tables. When the emperor is seated at his gold table, they bring him four gold dishes, each of which is brought on its own little chariot. One of these dishes, encrusted with pearls and rubies, they say belonged to Solomon son of David (peace be upon him); the second, similarly encrusted, to David (peace be upon him); the third to Alexander; and the fourth to Constantine. They are placed before the Emperor, and no one else may eat from them. They remain there while the Emperor is at table: when he rises, they are taken away. Then, for the Muslims, many hot and cold dishes are placed on the other tables, and the imperial herald announces: 'I swear on the Emperor's head that there is no pork at all in these dishes!' The dishes, on large silver and gold platters, are then served to the Emperor's guests.

Then they bring what is called an *organon*. It is a remarkable wooden object like an oil-press, and covered with solid leather. Sixty copper pipes are placed in it, so that they project above the leather, and where they are visible above the leather they are gilded. You can only see a small part of some of them, as they are of different lengths. On one side of this structure there is a hole in which they place a bellows like a blacksmith's. Three crosses are placed at the two extremities and in the middle of the *organon*. Two men come in to work the bellows, and the master stands and begins to press on the pipes, and each pipe, according to its tuning and the master's

[1] Liutprand, *Antapodosis* 6.8.

playing, sounds the praise of the Emperor. The guests are meanwhile seated at their tables, and twenty men enter with cymbals in their hands. The music continues while the guests continue their meal.[1]

Other excitements

An extensive section of the *Book of Ceremonies* is devoted to a calendar of festivals and grand dinners at the Palace, with the ritual and the guest list appropriate to each. The reader of this unique and very Byzantine compilation might be forgiven for concluding that dinner at the Palace was boring and predictable. That was not always true. Anna Comnena, who will have heard the story from her father Alexius I, is able to tell us all about the uncomfortable dinner that he and his brother Isaac enjoyed at the Palace, shortly before they risked their successful coup d'état in 1081. The reigning Emperor, Nicephorus III, had heard at that very moment that the city of Cyzicus, just across the Sea of Marmara, had fallen to the Turks. The brothers knew perfectly well that they were suspected of disloyalty but they did not know why the atmosphere at dinner was so charged or what the courtiers were muttering about. They were in terror of arrest or poisoning till one of the cooks, whom Isaac had wisely befriended, whispered the news. Hearing of this real disaster to the Empire they were, ironically, able to breathe a sigh of relief: they were not, after all, the focus of the Emperor's silent anger and were ready with sympathy and advice when he broached the subject.

Poison is never mentioned in the *Book of Ceremonies*. In the real world it was a serious concern. Simeon Seth's dietary manual suggests several reliable antidotes and prophylactics, the nicest perhaps being

---

[1] Ahmad Ibn Rustih, *Kitab al-a'lah al-nafisa*. The fourth description of Christmas feasting was written some time after 1261 in colloquial Greek; it appeared in *Gregorios o Palamas* (June 1933) pp. 240-247. For the grand dinner celebrating the feast of Epiphany see Constantine Porphyrogennetus, *Book of Ceremonies* 1.34-35 [esp. pp. 130, 135-6 Vogt].

'dried figs with walnuts and rue, taken before the main meal'. Anna Comnena tells us how at the palace her mother (the Empress Irene) was, as was proper for Byzantine ladies, modestly veiled and was very seldom heard to speak in public. On campaign, however, like it or not, she travelled with her husband and was always to be seen at his side. She was the only taster and guardian against poison that he could trust.[1] She also shows us that in 1095 a Crusader prince, Bohemond of Taranto, was wisely fearful of Byzantine poison and found his own way to deal with the threat.

Bohemond went off to the *Kosmidion*, where lodgings had been made ready for him and a rich table was laid full of food, including fish dishes of all kinds. Then the cooks brought in meat of animals and birds, uncooked.

'This seafood, as you see, has been prepared in our customary way,' they said, 'but in case that does not suit you we have here raw meat which can be cooked in whatever way you like.'

The emperor had instructed them to do and say exactly this ... The cunning Frank not only refused to taste any of the seafood: he pushed it away without even letting it touch his finger-tips. Saying nothing of his secret suspicions he shared it out among the others present with apparent generosity (in reality, as the reader will see, he was mixing them a cup of death, and so utterly despised those under him that he did not trouble to conceal his trick); meanwhile he told his own cooks to prepare the meat *à la Tarentine*.

On the next day he asked those who had eaten the fish dishes how they felt.

'Very well,' they replied: none of them was ill at all. In reply he let slip what he had kept secret till that moment:

'... I was afraid he might arrange to kill me by putting some deadly drug in the seafood.'[2]

[1] Simeon Seth p. 49; Anna Comnena, *Alexiad* 2.3, 12.3.
[2] Anna Comnena, *Alexiad* 10.11.3-4.

Such a banquet, generally without poison, delivered to the lodgings of an important guest with the Emperor's compliments, was no unusual honour. Bishop Liutprand of Cremona, kicking his heels unhappily in a city that had become hateful to him, tells us drily of a similar favour. 'The sacred emperor,' as he describes his benefactor with more than a hint of sarcasm, 'lessened my woes with a big gift,' and Liutprand's reader will not wait long to hear how big and how welcome this gift was. The Emperor had sent him 'one of his most delicate dishes, a fat kid of which he had himself partaken—proudly stuffed with garlic, onion, leeks, swimming in fish sauce'.[1] The Byantine dishes served to Liutprand were (he repeatedly complains) overloaded with garlic. This may well have been for the best of reasons. Byzantine dieticians were well aware of the health benefits of garlic, particularly for those with a 'hot constitution', and they had probably found sufficient reason to class Liutprand's constitution thus.

Having referred to the occasional excitements of dinner at the Palace, it would be fair to add that Byzantine diplomats, dining abroad during an embassy, sometimes encountered even greater excitement. A late sixth-century embassy to the Persian king Chosroes 'camped at Dinabadon, where Chosroes feasted the Roman and Persian leaders':

> When the dinner was already in progress, Bryzacius was led in chains into the middle, with his nose and ears mutilated. After the diners had made fun of him, Chosroes, to offer them a memorable dinner-time spectacle, signalled with his hand to his bodyguards (Persians do not speak while they are eating) to put the man to death. So they stabbed him to death. To follow this bloodshed, Chosroes gave his guests a further pleasure: after drenching them with perfume he wreathed them with garlands of flowers and told them to drink to Victory. And so his guests departed to their tents, describing

---

[1] Liutprand, *Embassy* 20.

everything that had happened to them at dinner. Bryzacius figured largely in their stories.[1]

Conclusion

The cuisine of the Byzantine Empire was a synthesis of what had gone before. There is the love of spices and exotic flavours so typical of Roman food. Beside this there is the emphasis on seafood and on local produce that emerges from the long tradition of classical Greek gastronomy. For Constantinople this means the produce of the Aegean, the southern Balkans, northwestern Anatolia and the Black Sea. But Byzantium was also unique, and even an unsympathetic observer can help us to grasp this uniqueness.

Becoming more elaborate as every day passes, our luxury now impels us to plaster our food with the aromatics of India. Nowadays the spice merchant seems to be working not for the physician but for the cook![2]

Unsympathetic Asterius certainly is: luxury offends him. His complaint seems strongly reminiscent of those made by the elder Pliny, author of the classical Latin *Natural History*, concerning the demand for spices in the first century AD. But in fact Asterius really has noticed something new. It had probably been true, in the Roman past, that except for a very few spendthrifts, and except for pepper, most of the spices that were imported from India at such enormous cost went into the medicine cabinet (or into divine worship and funeral rites). Gradually, however, the influence of the physicians was spreading. Both cooks and eaters took them more and more seriously. In one sense Asterius is wrong: the physician is still there in the background, setting the health agenda. In another sense he is right, because the

[1] Theophylact Simocatta, *History* 5.5.8-11. Translation after M. and M. Whitby.
[2] Asterius of Amasea, *Homilies* 1.5.3.

health aims are achieved, to a far greater extent than ever before, by adjusting the flavours and aromas – and thus by creating an astonishing and varied cuisine.

In truth, two influences had combined to produce the great range of powerful flavours that we can sense at the heart of this strange cuisine. One was the church calendar, with its numerous fast days on which both meat and fish were ruled out: the rich (including rich abbots and ecclesiastics) gave their cooks full rein to produce fast-day dishes as piquant and varied as could be conceived. We have seen what the *Prodromic Poems* have to tell us of this. The second influence was that of the physicians. By contrast with the earlier Greek dietary manuals, the Byzantine ones were written for non-specialists. Codification was complete: the effect of each ingredient could be stated, not only on the 'four humours' but on each section of the digestive system, beginning with the organs of taste. Thus spices and seasonings became ubiquitous, used both during the cooking process and at table to adjust the qualities and the attractions of each dish.

In reconstructing Byzantine cuisine we have luckily been able to look at non-Byzantine sources too. Medieval travellers to Constantinople did not always like the strange flavours they encountered. *Garos*, the venerable fish sauce, was an acquired taste. Most foreigners disapproved of retsina. But even strangers were seduced by the confectionery, the candied fruits and the sweet wines. Nearly all were enthralled by the pageantry of dinner at the Great palace. In its food and wine, as in its fabled wealth and its magic arts, the Byzantine Empire was a mystery and a legend in its own time. Something of the mystery remains.

Chapter 6

The Texts

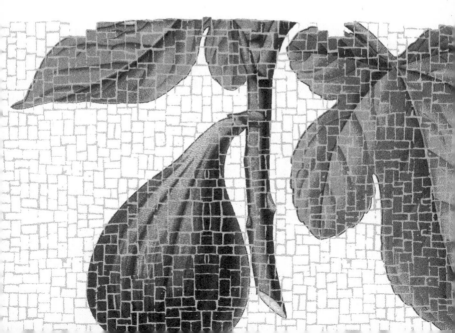

These short handbooks use the technical language of Greek humoral and dietary theory. This does not mean that they were intended for physicians alone (see page 48). The evidence suggests that numerous Byzantines – among those who had any choice of food at all – were more or less conscious of their 'constitution' and 'temperament' and gave attention to the good and bad effects of foods and drinks on these.

An important collection of texts of this kind was published (in Greek only) by Ideler in 1841–42. Some of these texts, including most of Ideler's collection, are now available on the *TLG* CD-ROM of classical Greek sources, published from the University of California at Irvine. In making the following translations I have occasionally consulted the original editions by Ideler and by Delatte (1939), but I have usually worked from the CD-ROM.

Text 1

The Eight Flavours

In this first short handbook, an unknown Greek nutritionist attempts to classify the flavours of food and to determine how flavour relates to dietary power. His work – totally at odds with modern Western dietary knowledge – is an essential starting point for understanding Byzantine views on how to choose foods, wines and aromas. He appeals constantly to the two elemental pairs, hot and cold, dry and moist. He takes for granted the four bodily humours, blood, phlegm, yellow bile, black bile: for more on these see chapter three.

In slightly differing forms this brief handbook is to be found included in the various manuscript compilations known to modern scholars as *Peri Trophon Dynameos* 'On the Power of Foods' and *De Cibis* 'On Foods'. The present translation is based on *Peri Trophon Dynameos*, pages 467–469 in Delatte's edition of that text, but incorporates (as indicated by footnotes below) selected variants from *De Cibis* section 1.[1]

[467] The nature and power of foods and drinks are known from their flavours. There are eight flavours: sweet, pungent, salty, sharp, oily, astringent, tasteless, melting.[2]

Sweet flavour is hot and moist. It is suited to those who have a well-balanced constitution, and increases the production of healthy blood. In the case of those with hot, dry, bilious constitutions it produces yellow bile. All juicy sweet fruits have less heat and dryness

[1] In the footnotes to this chapter the following abbreviations are used to identify various manuscript compilations. *DA*: *De Alimentis*. *DC*: *De Cibis*. *PTD*: *Peri Trophon Dynameos*. *PZT*: *Peri tes ek ton zoon trophes*.
[2] In *DC* the last two are given as 'acid, tasteless'.

than does sugar. In proportion with an increase in sweetness, in any food and drink, goes an increase in heat.

Pungent flavour has more heat and dryness than sweet flavour, and harms those whose constitutions are hot and dry. It lightens and dissolves phlegm, matures thick humours, and is helps those with cold and moist constitutions. [It produces thirst and appetite.][1]

Salty flavour is dry and [hot],[2] and creates thirst in in hot and dry constitutions. It cuts phlegm, and dissolves thick and unwholesome food residues in the stomach.

[468] The sharp flavour has a burning quality, as have pepper, pellitory, onions and garlic, all of which have great heat, and this harms hot and dry constitutions. Its exhalations produce headache and thin the blood. It helps those with cold and moist constitutions. It dissolves the moistness and thickness from the stomach and intestines, typical of cold and wet weather.

The oily flavour is moderately hot and moist. It is suited to those with a dry and hot temperament. It is unsuitable for those with a weak stomach, leading to loss of appetite and killing digestion. It is suited to dysenterics and to those with a dry temperament.

The astringent flavour, as of castor oil and the like, has a [dry][3] and cold temperament and is suited to those with a moist temperament. It is harmful to dry constitutions.[4] It is suited to persons the sinews of whose stomachs are porous from excessive moistness, and to those with bowel disorders.

Foods with moderately astringent flavour, such as quinces, pears, apples and the like, have moderate capability and aptitude to

[1] Added text from *DC*.
[2] The text reads 'moist', which is contradictory.
[3] Correction from *DC*.
[4] *DC* inserts at this point qualities attributed by *PTD* to the melting flavour (below): 'It strengthens the stomach, arouses its appetite, stops stomach pain, encourages stomach activity, and assuages thirst. A food with this quality is harmful to those with cold temperaments and constitutions: it weakens and harms their nerves. The acid flavour's natural dryness is suited to a cold and moist temperament. It is harmful to those with dry constitutions ...' The next sentence in the text is thus made to belong to the acid flavour.

encourage the activity of the stomach, bowels and liver and to encourage appetite for food. Taken before other food they inhibit the natural function; taken after other food they encourage it.

The tasteless flavour, as of white of egg, fleaseed and the like, is moist and cold and rapidly alters the constitution towards moistness. It is suited to those with a hot and dry temperament.

The melting flavour is cold and dry. It is suited to those with a rather hot temperament. It strengthens the stomach, arouses its appetite, stops stomach pain, encourages stomach activity [469] and assuages thirst. It is harmful to those with cold temperaments and constitutions: it weakens and harms their nerves.

Acid [flavour], through its natural dryness, cuts, breaks up and dissolves moistness.

Text 2

Categories of Foods

In the second handbook we get down to specifics. Here we are told the position of individual foodstuffs on the hot/cold and dry/wet axes, with additional information on their nutritional powers and their side-effects. Thus we begin to understand how to combine them to give an appropriate balance of nourishment to each individual.

This text is not to be found, at full length as translated here, in any single manuscript. It has been collected for this translation from related manuscript versions of varying fullness and coherence. This should not be seen as the reconstruction of a hypothetical, lost treatise, but as a gathering of knowledge that was collectively familiar to Byzantine dieticians. Nothing is added: every word translated below occurs in one or more of the manuscripts cited. Section [i] is based on *Peri Trophon Dynameos*, pp. 469–470, with selected variants from *De Cibis* 2 and with additions from *De Alimentis* 32–41. Sections [ii] and [iii] come from *Peri Trophon Dynameos* pp. 470–472, with selected variants from *De Cibis* 3–4. Section [iv] is based on *Peri Trophon Dynameos* pp. 472–474, with additions from *De Alimentis* 42–64. Section [v] is a translation of *De Alimentis* 65–75. Sections [vi] and [vii] are a translation of *Peri Trophon Dynameos* pp. 474–476. Section [viii] is based on *Peri Trophon Dynameos* pp. 476–478, with additions from *Peri tes ek ton zoon trophes*. Sections [ix] and [x] are translated from *Peri Trophon Dynameos* pp. 478–479. Section [xi] is translated from *Peri tes ek ton zoon trophes*. Within each section, square brackets and footnotes indicate passages taken from the secondary source texts.

[i] Food values of grains and legumes

Wheat has a high proportion of heat and is the best of all grains. It produces healthy, excellent blood.

Barley has a high proportion of coldness and its food value is less than that of wheat. It is not suited to those with a cold and moist temperament: it engenders excessive wind. It is suited to those with a rather hot constitution. Barley water (*ptisane*) is cold and moist. It helps in acute fevers and in diseases of the chest. It alleviates heat and thirst.

Rice is midway between heat and coldness and inhibits movement of the bowels; but if boiled with seasoning it becomes good for the bowels.

Broad beans have a high proportion of coldness, and cause gas and wind in the bowels and heaviness in the head; boiled with vinegar they inhibit movement of the bowels. [Eaten green, they add moistness to the constitution.][1]

Chickpeas have a high proportion of heat, and they too cause gas in the bowels; they bring on menstruation, increase the urine and encourage sexual intercourse. [Water from boiling chickpeas is good for those with kidney stones. If the chickpeas are roasted – it is the same with beans – they stop bowel movements and are more nutritious. When eaten fresh they add moisture to the constitution.

Lupins are indigestible and produce thick humours.

Fenugreek seed, steeped in water, sweetened, and sprouted, moves the bowels: this is the case whether the seed is eaten with fish sauce, or vinegar and fish sauce, or wine and fish sauce and olive oil. Eaten with fish sauce alone, it causes headache, but with wine and fish sauce and olive oil it does not. The water from cooking fenugreek, boiled and taken with honey, dislodges unhealthy humours in the stomach. It is good for the bowels.][2]

---

[1] Addition from *DA* 36.
[2] Addition from *DA* 37-39.

Lentils are cold and dry; they dry and cool the constitution and produce excess black bile. They also cause weak vision. Lupins are hot and dry. They are indigestible and bring on menstruation; but if sweetened in hot water they are a lighter food [and not so indigestible. The husk is astringent].[1]

Black-eyed peas are hot and moist in temperament. They produce wind in the bowels, move the bowels, bring on menstruation, increase the urine, cause nocturnal emission.[2] [Some people steep black-eyed peas, or *Lathyrus Ochrus* seeds, till they sprout and eat them as a starter, dipped in fish sauce: this is to move the bowels. The water from boiling black-eyed peas is nourishing when well boiled.

Grass peas are more nourishing than black-eyed peas or *Lathyrus Ochrus* seeds, but otherwise similar. They fill up those who eat them too quickly.][3]

Broomcorn millet is dry and not nutritious; it inhibits bowel movements.

Bread made from wheat is the best and [470] most nutritious of all foods. [Particularly if white, with a moderate use of yeast and salt, the dough kneaded midway between dryness and rawness, and with a little anise, fennel seed and mastic, it is very fine indeed. One with a hot constitution should include sesame in the dough. If wishing to add more moistness to the bread, knead in some almond oil.][4]

Frumenty, also called *amylon*, is cold and dry; it fills out the chest and neck. Made with ground almonds and sugar it relieves dysentery. [What peasants call *kourkoutin*, cracked wheat, is nourishing and produces phlegm if eaten to excess.][5]

---

[1] Additions from *DC* and from *DA* 35.
[2] The variants on this sentence in *DC* are typical of that text's tendency to euphemism: 'They produce wind in the bowels, promote nature, increase the urine, bring on menstruation, give bad dreams'.
[3] Addition from *DA* 40.
[4] The bracketed section has a faulty structure in *PTD*. It is translated from *DC*.
[5] Addition from *DA* 34.

[ii] On water drinking

Water protects the natural moistness of the constitution. It distributes the food to the whole body and to the veins. It is suitable for those with hot and dry temperaments, and is ideal in the hottest weather and in summer. Light, sweet water is the best of all waters, particularly if it has no bad smell. There are five kinds: spring water, well water, river water, rain water, lake water. Spring water that is pure and sweet is hot in winter, cold in summer, and is the best of all waters.

Salt water is extremely dry; likewise, water with an astringent flavour is drying and astringent. Hot water, if taken before food, dissolves phlegm and thins food residues. Washing in sweet water restores the bodily temperament. 'Vitriolic water'[1] dries up a sore, even if very moist, and alleviates thicknesses and moistnesses in the body.

[iii] On wine drinking

Wine made from ripened, fully sweet grapes is hot and wine made from unripe and not fully sweet grapes has less heat. White wine, too, is lower in heat. Red wine is thick and indigestible because of the excess of earthy substance in the black grape and because of its astringency. Golden, austere wine, midway between sweetness and astringency, is the hottest of all wines and the most nourishing: this type of wine is suitable for the old and for those with a cold temperament. Those with a hotter temperament are advised to drink light and white wine, while, for people who are exhausted, black, sweet and astringent wine is suitable because of their slow digestions. Young wine is more nutritious, and produces the full quantity of blood. Old wine is more rapidly digested, drier, and less nourishing than young.

[1] Water containing copper sulphate.

Wine heats the stomach, discharges the thinned product of digestion to the veins throughout the body, encourages digestion and thins food residues; it also rekindles natural heat and makes plenty of blood. Drinking wine to repletion, and continual drunkenness, harm certain parts of the body such as the liver, the brain and the nerves. They produce a tremor of the whole body and cause heavy and disgusting diseases: they cause heartburn, regurgitation, weakening of the eyes, general paralysis. Wine drunk in moderation restores the constitution and nourishes the body, in all age groups.

Wine made from raisins is excellent to drink. It has very great heat, and is suitable for those who eat a lot of meat.

Mead has more heat and dryness than any wine. It is suited to those with cold and moist temperaments and constitutions, and in cold weather and in cold climates. It is cleansing and purgative of thick and phlegmatic residues in the stomach. [472] It produces urine and encourages urination remarkably, and gives a good facial complexion. Some people mix in hot spices when making mead.

[iv] On fruits

[Figs and grapes are the best of all fruits, more nourishing than any others and less productive of bad humours so long as they are fully ripe. Grape pips should be removed before eating: they cannot be digested.][1]

Fresh figs have natural heat and moistness. The dried ones are extremely hot and dry: thus they produce a lot of blood and menstrual blood, move the bowels, produce gas, and harm the digestive system in those with a rather hot constitution. The harm is prevented if honey vinegar and fish sauce are taken after eating the dried figs. [When eaten with hyssop or pennyroyal they are very helpful in correcting a blocked or roughened digestive system. Those who eat them together with other foods are seriously harmed, but also

[1] Addition from DA 50.

effectively nourished, which is why in the ancient world they were given to athletes.][1] Figs also produce in the body digestive residues, lice and itches.

Grapes are hot and moist. As they increase in sweetness, so they increase in heat. White grapes have more heat than black: they nourish and thicken the body.

Dates have thickness and heat and are very nourishing. They produce headache and blockages of the digestive system; they produce a lot of seed and spermatic fluid.

Raisins produce good humours and are nourishing.

Sweet, ripe plums are lighter in moistness and coldness. Acid ones are colder, and also drier: they stop yellow bile and the overheating of the blood, they move the bowels, and assist in acute fevers. They are not suitable to the old or to those with moist constitutions.

Apricots have a moist and cold nature. They quickly decompose in the stomach and turn to decay, producing moistness, fevers and headache.

Cherries are cold and moist. They quench thirst and lessen yellow [473] bile and the heat of the constitution. They move the bowels. They often cause stomach ache and turn to black bile.

Peaches are moist and cold, and thus quench thirst. They suit those with a rather hot constitution. Because of their moistness they spoil the digestion of food and harm the sinews of the stomach. Their ill effects, as well as those of apricots and cherries, are prevented if one drinks austere wine or honey water, with ginger, after eating the fruit.

The zest of lemons is hot, the peel cold and indigestible, the flesh cold, watery and acid.

[Both medlars and sorbs are astringent and stop diarrhoea. Sorbs are the more astringent of the two, though with a more pleasant flavour.][2]

---

[1] Addition from *DA* 49.
[2] Addition from *DA* 55.

Sweet pomegranates are hot and moist, and are advisable in diseases of the thorax and lungs. Acid ones are cold and moist, soothing overheating in the body and quenching thirst.

Sweet apples have a moist and cold nature: they invigorate the liver and the heart. The acid ones quench thirst, encourage the digestion of food, alleviate yellow bile, and neutralize dangerous drugs of a hot nature.

Quinces are cold and dry. They invigorate the stomach and the liver, and help those with bowel disorders. Conserved with honey and spices they strengthen the digestion and the stomach and dissolve residues. [They are very astringent: similarly if their juice is boiled with honey to make a conserve. We are told the same of *strouthomela*.][1]

Pears are cold and moist. Acid ones tend towards coldness and dryness. If eaten after a meal they clean the food residues from the stomach. Eaten before the meal they stop the movement of the bowels, dry the excrement in the intestines and block its progress. Thus they invigorate the stomach and prepare it for food.

Sweet mulberries have a hot and moist nature and move the bowels. The sharp ones tend towards coldness and are suited to yellow bile.

Sweet melons predispose towards and produce 'cholera'.[2] They have a moist and cold nature: they quench thirst and cool the heat of the liver and stomach. They are unsuited to those with [474] cold constitutions. [They have a cleansing quality: they provoke urination, moisten the bowels and produce semen. When not fully ripe they act as emetics, especially if eaten in large quantity.

Watermelons are not as moist or as productive of bad humours as melons, and are not so diuretic or so effective as emetics. Although not as good to eat as other fruits, they are better to eat than melons.

[1] Addition from *DA* 53. '*Strouthomela*', literally 'sparrow-apples', refers to an ancient variety of quince. This variety (usually *strouthia*) is frequently mentioned in classical texts but was evidently no longer identifiable in Byzantine times.

[2] Meaning an excess of yellow bile.

Gherkins and cucumbers are also somewhat diuretic. If eaten to excess they eventually produce bad humours which cannot be converted to blood.

Olives give little nourishment, particularly the black ones. The green ones that are conserved as *kolymbades* are good to eat owing to their astringency and arouse the appetite. Those conserved in vinegar are especially suitable.][1]

Acorns are cold and dry; thus they open the bowels and the bladder.

Chestnuts are more nourishing than acorns, and produce intestinal wind. They are hot and moist.

Walnuts are hot and dry. They heat the body and cause headache. They assist those with cold constitutions and also combat dangerous drugs and venoms of a hot nature. [Walnuts are better to eat and more digestible than hazelnuts, and particularly if eaten with dried figs. Dried walnuts, steeped and shelled, are just as good as green ones.][2]

Almonds have moderate moistness and heat. Eaten with sugar they help in diseases of the chest and neck, the kidneys and bladder. [Bitter almonds have the power to cut through thick and sticky humours.

Jujubes have little nourishment. They are good for the liver.][3]

Pistachios are hot, tending towards dryness. They help with blockage of the liver, encourage urination and break up bladder and kidney stones.

Hazelnuts are not as hot as walnuts. They are good for those with a cold constitution and in combatting dangerous drugs.

Pine kernels heat the constitution. They encourage urination and help in cases of kidney and bladder disorders.

Sesame is hot and moist. It moves the bowels, kills the appetite for food and relaxes the stomach. It is good for dysenterics.

[1] Additions from *DA* 45-47, 57.
[2] Addition from *DA* 58.
[3] Addition from *DA* 59-60.

[Hemp seed is indigestible and not good to eat. It produces headache and bad humours. It is fairly heating.

Gourd provides a little moist and cold nourishment to the body which is good for the bowels. If cold, as when they cut and dry it and eat it dried in winter, it produces raw humours.

Capers break up phlegm in the digestive system and stop excretion, when eaten before other food, whether in honey vinegar or in oil and vinegar.][1]

Carobs are hot. They stop excretion and purge the intestines.

Manna has a moderate temperament, tending a little towards coldness: it stirs unhealthy blood and cools the heat of the stomach.

[v. On vegetables]

[65–71] Wild greens are extremely productive of bad humours. All vegetables produce blood in small quantity, and containing bad humours. Lettuce has these qualities less than other vegetables, and is least nourishing. Endive is second after lettuce; it is mucilaginous, and for this reason good for the bowels, when eaten with olive oil and fish sauce. It is moderately digestible. Beet is not good to eat in quantity, but it dislodges residues and so is good for the bowels. It is helpful in blockages of the liver and spleen, and particularly if eaten with vinegar or mustard. Celery is diuretic and better to eat than other vegetables. It is sometimes pleasant to eat it raw. Rocket is very heating. It produces semen and awakens the appetite for sex. It causes headache. Asparagus of all kinds is good to eat, diuretic, and not without nourishment.

[72–75] Grape-hyacinth bulbs are good to eat, particularly in vinegar, eaten with olive oil and fish sauce. Carrot is diuretic, but indigestible. Truffles are indistinct and watery in flavour. They are comparable to mushrooms. The nourishment they provide is phlegmatic and cold, and, in excess, productive of bad humours. Radishes,

---

[1] Addition from *DA* 43-44, 63.

along with their heat, are productive of thin humours. The bitter quality is uppermost in them, as also in leeks, garlic and Levant garlic.

[vi] On medicinal plants

Roses are cold and dry. They stop headaches caused by heat and they invigorate the stomach. They also help with overheating of the liver.

Violets are moist and cold. They stop headaches caused by yellow bile and they are soporific.

Myrtles are cold and dry. They invigorate the member when impotent and they stop movement of the bowels.

All kinds of basil are hot [475] and dry. They invigorate the heart and cure pains in the head caused by coldness.

Marjoram is hot. It helps with pain in the kidneys, encourages urination, stops pain in the bowels. A decoction of marjoram helps in dimness of the eyes.

Water-lilies are cold, moist and soporific. They stop heat headaches and help with all diseases caused by heat.

The 'white violets' called in Arabic *zambag-iasmin* [*Jasminum Sambac*] are hot. They stop pain in the head caused by coldness and invigorate the head. The oil made from them helps with cold and thick winds and is good for the kidneys.

Narcissus is cold, but with the power of jasmine. Its root, as a decoction, is a safe and easy emetic.

Calamint is hot and dry. It helps with pain in the kidneys and bowels. The scent of it stops cold headaches.

White lilies are hot and relaxing. The medicine made from them dissolves cold winds.

Wild chamomile is hot and relaxing. It dispels thick winds, just as white lily does.

[vii] On aromatics

Musk is hot and dry by nature. It is suited to those with a moist and cold temperament. It dissolves aching of the head caused by phlegm. It also helps with weakness of the heart, heartburn and dysuria. It is not good for those with a hot temperament.

Ambergris is hot by nature and invigorates the brain. It cheers the heart and the stomach.

Camphor is moist and cold. It helps with heat diseases of the head and body. In those who take too much of it [476] it causes sleeplessness. It cools the kidneys, reduces the seed and causes incurable diseases of the genital parts.

Sandalwood is cold and dry. It helps in heat diseases of the liver, invigorates the liver and cools any disproportionate heat in that organ.

Aloeswood is hot and dry. It helps in weakness of the head and stomach, and in excessive cold of the stomach, and in blockage of the liver and urinary system caused by coldness and moistness.

Saffron is cold and dry. It is bad for the stomach; it causes pain and heaviness in the head, and is soporific. It cheers the heart.

Cloves are hot and dry. They strengthen the stomach and the heart.

Nutmeg is hot and dry: it shares the dietary effects of cloves.

Attar of roses is cold and moist. It stops pain in the head caused by heat and by excessive drinking, invigorates the heart and helps with dysuria.

[viii] On various kinds of meat

Meat is more nourishing than any other food and makes the body healthy. Those who eat meat regularly and drink wine regularly should therefore be bled. The meats of different animals vary in their effects.

Beef is cold and dry. Veal is moderately hot and moist. Goat is cold and dry: meat of females is better than that of males, while kid is moderately cold and moist. Mutton is hot and moist by nature: one-year-old animals are better, and castrated males the best of these; lamb is particularly moist. Pork is high in moistness and relatively low in heat: this meat produces plenty of moisture in the body and a good deal of phlegm, but its moisture is neutralized if roasted and eaten with pepper or mustard.

[477] Wild goat is indigestible and produces black bile. Deer is hot by nature, light, and produces black bile: meat with fat is better. Gazelle is hot and dry, indigestible and not nourishing. Hare is cold and dry by nature, and produces black bile. Bear is cold, not nourishing, indigestible: it causes tremors and weakness in the sinews. Buffalo is cold, indigestible, heavy, not nourishing, and altogether unhealthy: those who eat it frequently develop leprosy, elephantiasis, diseases of black bile and other disgusting illnesses.

That of the domestic hen is the best and the lightest of all meats. It produces pure, healthy blood. Chicken is particularly light and digestible, and is suited to those recovering from illness. The meat of older birds is dry by nature. Chicken soup cures coldness in the intestines.

Duck has more of the heat and thickness of buffalo meat and produces a great deal of excrement. Crane is particularly indigestible and thick by nature, and produces good blood. Pigeon is hot and dry by nature: the meat of young pigeons is hot, moist and indigestible. The meat of peafowl tends towards coldness: it is light and quickly digested. The meat of small birds is hot and moist: it helps those with a cold temperament.

The heads of all animals are thicker and heavier than other parts of the body and particularly nourishing. Brain creates heaviness in the stomach and tends to be emetic: it should be eaten with pepper or mustard. [Bone marrow is sweeter and pleasanter to eat than brain, but it too may be nauseous and emetic. If well cooked it is nourishing.][1] Udders are cold, slow in digestion and very nourishing, suiting those with a hot stomach. [478] Liver is hot, slow in digestion and very nourishing. [Spleen] produces melancholic and unhealthy blood. [Lung is spongy and easily digested, but not

[1] Addition from *PZT*.

nourishing and productive of bad humours. Heart is coarse and indigestible, but, if well cooked, nourishing and not productive of bad humours.] Intestines [also womb and tripe] are cold, indigestible and produce phlegmatic blood.

Muscle meat produces blood with little heat: red meat, with no fat, produces light, healthy blood; meat with fat produces moist blood.

The extremities of animals are light, quickly digested, and produce thin blood. [Pigs' trotters are the healthiest, followed by snouts, followed by ears. Tongue is spongy and with little blood. Testicles produce bad humours.][1]

[ix] On eggs

Those of domestic hens are the best of all eggs; those of partridges are just as good. All those of ducks and peahens are heavy and indigestible. Those of small birds are hot and lacking in nourishment.

Yolk or yellow of egg is moderately hot. The white is cold and indigestible; it helps in roughness of the chest and lungs and is strengthening. Taken with vinegar it stops the bowels.

[x] On milk

Milk is cold and moist, so it thickens the body, and helps in cases of consumption, cough when there is no fever, and burning of the urine. It does not help those with fever or headache or intestinal obstruction. Fresh milk and curds give moisture to the intestines; they help with pain in the head and heat of the stomach. Whey has the power of breaking up obstructions, so it is taken by those who need a medicine to purge the digestive system.

Butter is moist and midway between hot and cold. It is suited to those with a rather hot temperament. It alleviates roughness of

[1] All bracketed additions in this section are from *PZT*.

the chest and [479] helps with pain in the kidneys and burning of the bladder. Young cheese without salt is nourishing and good to eat; it is easy to digest, builds up the flesh, is relatively soothing to the bowels. Other cheeses are all bad, except those made from buttermilk.

[xi] On fish

Grey mullet is rather unhealthy in that it customarily feeds on mud; fish from the deep sea would be better; those from lakes even worse, but fish that come from rivers are better again, especially if swift-flowing.

Oily fish are not so easy to digest. They are poor eating and produce bad humours.

Bass produces rather light blood, as do other fish. Apart from this it is not a bad food.

Red mullet has coarse, friable flesh and for this reason gives more nourishment than other fish, when well cooked. Good are the red mullets that feed in clear water, where there is no weed.

Inshore fish offer healthy and easily digested nourishment. Other fish produce poor blood; these produce well-balanced, good blood.

The goby is one of the best. Those of sandy shores and rocky headlands are pleasant to the taste; they are easy to digest, to assimilate and to convert to good humours. Those of lakes and of river mouths, or lagoons, are unhealthy, especially if crabs live there. Similarly, all fish from such locations are bad.

Coarse-fleshed fish are indigestible, not only in the stomach but also when the food reaches the veins and other parts. Of soft-fleshed fish, the heaviest are the weever, piper, rascasse, grouper and large red mullet.

Common to all shellfish is that there is a salty humour in the flesh, and this provokes bowel movement. Some have more of it, some less. Oysters have softer flesh than the rest; all the others are less digestible, and some of them coarse-fleshed. They are best given to those who are wasting nourishment owing to bad humours in the stomach, whether originating there or deriving from the liver. From shellfish comes a great deal of the so-called raw humour. When soft-fleshed shellfish are boiled, much of the salty humour is taken off; the flesh then becomes difficult to excrete and constipating, but drinking the cooking liquor provokes bowel movement. They include oysters, mussels, winkles, cockles and scallops.

Crustaceans are also difficult to digest, but nourishing. When boiled – like oysters – they are constipating, and resemble the coarser-fleshed of shellfish. They include lobsters, crabs [*karkinoi, pagouroi*] including river and sea crabs, crayfish and all other such creatures with a light shell.

Soft-bodied seafood is coarse-fleshed and indigestible, but very nourishing when digested. These foods, too, produce a great deal of raw humour. They include octopuses, squid, cuttlefish, curled octopuses and the like.

Cartilaginous fish have sweet, soft flesh, which is good for the bowels, digestible and moderately nourishing. Such are electric rays and sting-rays. Skates, rays and monkfish are less digestible, but more nourishing, than electric rays and sting-rays.

There are no other fish in regular use among us except *yska* [catfish?], tuna. These are all productive of bad humours and excrement. They are to be eaten pickled or salted.

Text 3

Humoral and Dietary Qualities of Foods

The purpose of the third handbook in this collection is to ease the task of the physician or the self-prescriber by indexing foods according to their dietary properties.

This treatise appears, in similar form, in two manuscript compilations. The translation of the sections here numbered [i] to [xxv] is based on *De Cibis* 5–25.[1] This in general gives the fullest and most coherent text, but it is incomplete at certain points; therefore selected variants and additions are included, as indicated by footnotes, from *De Alimentis* 1–24. Sections here numbered [xxvi] to [xxxi] are a translation of *De Alimentis* 25–31.[2]

[i] Foods that produce good humours

[5] Of all foods the one that is most productive of good humours is best quality milk, particularly from healthy animals, and if drunk immediately after milking. It should be taken before any food or drink, and nothing else should be eaten until it has been digested and passed through. If even a little of anything else is mixed with it, it goes to decay and so does the milk. A good way is to drink it early in the morning, freshly milked, to eat nothing with it, and to walk quietly about. Initially it moves the bowels, but then gives nourishment; it is not itself excreted but settles the digestion.

To a less degree than milk, hens' eggs are also productive of good

---

[1] *De Cibis* 1-4 is a curtailed version of the two preceding texts.
[2] *De Alimentis* 32-75 is a version of text 2 'Categories of Foods'.

humours, whether lightly boiled or simply drunk raw; goose eggs are not so good.

The meats that are most productive of good humours are those of the domestic hen and of the pheasant, and the testicles of cocks. Similarly [the meat of] other birds, I mean partridge, francolin, pigeon, thrush, blackbird, and small birds including wrens. Coarser, less digestible and more sinewy than these is the meat of the peafowl and turtle dove; even coarser that of the wood pigeon, duck and crane; more productive of excrement that of geese, swans and bustards. Of all such, meat that is more productive of good humours comes from birds that are not yet full grown [and fattened;][1] that of both old and very young birds is harmful. The very best is of domestic hens and pigeons that feed in the wild, and in general of free range birds that are fed on relatively dry foods and breathe good fresh air: one should prefer the meat of these, particularly if with tender flesh, from well-kept animals that have been fed to repletion, and one should eat sparingly of others. Kid is the best meat of any of the caprines: it is more harmful if cooked with the skin.

Deep sea and inshore fish, including grey mullet (the best of all of these) and bass; also cartilaginous fish, and gobies, and dogfish, and the rest, except that large red mullet are rather coarse. Moderately productive of both good and bad humours are guitar-fish, sole, plaice. Of all fish the very best are those with a certain stickiness of texture and with a certain unpleasantness in their taste.

Among quadrupeds the meat of well-fattened young pigs, such as are between one and two years old, with the udders and the trotters; less good, the snout and the ears. But the meat of wild animals is more productive of good humours than that of domestic ones.

Well-made white bread; emmer gruel, or the gruel of roughly pounded wheat; hulled barley well boiled. Among legumes, beans. Among fruits, ripe figs and ripe grapes briefly hung. Dried figs, if rapidly dried, produce good humours; if slowly dried, they produce

[1] Addition from *DA*.

bad humours in the stomach. They are excellent if eaten with walnuts, but those who eat fresh or dried figs with other foods are rather harmed. Chestnuts do not produce bad humours, but they are indigestible; once baked, however, they are digestible. Pistachios and almonds may be taken from time to time.

Among vegetables, lettuce, and to a lesser degree endives, [mallow, boiled gourd if not overcooked.]¹

Among wines, those that have a good bouquet and are easy to drink.

[ii] Foods that are digestible

[6] Bread that has been well kneaded and well baked, with proper amounts of salt, flour and water.

[All inshore fish, goby, ray, sting-ray.]

The meat of birds such as partridge and francolin [is not very digestible: nor that of] pigeon, capon, chicken and pheasant. The wings of geese are digestible [and also those of chickens]. Most digestible are [the wings of] plump young birds, scrawny and old ones least so. The livers of geese fattened on cream; the testicles of birds similarly fattened.

Calves are better than older cattle, kids are better than older goats; in both cases, best of all if they have grazed in dry places.

[Soft-boiled eggs; raw eggs.]

Among vegetables [lettuce, endive,] mallow and boiled gourd [if not overcooked. Walnuts are more digestible than] hazelnuts.

Sweet wines, drunk before the meal, are better than austere ones.

But all foods that are pleasant to eat are more digestible than those that are unpleasant.

[iii] Foods that are indigestible

[7] Goat meat, beef, venison: the worst of these is the meat of billy-

¹ Addition from *DA*; similarly, as indicated by square brakets, in sections ii to vii.

goats, likewise that of rams and of bulls. All meat of older animals is indigestible, including offal: trotters, tripe, womb, heart, liver, ears, kidneys, all vital organs, brain, tail, and (when not castrated) testicles.

Geese (except the wings), wood pigeons, thrushes, blackbirds and all meat of small birds that is coarse; and more especially turtle-dove, duck; and most of all peafowl and bustard; and the intestines of all birds.

Snails.

Yoghourt; mature cheese.

Shellfish, lobsters, crabs [*pagouria, karkinoi*], crayfish, shrimps, octopuses, cuttlefish, curled octopus, squid, skate, ray, monkfish, weever, gobies, rascasse, red mullet, grouper, pagres.

Hard-boiled eggs, oeufs en cocotte, fried eggs.

Boiled wheat, broad beans, *Lathyrus Ochrus*, the pods and the seeds of black-eyed pea, grass pea, chickpea, rice, lupin, [broomcorn millet, lentils, sesame, chestnuts.

Apples, pears, figs,] unripe sorbs, acid grapes, dates of any kind, carobs, lemons (except the peel), undercooked turnip, undercooked grape-hyacinth bulbs, carrot and all vegetable roots, and leaf vegetables too with the exception of lettuce and endive.

Thick and young wines are indigestible; water even more so.

[iv] Foods that are good to eat and strengthening

[8] Relatively astringent dates, [apples,] quinces, [green] olives, *kolymbades*, and even more so olives preserved in vinegar, astringent raisins, bunches of grapes put up in jars, walnuts with figs.

[Artichoke,] mustard, radish, boiled turnips [thoroughly cooked], cress, young shoots of butcher's broom, grape-hyacinth bulbs [which also serve as appetizer, capers].

Lemon peel taken as digestive.

Astringent wine.

Absinthe and aloes.

[v] Foods that are difficult to eat

[9] Beet, which causes stomach ache when too much is eaten.

Undercooked turnip is difficult to eat, but if well cooked it is easy to eat.

Blite, orach unless eaten with vinegar, [fish sauce] and olive oil, [fenugreek,] sesame.

Cold milk gives acute pain to those whose bowels are in a cold condition; those in a hot condition it turns to smoke in the stomach.[1] It is harmful to those with fever.

Melons, if not fully ripe, fill up those who are choleric. Rather than breaking down, however, they are useful as an emetic, if eaten in quantity, as long as one of the foods that produce good humours is not eaten with them.

Brain is difficult to eat, and has an emetic effect, as does bone marrow. Black, astringent wine has a pleasant acidity and has an emetic effect, [whether it is young or mature.]

[vi] Foods that break up residues and clear the digestion

[10] Barley, fenugreek, watermelon, sweet raisins, broad beans, chickpeas (especially black gram), capers (especially if eaten as a starter with honey vinegar or oil and vinegar), beet liquor and beet itself if eaten with mustard or vinegar, sorrel, grape-hyacinth bulbs, onions, garlic, [leeks, Levant garlic]. These, boiled two or three times, lose their sharpness.

Cream also thins the residues.

Figs break up the residues: hence, when eaten by those with kidney diseases, they often produce sandy urine.

Dried figs, almonds, pistachios, cabbage, honey, honey vinegar.

Light wines: if the humours are cold, old and watery wines constipate.

If there is a blockage, take fish sauce with water, and fine, light,

[1] Cf. Galen 6.691, 6.706, 8.37; Oribasius 10.19.4.

white wines, and cooked onion and garlic. As flavourings, and especially in winter, use pepper, oregano, savory, pennyroyal and mustard. Rocket, celery, parsley, radish, mint, five-spice mixture, dill, cumin, anise, carrot: all these flavourings will go with the foods mentioned.[1]

[vii] Foods that block the digestion

[11] Milk that has only a little cream is not healthy if one takes too much of it, since it harms the kidneys and produces kidney stones. Fresh and dried figs, taken after the meal, block the liver; but, mixed with oregano, hyssop or pepper and eaten before the meal, they are particularly healthy. Honey water is unsuitable to those with weak digestions. Fresh dates, and anything made with pasta or durum wheat, block the digestion, enlarge the spleen and also cause kidney stones. Wheat meal with milk, and sweet types of wine, block the digestion and build up intestinal wind.

[viii] Foods that move the bowels

[12] The first water from boiling lentils, [also from cabbage,] especially if flavoured with olive oil or fish sauce. Cooking liquor from hard-shelled seafood, such as lobsters, crabs and the like: if, after cooking them, you flavour the liquid with olive oil or fish sauce, as explained, or with pepper, it will loosen the bowels. Similarly the cooking liquor of sea urchins, shellfish and snails, also of old domestic fowls. Wholemeal loaves, because they contain a lot of bran. Water from cooking fenugreek, boiled with not too much honey, is useful; it purges all who have unhealthy humours in their digestive tract. Only a little honey is wanted in the boiling, because of its pungency. *Kolymbades* olives with fish sauce, taken before the main course. Cream with a little of the best honey. If you want to make the suggested liquids more strongly purgative, add plenty of

[1] Another version of this paragraph in *DA* 1. The text as translated draws on both versions.

salt. The meat of very young animals purges better than that of old ones. Beet, sorrel, garden mercury; also the liquor from boiling these, with salt. Young cheese with honey. Orach, blite, gourd, melons, figs, juicy sweet grapes, mulberries, any of these taken without any addition and eaten before food will purge the bowels. Eaten afterwards they will also eliminate any bad humours found in the system. The gourd does likewise, as do green walnuts, and also dry walnuts that have been steeped in water and shelled. Fresh plums, and dried plums steeped in honey water, whether they are eaten by themselves or taken together with the syrup, purge effectively. Drinking sweet wine [on an empty stomach] and not immediately taking a meal, but allowing it to work for a while. Fresh cherries, apricots, fresh peaches and all fresh juicy fruits, because they prepare the system for purging, but also because the humoral quality of these foods is in the middle of the range and they have no bitterness or alkalinity.

[ix] Foods that settle the digestive system

[13] Astringent dates, astringent raisins, unripe mulberries, blackberries, the fruit of the azarole; more so, myrtle berries, sloes. Astringent apples, whereas the sweet ones, and those that are rather sweet than sharp, move the bowels: the same is said of pomegranates and of pears. Milk, once it has been boiled and the cream taken off. Lobsters, crabs [*pagouria, karkinoi*], crayfish, if boiled and the liquid drained off, get the digestion under control; similarly with oysters, mussels and the like. Lentils and cabbage, boiled twice, then (in both cases) returned to the second water and boiled vigorously till they soften; the cooking water from these also settles. Rice, broomcorn millet, [foxtail millet.][1] Fried eggs. Astringent wine, white wine.

[x] Foods that produce bad humours

[14] Bad humours are not all of one kind: some foods are more phlegmatic, some more bilious, some more atrabilious. All such

[1] Addition from *DA*.

foods are best avoided, even if they are good to eat, in case over time bad humours are stored in the veins, and from this small beginning putrefaction may cause dangerous fevers. The following produce bad humours.

The meat of sheep and goats, equally if it has a sharp taste; that of billy-goats and rams is worst, also of bulls, while that of castrated animals is the finest. Old animals are much worse than young ones. Hare meat produces very thick blood. The meat of oxen and sheep is better for producing good humours. The meat of deer fawns produces bad humours. So do the testicles of fully grown animals, except cocks; so does brain of all animals, and spinal marrow, and spleen. So does liver, a little more than these; and worst are the vital organs of animals.

Productive of bad humours are fried eggs, mature cheeses, grape-hyacinth bulbs, mushrooms, fenugreek, lentils, einkorn, oats; [emmer, which is between wheat, einkorn and oats;][1] foxtail millet, broomcorn millet; no such foods produce good humours.

Among fish, gobies, dogfish, rascasses, groupers, red mullets that feed on shrimps, all large fish.

All fruits: fresh figs are a little more productive of bad humours than the rest; so are grapes. Dried figs in excess. Unripe pears.

Artichokes, particularly when they become coarse, cucumbers, melons. Gourds are the best of these if they are fully ripe.

No greens produce good humours. Midway between good and bad are lettuce and endive; after these mallow, orach, purslane, blite, sorrel. Vegetable roots, if sharp-flavoured, produce bad humours: onions, leeks, garlic, cabbage stalk, carrots, turnips, grape-hyacinth bulbs unless well boiled. Onions, leeks, garlic and Levant garlic lose their bad humours if boiled twice. Wild greens are productive of bad humours in the extreme, including dandelion, sow-thistle, chicory and the like.

Thick wines, austere and with poor aroma.

---

[1] Addition from *DA*.

[xi] Foods that produce phlegm

[15] Fibrous parts of animals, such as the feet and the skin, brain, lungs, spinal marrow. Lamb. Mushrooms, meat of hard-shelled seafood and of cephalopods. Unripe apples.

[xii] Foods that produce black bile

[16] Meat of oxen and of goats, and in particular the meat of bulls and of billy-goats, also hares, [wild boar.] Salt meat of quadrupeds. Among seafood, tuna; winkles. Among vegetables, cabbage and the young shoots of trees prepared in brine or vinegar and brine. Lentils are more productive of black bile than any other legume. Also wheat bran and that of einkorn, broomcorn millet, [foxtail millet,][1] vetch. Thick and black wines.

[xiii] Foods that produce bile

[17] Carobs, artichokes, honey (but they reduce bile in hot constitutions). Sweet wines.

[xiv] Foods that produce thin humours

[18] Durum wheat bread and durum wheat itself and trakhanas. Animal offal, the bones, ears, snouts, neck; fresh pork and caprine meat. Equally, grape-hyacinth bulbs, [cucumbers,] semi-dried dates.

[xv. Foods that produce raw humours][2]

Fresh dates. Turnips. The flesh of hard-shelled seafood after long boiling, discarding the cooking liquor; also soft-bodied seafood such as octopuses, cuttlefish, squid, curled octopus; also larger fish including tuna, scad, swordfish. Animal offal: intestines, tripe,

---

[1] Additions from *DA*; similarly, as indicated by square brackets, in sections xiv to xxiv.
[2] In *DC* at this point some headings are missing and some appear to be misplaced. 19 is headed 'Foods that produce raw humours'. 20 is headed 'Foods that produce clammy humours'. The headings of sections [xv] to [xviii] in the translation are taken from *DA*.

womb. Yoghourt, [young cheeses, lupins, grapes: when they control the digestion] these produce cold humours also.

[xvi. Foods that are not windy]

Cumin, seed and root of lovage, linseed, hemp seed, roasted broad beans, grape-hyacinth bulbs, boiled, in olive oil and fish sauce and eaten with vinegar. Honey if skimmed. Honey vinegar, in order also to open the lungs. Barley bread.

[xvii. Foods that are windy]

[19] Chickpeas, lupins, black-eyed peas, *Lathyrus Ochrus*, broomcorn millet, broad beans, fresh dates. Milk, especially cold. Grape-hyacinth bulbs if undercooked. Honey if boiled. Wines that are both sweet and austere. Figs, both fresh ripe and dried.

[xviii. Foods that produce thick humours]

[20] Bread baked in the clay oven, must-cakes, pasta, cakes. Black-eyed pea pods, lupins, [roasted broad beans, sesame.] Shark-like fish, cuttlefish, octopuses, oysters, mussels, scallops, fan-mussels, horn-shells, clams, razor-shells, eels, winkles. Venison, caprine meat, beef, hare, pork. Liver, kidneys, testicles, brain, [spinal marrow,] udder, tongue. Fully boiled milk, cheeses of all kinds, yoghourt, hard-boiled eggs; more so, oeufs en cocotte cooked till they are hard; still more so, fried eggs. Chestnuts, acorns, grape-hyacinth bulbs, turnips, truffles. Arbutus fruits,[1] slightly unripe figs, the flesh of lemons, gherkins, melons, ripe apples. Sweet wines; more so, fresh must and concentrated must.

---

[1] Instead of *koumara* 'arbutus fruits' *DA* has *koneion* 'hemlock'. This is surely an error, because poisons do not otherwise occur in these texts. The scribe was perhaps not familiar with the word *koumara*. For the following item *DC* has 'rather ripe figs'. At the end of the sentence, in place of 'melons, ripe apples' *DA* has 'cucumbers, apples not yet ripe'.

[xix] Foods that are especially nourishing

[21] Pork. Beef. Brain, testicles, heart, spinal marrow and other marrow. Chicken wings, and the wings of geese and other birds. The coarser of hard-shelled seafood, including horn-shells, winkles, lobsters, crabs [*pagouria*], shrimps, [crayfish,] octopuses, cuttlefish, squid and the like. Electric ray, sting-ray, skates and rays, monkfish, red mullet. Durum wheat bread and white flour bread, boiled wheat, durum wheat, broad beans, chickpeas, black-eyed peas, *Lathyrus Ochrus*, fenugreek, [lablab beans,] grape-hyacinth bulbs twice boiled. Skimmed honey; well-boiled honey water. Lupins, chestnuts, lentils. Sweet dates, sweet and 'oily' raisins. Acorns. Turnips. Thick wines, rosé wines: more than these, black, sweet and thick wines; and astringent wines.

[xx] Foods that are least nourishing

[22] The extremities of animals; the womb, intestine, tripe, tail, ears; the fat. In general all kinds of birds are less nourishing than quadrupeds, and all kinds of old animals by comparison with those that are still growing. Fish as food produces very light blood. Among hard-shelled seafood, those with soft flesh, such as oysters. Barley bread, bran bread, wholemeal bread, [but also 'washed' bread, frumenty;] oats, broomcorn millet, foxtail millet, rice, fresh broad beans. Mulberries, almonds, pistachios, cornels, plums, peaches, aubergines, apricots, sloes, [black olives, hazelnuts and especially filberts, walnuts, jujubes.] Capers, beet, sorrel, dock, purslane, radish, turnip, mustard, cress, asparagus [of all kinds], carrot. Onion, garlic, leek and Levant garlic, raw, provide absolutely no nourishment, but a very little if boiled two or three times. Pomegranates, pears, gourds. Raisins if astringent and not 'oily'. Figs are more nourishing, but they make the flesh spongy and porous, as do grapes; grapes are less nourishing than figs.

[xxii] Foods that produce excrement

[23] Wood pigeons; geese, except the wings. All vital organs including liver, spleen, [kidney,] tripe, womb, intestine, spinal marrow, brain. Birds that feed in lakes. Chickpeas, fresh broad beans. Piglets; mutton and the meat of all animals pastured in wild country. River and lake fish, fish that feed on mud, shark-like sea creatures.

[xxiii] Slimming foods

[24] Garlic, onions, leek, cress, mustard, pepper, oregano, mint, hyssop, pennyroyal, Cretan thyme, Roman hyssop served fresh, rocket, celery, parsley, radish, cabbage, beet, golden thistle, fennel, coriander, rue, dill, cumin, capers, anise, carrot seed. Barley. Inshore fish. Birds that feed on dry land, the smaller birds and mountain birds: starlings, thrushes, blackbirds, partridges, wrens; small birds caught in vineyards, pigeons fed in their towers. Among deep sea fish, sting-rays and [electric rays have the same effect, also sole, brill; larger animals and birds, to be eaten one day after slaughtering; salt meats if tender.][1] The more succulent and juicy of fruits, dried figs with walnuts, pistachios, slightly bitter almonds. Olives are moderately slimming. White and light wines. Cream is helpful to slimming and to a light diet, and honey vinegar is especially so.

[xxiv] Heating foods

[25] Boiled wheat and bread made from wheat, including leavened bread. Fenugreek. Sweet dates, sweet apples, sesame, hemp seed, sweet grapes. Celery, rocket, radish, turnip, mustard, cress, carrot. Garlic, [onion, leek, Levant garlic. Mature cheese.] Sweet wines; yellow wines and old wines are even more heating.

---

[1] This sentence is fuller and apparently more coherent in *DA* and is translated from there.

[xxv] Cooling foods

[25] Barley, however cooked; broomcorn millet. Truffles, well-cooked gourd, melons, watermelons, gherkins, cucumbers. Plums, sycomore figs, acid grapes, astringent raisins, astringent apples, acid pomegranates. Lettuce, endives, purslane, myrtle berries, water, watery wine. White, austere, thick and new wines are noticeably cooling, as is vinegar. Midway between heating and cooling are 'washed' loaves, frumenty, wine-flavoured grapes.

[xxvi] Foods that dry

[26] Lentils. Cabbage, which for this reason also clouds the eyes, unless the eyes as a whole are particularly moist; cabbage stalk is not as drying as the leaf. In the case of other vegetables the stalk is drier than the rest. Radishes, turnips, mustard, linseed. Bitter vetch, twice boiled and thoroughly sweetened in water, becomes a drying food.

White foods are better, and what is baked and fried; also foods that are dressed with wine and fish sauce are drier than those that are not; also those seasoned with seeds or flavoured with five-spice mixture, caraway, pennyroyal and the like.

[xxvii] Foods that moisten

[27] Boiled barley, gourd, melons, watermelons, gherkins and cucumbers, green walnuts, plums, sycomore figs, mulberries, lettuce, endives, purslane, mallow, blite. Orach is moistening, as is lettuce seed and the seeds from a poppy head, fresh broad bean and chickpea, water.

[xxviii] Foods that are easily broken down

[28] Peaches, aubergines, apricots and all fruits if they are not too quickly expelled: hence they should be eaten before other foods,

when they will be quickly assimilated and lead the way for other food. If eaten afterwards they are themselves wasted and they waste other food along with themselves.

[xxix] Foods that are slow to break down

[29] Winkles, horn-shells, lobsters, crayfish, crabs [*pagouroi*], shrimps, fan-mussels: these are recommended to those who fail to absorb their food through excess of bad humours. Boil two or three times in purest water, replacing with new water when the first becomes briny.

[xxx] Foods that are slow to excrete

[30] Anything made with pasta and durum wheat flour is slow to excrete. Roasted broad beans, white bread, lentil without the shell. Brain, spinal marrow, liver, foie gras, heart. Oeufs en cocotte, hard-boiled eggs, and even more so fried eggs. Lupins, black-eyed peas, sesame, acorns. Underripe apples and pears, carobs. Sweet wine and particularly astringent wine, and water.

[xxxi] Foods that hurt the head

[31] Mulberries, blackberries, juniper berries, hemp seed, dates. Rocket, fenugreek, linseed. Yellow and austere wine. All aromatic wines affect the head and the nerves, while watery wine affects neither. Milk. Plums. Saffron. Walnuts. New wine. Chestnuts. Leeks, onions, garlic. Tarragon. *Phoukas*.[1]

[1] Vinegar-and-water, and perhaps beer: see pp. 84-5 and glossary s.v. *phouska*.

Text 4

A Dietary Calendar

The daily regimen involves not only the choice of foods and drinks but also their quantity and the frequency of meals: it involves exercise, sexual activity, baths, massage, the use and selection of soaps and lotions and other medicaments. All of these will vary depending on the climate and the seasons. It was therefore necessary to develop a general monthly regimen which anyone might follow, and that is the purpose of the fourth and last of these dietary handbooks. The individual Byzantine reader, and most particularly the physician of any well-paying Byzantine patient, would naturally regard this as no more than a general guide, to be adjusted to the individual constitution.

Several versions of this 'Calendar' exist, some of them attributed to a certain Hierophilus the Sophist. This is a translation of the version published by Delatte in 1939. Other versions were published by Boissonade, in 1827, and by Ideler, in 1841-2 (see bibliography).

[i] January

January: sweet phlegm. Take three small doses of fine and very aromatic wine, but not too quickly. Take no food for three hours. Food should be roast lamb served hot, or roast sucking pig, and gravies spiced with pepper, spikenard and cinnamon; seasonings including Eastern caraway, pepper and spices; when roasting pork, baste it with honeyed wine; also eat pigs' trotters and head, jellied, with vinegar. Among birds, chickens, white and *brakata* pigeons[1]

[1] 'Breeched' pigeons, a domestic variety.

(these are the best kinds) roasted, accompanied by spicy gravy and served hot; also quails and wrens: these if from the wild, being tough, should be well boiled and served hot. Among fish, sar [*Diplodus Sargus*], fried; also daurade, which like the preceding should be flavoured with spiced sauces. Among vegetables, cabbage and turnips, carrots, leeks, wild asparagus, butcher's broom, bryony shoots, to be dressed with olive oil and fish sauce; and their cooking liquor, to be drunk flavoured with spices. The cabbage is to be cooked with oil and fish sauce. Garlic suits all constitutions this month, cooked in pure olive oil. Those of robust constitutions may also take a 'dry soup',[1] with pepper, spikenard, cinnamon, cloves, a little of the best storax, and just enough honey. Among garden herbs eat rocket, leek, celery and little radishes, also rue, mint and lovage. For dips use mustard, aloes, cumin and *oinogaron*. Among pulses, grass peas and *Lathyrus Ochrus*: they are to be seasoned with oil and ground cumin. Among fruits, raisins, almonds, pistachios and pine kernels; those of robust constitutions may take quince marmalade and a little lemon; pomegranate, pear, dates, cream blended with honey and spikenard and cinnamon, and durum wheat gruel.

Four baths in the course of the month; soap with sodium carbonate diluted in wine. Make a compound skin lotion by mixing 3 lb. weight aloes, 1 lb. myrrh, 2 egg yolks; combine these and apply to the skin. This is the quantity per person. Apply it before you enter the bath,[2] and have three bucketfuls [of water] poured over you, then sweat, then go into the open air and sponge the ointment off thoroughly. After washing the ointment off, rub down with cooling wine and egg yolks mixed with hot rose oil, then make love.

---

[1] One flavoured with ingredients that are 'dry' in terms of humoral theory.
[2] The versions edited by Ideler and Boissonade specify 3 drams of aloes, 1 dram myrrh, and instruct that the lotion is to be applied after bathing.

[ii] February

During this month no beet and no wild vegetables must be eaten at all, and among fish no corkwings, and no vegetable soups must be drunk except leek, celery, dill and garlic. Sauces and spices and old and aromatic wines should be taken in moderation. Meats may be eaten as in the previous list, also so-called crustacea, including oysters, crabs, lobsters, mussels, scallops and the like. Among fish, groupers, wrasses, sparaillons, parrot-wrasses, *stromataioi*, gobies; flavour with mustard. Dips and fruits as for January. Garden herbs and vegetables as for January; also baths, ointments and love-making as prescribed above.

[iii] March

Sweet flavours are advisable in food and drink, but in moderation: all excess is inimical to health, but small quantities are safe. Sour and bitter foods should be avoided. All kinds of fish may be eaten except those without scales; bass and grey mullet may be eaten frequently. Among pulses, emmer groats well boiled, rather watery, flavoured with honey, spikenard and cinnamon, eaten with the most aromatic of wine. Soak broad beans and boil them thoroughly with salt and good green olive oil. Also take fenugreek seed, well boiled, cold, seasoned with honey, spikenard and cinnamon; you should wash the fenugreek, rub it in the hands, then boil it until partly boiled down. If it boils down completely it becomes indigestible, constipating and bad for the bowels, but if it is not fully boiled down the same liquor, with the same bitterness, does not block the bowels. Honey will relieve its bitterness. Grass peas and *Lathyrus Ochrus*, ground; those with robust constitutions may take black-eyed peas, well boiled, with honey vinegar. Among vegetables eat beet, mallow, orach and all kinds of asparagus and mushroom, but not bryony or butcher's broom shoots, because these are bitter. Among conserves eat green olives in brine [*kolymbades*] and olives in honey vinegar, but only from time to time. Sour foods should not be eaten, only sweet. Among fruits those already listed, with dates as wanted. Your sweet wine should be *konditon* including pepper, cinnamon, spikenard and cloves.

Six baths in the course of the month: for three of these, on Tuesdays, anoint with oil but no myrrh or aloes; for the other three, wash with water, on Fridays. Light, aromatic wines of the colour of olive oil. Moderate sex.

[iv] April

This month one should avoid radishes, mint, capers, pepper, basil, savory and all bitter flavours. Among meats choose those that are rich and well-fleshed: lambs that are grass-fed, not suckling, but that have been suckled by their mothers, and they may be young males or castrated; suckling kids: lean meat well boiled. With this take gravy moderately spiced with spikenard, green coriander and a little pepper, and the fruit of safflower because it relaxes the bowels. Avoid pork. Among birds, eat hens, male chickens, white pigeons, ducks and geese; lean meat well boiled. With this take gravy moderately [spiced]. Serve sweetened, while still hot. Sweet food and sweet drinks are the rule. Among fish, bass, *syakia*, daurade, pagre in a little well-spiced sauce; wrasse, perch, gurnard, scad, oblade, and to speak simply all tender-fleshed scaly fish are to be eaten fried, with a little spiced sauce, no excessive quantity. Avoid all dried pulses, but fresh pulses may be eaten with the meats listed above. Among vegetables eat orach, dill and coriander, all green, and lettuce, which requires moderate dressing in squill vinegar.[1] Also eat boiled garlic cloves with olive oil and salt, and a little leek. Avoid all dried fruits. Drink highly aromatic, anise-flavoured, and white wines.

Inhale the scents of violets, roses, lilies, wild chamomile and all aromatic flowers, and among 'dry' scents those of musk and attar

---

[1] Squill root (*Urginea maritima*), now often said to be poisonous, was once important in Byzantine cuisine and medicine. See Stannard 1974; Jeanselme and Oeconomos 1923.

of roses. Moderate love-making. Eight baths in the course of the month; soap with Gallic soap. Apply a skin lotion once in the month, with no aloes; it should contain musk, three egg yolks and rose oil.

[v] May

May governs the black blood. Avoid anything dry, anything that produces bad humours, anything glutinous like extremities, offal and fibrous parts. Eat the meats prescribed for April. Eat salt and dried fish; avoid the young of the sea, and follow the previous month's rules for food and bathing. Among vegetables eat asparagus shoots, 'dry soups', pulse soups, porridges, watered fish sauce, fenugreek. Avoid everything dry, salty and sour. Take moderately sweet food and sweet drinks, and follow the prescriptions for April.

[vi] June

June governs the hot blood. [On rising] swallow three small doses of cold water, slowly, and then fast until the third hour. Choose all relatively cold foods, in moderation, and avoid the more bitter and dry flavours such as pepper, cloves, cinnamon and spicy products. Among garden herbs garlic, onion, leeks, radish, rocket, cress, mustard and chopped oregano, mint.[1] Savory and butcher's broom to be avoided. Among meats, rich lamb or kid: prefer the meat of male animals, and do not take any fat. They should be pastured or milk-fed lambs: no spicing is required at all except coriander, spikenard and anise. Take oregano moderately. Avoid drinking any kind of soup. Among birds, eat hens, chickens, young *brakata* pigeons, roasted and served hot. Take aromatic and anise-flavoured *kondita* and light wines with hot water, not old or deeply-coloured

---

[1] Herbs in this list beginning with garlic are recommended; those in the following list ending with butcher's broom are to be avoided (as if anyone would dream of eating butcher's broom shoots in June!) but it is not clear where the full stop separating the two lists should be placed.

wines. Among fish, eat all the rich-fleshed ones including wrasse, perch, gurnard, sparaillon, daurade, grouper, gobies and all soft-fleshed fish. Avoid bass, grey mullet, corkwing, red mullet, rascasse, pagre, lobster, crab and all hard-shelled and coarse-fleshed seafood. Dips should be based on honey vinegar. Fish soups should be spiced with spikenard, anise and coriander; fried fish only moderately [spiced]. Lettuce, endive, white celery, dressed with squill vinegar, to be taken moderately: copious amounts of lettuce dim the eyesight. Among fruits eat 'white' cherries and cucumbers, moderately. Anything not listed should be avoided this month.

Eight baths in the course of the month: no skin lotion at all this month. Ointment and soap, of the same ingredients, until the 21st of the month. No love-making.

[vii] July

July governs the yellow bile. This month one should avoid sexual activity, excessive food of all kinds, stress and excessive drinking.[1] As prescribed for June, eat, in moderation, rich kid meat from castrated animals, hare, gazelle, deer, turtle doves and wood pigeons; always eat these with some vinegar. Garden herbs as for June. Among fish eat the rich-fleshed kinds such as corkwing, wrasse and all rich-fleshed and moist fish. [Conserves] in honey vinegar and in fish sauce and vinegar. Among fruits choose the moister ones such as melons, green figs eaten with salt, any grapes except the black ones, pear, apple, plum, peach and all that are moist to eat; avoid other fruits. Light wines: eat sparingly but take plenty of wine, also rose wine. Do not take any vegetable soups except carrot, flavoured with honey and spikenard.

Eight baths in the course of the month; wash briskly, using a lotion incorporating Cimolian fullers' earth. Do not use purges.

---

[1] The versions edited by Ideler and Boissonade add that siestas, snacks and dried fruits are also to be avoided, explaining that all these things cause biliousness.

[viii] August

August governs the green bile. During this month avoid glutinous vegetables with thick juices, such as mallow and all wild greens: eat beet, blite and gourd. Among meats take lamb and castrated kid, with hare and gazelle till the 15th of the month; lean meat, served hot with honey vinegar. All hens, chickens and pigeons may be eaten without danger. Among [fresh] fish, flatfish and rich-fleshed kinds should be taken, occasionally with a mustard dip. [Salt and pickled fish, and also dried fruits, should be avoided. Take fresh fruit, including figs, grapes, pears, yellow plums, ripe peaches and the like. Among vegetables, all hot and dry types should be avoided,][1] such as rue, savory, garlic, leeks, cress, radish and mustard.

Four baths in the course of the month.

Among conserves use capers, green olives in brine [*kolymbades*], olives in honey vinegar, almonds. Black olives must be avoided. Light and aromatic wines and rose wine.

[ix] September

September governs the black bile. All kinds of bitter foods should be eaten, in particular boiled leeks, fresh leeks, leek soup, boiled garlic, raw garlic and garlic in a spicy sauce. Among meat, lamb; [among] birds, pigeons and geese and quails (chicks and hens), ducks and wood pigeons and turtle doves and partridges; beef, along with deer, gazelle, fallow deer, hare and wild boar should be avoided. Among fish, grey mullet, corkwing and all scaleless fish may be eaten; only salt fish is to be avoided. Among pulses broad beans, lentils and grass peas are to be avoided; others may be eaten. All kinds of asparagus and cèpes de Bordeaux[2] may be eaten. Among fruits,

---

[1] The missing text is supplied from the version edited by Ideler.

[2] The Greek is *amanitai leukoi* 'white mushrooms'. This species is similarly named in several modern languages and is found from August to September (Davidson 1999 pp. 152, 523 with reference).

white grapes, wild pears as they ripen, sweet apples, green figs, peaches of both kinds (downy peaches and nectarines), pomegranates, dates, quinces may all be eaten. Among dry fruits, pistachioes, walnuts, almonds and pine kernels. Drink white and olive-oil-coloured wines and rose and wormwood wines.

Eight baths, using lotion. Make love.

[x] October

October governs light [phlegm]. All kinds of bitter foods should be eaten, particularly leeks and spicy leek soups. Avoid all fish, glutinous vegetables, and all salt meat.[1]

[xi] November

November governs the watery phlegm. This month there must be no baths or anointing: if necessary, just two baths. Among meats, no deer or goat or wild boar or wild goat. All other meats of animals and birds may be eaten, lean, served hot, boiled and spiced; including sucklings. Among fish eat any except the more watery ones, corkwing and gobies, but do not eat scaleless fish. In using spices prefer the bitter tastes. Leek and mallow are good to eat, and all dry foods. Old, light, aromatic wines. Take fenugreek soup occasionally. Make love.

---

[1] The versions edited by Ideler and Boissonade are much fuller here. Ideler's adds: 'Firstly, all food should be either boiled or raw; and drink the cooking liquor. Boiled garlic, spiced: spikenard, pepper, cinnamon and cloves. This to accompany food. Among meats, lamb, chicken, pigeon, geese, quails, corncrakes, and suckling animals. Avoid ducks, woodpigeons, turtle doves, fallow deer, wild boar, hare. Among fish, avoid grey mullet, anchovies, red mullet, and all scaleless and all salt fish; all others can be eaten. Among pulses, avoid broad bean, lentil and grass pea: eat others. Among vegetables, avoid cabbage and turnip: eat others. Eat all kinds of asparagus and cèpes de Bordeaux. In fruits, eat white grapes, ripe wild pears, sweet apples, green figs, medlars, peaches, dates, pomegranates; in dried fruits, walnuts, pistachios, almonds, pine kernels and hazelnuts, but avoid bay berries. White and olive-oil-coloured wine and wormwood and rose wine.'

[xii] December

December governs the salty phlegm. During this month do not eat cabbage or *serizon*[1] or *skimbron*.[2] Meats just as for November, similarly with fish, vegetables, pulses, wine and leek soup. Take fenugreek soup in moderate amount, young green olives in brine [*kolymbades*], olives in honey vinegar.

Eight baths, using an ointment containing aloes and myrrh. Wash off with wine and sodium carbonate. Make love.

[1] Possibly *seris*, which would mean 'endive' or 'chicory'.
[2] For the unknown *skimbron* the version edited by Boissonade has *sisymbrion*, classical Greek for 'water mint'.

Chapter 7

Instructions and Recipes

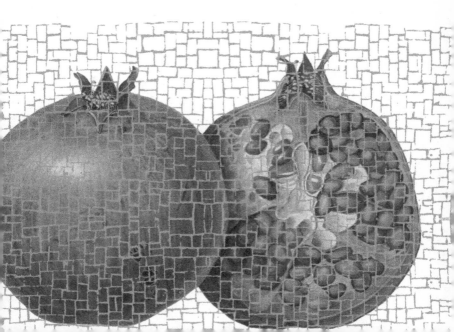

These few recipes have been selected because they are clearly linked with Byzantine Constantinople. Anthimus was a Byzantine physician in exile: he wrote for a Frankish king, but drew on his fond memories of Mediterranean foods (note the reference to the fine fish and scallops available 'at home'). *Apicius*, the Roman recipe collection, is quoted for a few dishes that are known from other sources to have been available at Constantinople. The *Geoponica*, compiled in Byzantium from classical Greek and Roman sources, is likewise used for recipes that are known to have continued in use in Byzantine times.

Three menus

First comes the baked dish, the little *pisi* in their stew. Second, the saucy one, a hake weighed down with gravy. Third, the sweet-and-sour, the saffron dish, with spikenard, valerian, cloves, cinnamon, and little mushrooms, and vinegar and unsmoked honey, and in the midst a big golden gurnard and a grey mullet, three hands' breadths, with the roe, from Rygin harbour, and a fine, well grown, first quality dentex – O let me munch on the bits in the bowl, let me sup at their sauces, let me make off with four cups of the Chian wine, let me find a sufficiency, let me be satisfied! Fourth the grill and fifth the fry-up: chopped morsels from the middle; red mullets (with their moustaches); a double-sized deep pan of big sand-smelts; a flounder, nicely grilled on its own, with fish sauce, sprinkled from top to tail with caraway; and a steak from a big sea bass.

Prodromic Poems 3.147–163 Hesseling.

They munch angler-fish, we have our Lent Soup. They drink their Chian till they can take no more, we have Varna wine cut with water. They have the sweet wine after the table wine, we have some nice water after our one-course meal. They have white bread, we have bran bread. They have a mousse after their sesame sweetmeat; we have wheat gruel with the wheat filtered out. They have second helpings of fritters with honey … They have spoon sweets, we get castor oil seeds …

Prodromic Poems 3.311–320.

Three recipes for meat

Meat is more nourishing than any other food and makes the body healthy. Those who eat meat regularly and drink wine regularly should therefore be bled.

Peri Trophon Dynameos p. 476
(see text 2 section viii above).

Beef can be stewed, or boiled in a pot and served with a sauce … Boil it in fresh water, enough that you need not add water during cooking. When the meat is boiled, put in a casserole about half a cup of sharp vinegar, some leeks and a little pennyroyal, some celery root and fennel, and allow to cook for one hour. Then add half as much honey as you had vinegar, or make it sweeter if you like. Cook over a low heat, stirring the pot frequently with your hands so that the sauce is well mixed with the meat. Then grind 50 peppercorns, half a *solidus* each of putchuk and spikenard, one *tremissis* of cloves. Carefully grind all these spices together in an earthenware mortar, adding a little wine. When well ground, add them to the pot and stir well. Allow time for them to lose some of their individual force and to blend their flavours into the sauce before it is taken off the fire. If, besides honey, you have must or concentrated must, you may choose any of the three to add as directed above. Do not use a copper; the flavour is better if cooked in earthenware.

Anthimus, *Letter on Diet* 3.

Sucking pigs are very good and suitable stewed. Or, served in sauce after roasting in an oven (so long as the heat is not high enough to burn them: they should be as if baked); the sauce is a simple honey vinegar, made on the spot, two parts honey to one part vinegar. Or, cooked in an earthenware pot; in that case the meat is dipped in this sauce as it is eaten.

Anthimus, *Letter on Diet* 10.

Hares, if they are quite young, can be taken with a sweet sauce including pepper, a little cloves and ginger, seasoned with putchuk and spikenard or tejpat leaf. Hare is an excellent food, good in cases of dysentery, and its bile can be taken, mixed with pepper, for earache.

Anthimus, *Letter on Diet* 13.

Dried meat: Apokti

Apokti is mentioned by Constantine Porphyrogennetus, *On Ceremonies* p. 464 Reiske. This modern recipe for *apokti*, cured loin of pork, is reported by Diane Kochilas from Santorini:

Once the loin is trimmed, it is salted for a day, then steeped in vinegar for three days. It is removed from the vinegar, then patted dry and rubbed with cinnamon. It is left for five or six hours with the cinnamon rub, so that the spice adheres to the meat. Then it is rubbed with ground black pepper, dried savory, and more cinnamon and hung to dry for several weeks.

Diane Kochilas, *The glorious foods of Greece* (New York: Morrow, 2001) p. 311.

Smoked sausage: Loukanika

Lucanica similarly: crush pepper, cumin, savory, rue, parsley, mixed herbs, bay berry, fish sauce, and mix in well-beaten meat, rubbing it well into the mixture. Then, adding fish sauce, whole peppercorns, plenty of fat, and pine kernels, stuff into an intestine (pulled as thin as possible) and hang in the smoke.

Apicius 2.4 [61 André].

One-pot meal: Monokythron

After all these dishes have been served comes in a nice *monokythron*, slightly blackened on the top, preceded by its aroma. If you like I'll tell you all about this *monokythron*. Four hearts of cabbage, crisp and snowy white; a salted neck of swordfish; a middle cut of carp; about twenty *glaukoi*; a slice of salt sturgeon; fourteen eggs and some Cretan cheese and four *apotyra* and a bit of Vlach cheese and a pint of olive oil, a handful of pepper, twelve little heads of garlic and fifteen chub mackerels, and a splash of sweet wine over the top, and roll up your sleeves and get to work – just watch the mouthfuls go.

Prodromic Poems 3.178–186 Hesseling.

Soufflé: Aphraton

Greek has the name *afrutum* [*aphraton*] for what is called *spumeum* in Latin. It is made from chicken and white of egg. You must take a lot of white of egg so that your *afrutum* becomes foamy. It should be arranged in a mound on a shallow casserole with a previously prepared sauce, based on fish sauce,[1] underneath. Then the casserole is set over the coals and the *afrutum* cooked in the steam of the sauce. The casserole is then placed in the middle of a serving tray, and a little wine or honey poured over it. It is eaten with a spoon or

[1] The text and meaning are uncertain.

a small ladle. We often add fine fish or scallops to this dish, because they are very good and also common at home.

Anthimus, *Letter on Diet* 34. Translation after Mark Grant.

Fish sauce: Garos

Liquamen is made thus. Fish entrails are put in a pot and salted; and little fish, especially sand-smelt or small red mullet or sardine or anchovy, or any small enough, are used whole; and left to pickle in the sun, stirring frequently. When the heat has pickled them, the liquid is extracted thus: a deep close-woven basket is inserted into the centre of the jar containing these fish, and the liquid flows into the basket, and so *liquamen* is obtained, filtered through the basket. The solid residue makes *alix*.

The Bithynians make it thus. They take preferably small or large picarel, or, if none, anchovy or scad or mackerel, or perhaps *alix*, or a mixture of all these, and put them into a baker's bowl of the kind in which dough is kneaded, and knead in 6 Italian pints of salt to one peck fish so that they are well mixed with the salt, and leaving it overnight put it in an earthenware jar which they leave uncovered in the sun for 2 or 3 months, occasionally stirring with a stick, then extract the liquid, cover and store ...

A better *garos*, called *haimation* 'blood sauce', is made thus. Take tunny entrails with gills, fluid and blood, sprinkle with sufficient salt, leave in a jar for two months at the most; then the jar is pierced, and the *garos* called *haimation* flows out.

Geoponica 20.46.

Two ideas for fenugreek seed

Take fenugreek seed, well boiled, cold, seasoned with honey, spikenard and cinnamon. You should have washed the fenugreek, rubbed it in the hands, then boiled it until partly boiled down. If it boils down completely it becomes indigestible, constipating and bad for the bowels, but if it is not fully boiled down the same liquor, with the same bitterness, does not block the bowels. Honey will relieve its bitterness.

Hierophilus, *Dietary Calendar* March.

Fenugreek seed, steeped in water, sweetened, and sprouted, moves the bowels: this is the case whether the seed is eaten with fish sauce, or vinegar and fish sauce, or wine and fish sauce and olive oil.

De Alimentis 39–40.

Five recipes for table olives

The green ones that are conserved as *kolymbades* are good to eat owing to their astringency; they arouse the appetite. Those conserved in vinegar are especially suitable as food.

De Alimentis 57 (see text 2 section iv above).

How to preserve best olives (Florentinus). Taking large perfect olives, picked by hand, cut them round with a sharp reed and put them in a new jar, not yet pitched, sprinkling on top a very little salt, and when it has dissolved have ready another jar, with honey if available, if not, *epsema* and a lemon leaf, and put the olives into this marinade so that it covers them. Some add fennel seed, caraway, parsley seed and dill to this marinade, and make a quite remarkable olive conserve, which is unfamiliar to many.

Conserve in oxymeli (the same). Take long ones with their stalks, best quality of course, black and unbruised, wash in cold water and dry on wicker mats; then put them in a bowl and pour olive oil on them and sprinkle on fine salt, one choenix to 9 choenices of olives; move them gently with the hands but do not let them bruise; then put them in a jar, pour in *oxymeli* so that it covers them, top with fennel fronds, and store.

Conserve in must (the same). Picking white olives they soak them in sea water for 6 days. Then they put them in a jar and pour fresh must in, but they do not completely fill it or the must would overflow in fermenting; after fermentation they seal it. Others put in a handful of salt before the must, and then the olives, and seal when it has fermented …

Bruised olives (Didymus). Take relatively unblemished olives, before they turn in colour. Bruise them on a wooden surface and put them in hot water. Then put them in a basket, press them down, and add salt not finely ground. Next day fill a jar with them, adding a handful of salt and covering with fronds of fennel. Others, after bruising, remove the stones, sprinkle with ground salt, cumin and fronds of fennel, then add good quality must and seal.

Kolymbades (Didymus). For '*kolymbades*' take large olives with their stalks, when full-grown and about to turn dark, and take care they do not bruise one another by being carried in too large a jar. Wash them, a few at a time, in cold water and put them for a day in wicker baskets in the shade to dry, turning them carefully so that they dry evenly. Then put in the bottom [of a jar] a handful of crushed salt and 4 choes of second brine [?] with 3 cups vinegar and add 20 choenices of olives, and when the jar is full, agitate it. The liquid should reach the top; add fennel fronds and seal. We say the brine is to be put in first so that the olives will not be bruised as they are added. Others, picking [olives] with their stalks, put them in a jar containing sea water and leave for 5 or 6 days, take them out, and put them in jars of brine and seal. This is all done before winter starts.

Geoponica 9.28–33.

White bread

Bread made from wheat is the best and most nutritious of all foods. Particularly if white, with a moderate use of yeast and salt, the dough kneaded midway between dryness and rawness, and with a little anise, fennel seed and mastic, it is very fine indeed. One with a hot constitution should include sesame in the dough. If wishing to add more moistness to the bread, knead in some almond oil.

De Cibis 2.

Tragos, traganos, modern trakhanas

Making tragos. 'Alexandrine' wheat[1] is to be soaked and crushed and dried under hot sun; then repeat the process, until the membranes and the fibrous part are detached. Good local emmer can be dried and stored as tragos in the same way.

Geoponica 3.8.

In modern preparations of *trakhanas*, milk or yoghourt is incorporated with the cereal (cracked grain or flour) as it is drying. The product is shaped into small lumps, and, once fully dry, can be bagged and stored for many months. To eat, it is boiled in water or broth to make a sour soup.

Twelve spiced wines

Your sweet wine should be *konditon* including pepper, cinnamon, spikenard and cloves.

Hierophilus, *Dietary Calendar* March
(see text 4 section iii above).

To make rose wine. When you are pure of pullution, pick rose petals and add them to your chosen quantity of very old wine, not in

[1] 'Alexandrine' wheat was emmer grain as imported from Egypt.

excessive amount but moderately. Stir them each day with a sharp reed till they fall to the bottom of the jar. Seal tightly so that no air can enter and leave for thirty days. Then strain the wine, and add one pint of honey, blending carefully, to each five pints of wine. Allow to mature for thirty days; then use.

Another way to make rose wine, using a conserve. Pick rose petals, add 7 pints honey and leave for a year. Mix one pint of the rose concentrate and five pints of new honey and, stirring, add 10 pints fine wine.

Rose cordial. Best honey 30 pints, rose petals 10 pints, spring water 60 pints. Heat the water to boiling, remove the pan from the fire, add the roses. Cover the pan till cooked. Heat the honey separately and skim it. Strain the rose petals off and add the honey to the rosewater.

Another rose wine. First quality wine 21 pints, honey 8 pints, rose petals 3 pints. Steep the roses in the wine for 15 days. Strain the wine. Boil and skim the honey and blend it with the rose wine. Seal carefully and store.

Another very good rose wine. Honey 7 pints, wine 21 pints, rose petals 2 pints. Crush the rose petals thoroughly and allow to steep in the wine for 15 days. Strain off the rose petals. Boil the honey. Blend the two liquids, seal carefully and store.

Violet wine. Honey 7 pints, wine 21 pints, 240 bunches violets.[1] Separate the flowers, steep them in the wine for 30 days, strain them off. Boil the honey, blend the two liquids, seal carefully and store.

Chamomile wine. Ascalon wine 21 pints, honey 7 pints, wild chamomile seeds 7 ounces. Steep the seeds in the wine for 30 days. Strain. Boil and skim the honey, blend the liquids, seal and store.

---

[1] Asparagus was also measured in bunches. How many violets were there in a bunch?

Excellent *konditon* for bladder stone. Honey 1 pint, wine 5 pints, pepper 1 ounce, burnet saxifrage 4 scruples, spikenard 4 scruples, cubebs, ginger, spignel, hazelwort, cassia, stone parsley, parsley, yellow flag, gentian, carrot seed, 4 scruples each. Combine the dry ingredients with the skimmed honey and the wine and leave in a jar for 10 days to mature.

Konditon. Honey 10 pints, first quality wine 30 pints, pepper 1 ounce. Grind the pepper and mix into the wine. Skim the homey, blend with the wine, seal and store.

Anise wine. Honey 10 pints, first quality white wine 30 pints, anise 5 ounces; to ginger-grass 16 [scruples?] take saffron 12 [scruples?]; mastic 16 scruples. Grind the spices, combine with the wine. Skim the honey, combine with the rest. Seal and store.

Storax wine. Honey 20 pints, storax 1 pint, wine 6 pints. Skim the honey, grind the storax and mix the two. Add the wine to the honey while it is still in the mortar, and take in your hand and use.

Wormwood wine. To 50 pints of wine add ½ ounce putchuk, ½ ounce tejpat, ½ ounce amomum, ½ ounce cassia, 10 pints honey. Steep wormwood, the fresh herb, in a little wine, strain, and judge by your taste how much of the resulting liquid to add to the other ingredients.

Oribasius, *Medical Collections* 5.33.

Chapter 8

A Phrase-Book of Byzantine Foods and Aromas

The language of Byzantine food

This phrase-book includes words and phrases used by Byzantine authors when talking of the food of their own time, and adds a few expressions used by contemporary authors in other languages who happen to be talking specifically of the food of Byzantium.

Educated Byzantines were taught to write good classical Greek – a language that was a thousand years old and more in their time. A few of them did. A few chose to write in something close to their everyday speech. All were intimately familiar with the Greek of the Bible and were much influenced by it. Most of them mixed these three registers (whether or not they knew they were doing so), especially when they wrote about matters of everyday life such as food and drink. This phrase-book does the same. It thus reflects the linguistic competence of a cultured Byzantine. So do its spellings, varying as wildly as did those of Shakespeare.

Byzantine authors were of course aware – they encountered the problem every day – that many words which they read in classical books and used in their own carefully written compositions differed totally from the words they used in conversation. Intelligent and learned as they were, they could only attribute the differences to the even greater intelligence and learning of classical writers:

The authors of the old farming books, being highly educated, did not use our everyday names of fruits. They use terms like 'Royal nut', or 'Pontic nut', or maybe 'Zeus's acorn'. It is necessary for us to explain these and other old terms. 'Royal nut' is what we call simply *karyon* 'walnut'. 'Pontic nut' is our *leptokaryon* 'hazelnut'. 'Zeus's acorn' is *kastanon* 'chestnut'. 'Cuckoo-apple' is what we call *damaskenon* 'plum'. The 'Armenian apple' is the *berikokkon* 'apricot'. The *terminthos* is what we call *terebinthos* 'terebinth fruit'.

Geoponica 10.73.

By at least one Byzantine author this attractive, historic term 'Royal nut', which in classical texts means 'walnut', was put to work in a completely new sense, 'nutmeg' (see *karyon basilikon* below).

The phrase-book

Agelada, cow, *Bos Taurus*: Demetrius Chomatianus p. 542 Zepi. *ageladia ypomoskha*, suckling calves: Constantine Porphyrogennetus, *On Ceremonies* p. 464 Reiske.

Agiozoumin, agiozomin, monastery soup: *Prodromic Poems* 3.290–325b; *Typikon of Kosmosoteira* 33 Petit.

Agouris, verjuice, juice of unripe or wild grapes: Agapius, *Geoponicon. omphake agourida legetai* [earlier equivalent]: *Lexikon ton Sarakenon* 245.

Agria lakhana, agriolakhana, wild greens: *De cibis* 22; *De alimentis* 65; *Peri trophon dynameos* 479.

Agriaiges, wild goats: Hierophilus, November.

Agriokhoireia, wild boar meat: *De alimentis* 12. French *venesun de sengler*: *Voyage de Charlemagne* 410.

Agriomaioulion, dandelion, *Taraxacum officinale*: *De cibis* 14.

Agriomelintzana, agria mazizone, garden nightshade, *Solanum nigrum. trykhna esti en oi koinoi agrian mazizonen phasin* [classical equivalent], *trykhna* are what are called 'wild aubergine' by ordinary people: *Scholia on Theocritus, Idylls* 1.37.

Aiges, goats, *Capra spp.*: *De cibis* 6. *aigeia krea*, goat meat: *De cibis* 7, 20; *Peri trophon dynameos* 476. *ton aigon ta lipara galaktophora brephe*, fat milk-stuffed suckling kids: Constantine Manasses, *Moral Poem*.

Aimatia, black puddings. *aimatia: allantia, aimatia: zomos melas* [two possible classical equivalents]: *Etymologicum Magnum*; Photius, *Lexicon*; *Suda*.

Akoron, yellow flag, *Iris pseudacorus*: Oribasius, *Medical Collections* 5.33.

Akra. ta akra ton zoon, feet, trotters: *Peri trophon dynameos* 478; *De cibis* 22.

Akrides, locusts, *Schistocerca gregaria* [an unattractive food]: *Prodromic Poems* 2.103; Mai in *Nova Patrum Bibliotheca* vol. 6 p. 407.

Akrodrya, tree fruits: Agapius, *Geoponicon*.

Alektorion, alektoris, alektryon, alektoropoulon, cock, capon, chicken: Hierophilus, August; *De cibis* 5. *ai alektorides egoun ai ornithes* [alternative terms]: *De alimentis* 2. *ta mikrotera alektoreia*, young chickens: *Peri trophon dynameos* 477. *alektoridas trieteis esphagmenas kai liposas dyo ... ton polounton to enkeimenon autais stear ypokhalonton dia gastros epi tous merous exo*, two three-year hens freshly killed and sleek ... the salesmen having loosened the fat of their bellies and tucked their legs into it: *Timarion* 46.

Alepia, alepida, scaleless fish: Hierophilus, March, November.

Ales, alas, salt: Simeon Seth p. 25; *Peri trophon dynameos* 469; *De cibis* 12. *ales pleistoi kai kallistoi ton apantakhou*, the most plentiful and finest salt in the world [it comes from Aenus]: Critobulus of Imbros 2.12.7. *alatia diaphora*, various spiced salts: Simeon Seth p. 25.

Aleuron, areurion, bread-wheat meal, *Triticum aestivum*: Maurice, *Stratagems* 7B.17.37; Constantine Porphyrogennetus, *On Ceremonies* p. 658 Reiske. *aleura meta galaktos*, wheat meal with milk: *De cibis* 11. *athera: eidos poltariou paidiois o legousin alebraia*, 'athera': a kind of porridge for children, now called 'alevrea': *Glossae Jatricae*.

Alix, emmer groats, *Triticum dicoccum*. *alix diephthos kai ydaresteros kai karykeutos dia melitos stakhous kai kinamomou*, emmer groats well boiled and rather watery, seasoned with honey, spikenard and cinnamon: Hierophilus, March.

Alix (Latin *allec*), fermented fish paste: *Geoponica* 20.46.

Almaia, pickled cabbage: Nicetas Choniates, *Chronicle* p. 57 van Dieten.

Alme, almyris, brine: *De cibis* 16; Oribasius, *Medical Collections* 4.3.3. Latin *salimoria*, cooking brine: Anthimus 29, 43. Latin *salsugo*, salty water, brackish water: Liutprand, *Embassy* 13.

Aloe, aloes, *Aloe Perryi*: Theophanes, *Chronicle* AM 6118; *De cibis* 8; Hierophilus, January. Latin *alohe*: Justinian, *Digest* 39.4.16.7.

Amanitaria, amanitai, mushrooms: *Prodromic Poems* 2.39, 3.151; *De cibis* 14; Hierophilus, March. *dei synepsein toutois apidia*, pears should be cooked with these: Simeon Seth p. 22.

Amanitai leukoi, 'white mushrooms', cèpes de Bordeaux, *Boletus edulis*? Hierophilus, September. See text 4 section ix and footnote 73.

Ami, ajowan, *Trachyspermum Ammi*: see *nanakhoua*.

Aminios, a grape variety: *Geoponica* 4.1.3, 5.17. *gleukos aminaion*, Aminian grape juice: Alexander of Tralles, *Therapeutics* vol. 2 p. 431.

Amomon, bastard cardamom, *Amomum spp.*: Oribasius, *Medical Collections* 5.33. Latin *amomum*: Justinian, *Digest* 39.4.16.7.

Ampar, ambar, ambergris (secretion of *Physeter macrocephalus*): Constantine Porphyrogennetus, *On Ceremonies* p. 468 Reiske; *Book of the Eparch* 10; Simeon Seth p. 26; Pseudo-Galen, *On Similar Remedies* p. 547. *amparatitzin*, tiny bit of ambergris: Tzetzes, *Letters* 59 Leone.

Ampeloprasa, Levant garlic, *Allium Ampeloprasum*: *De alimentis* 6, 75. *ampeloprasa oma*, raw Levant garlic: *De cibis* 22. *ampeloprasa dis epsethenta*, Levant garlic twice boiled: *De cibis* 14, 22.

Amygdala, almonds, *Amygdalus communis*: Constantine Porphyrogennetus, *On Ceremonies* p. 463 Reiske; Hierophilus, August, September. *amygdala pikra*, bitter almonds: Simeon Seth p. 20; *De alimentis* 59. *ton amygdalon ta ypopikra*, slightly bitter almonds: *De cibis* 24. *amygdala glykea*, sweet almonds: Simeon Seth p. 21. *amygdala khloroutsika*, young green almonds: *Prodromic Poems* 2.65b. *amygdala tetrimmena*, ground almonds: *Peri trophon dynameos* 470. *amygdala esthiomena meta sakkhareos*, almonds eaten with sugar: *Peri trophon dynameos* 474. *elaion ton amygdalon, amygdelaion, amygdalelaion*, almond oil: Simeon Seth p. 21; *Peri trophon dynameos* 470; *De cibis* 2. *elaion ton amygdalon pikron*, bitter almond oil: Simeon Seth p. 21. *khylos ton amygdalon proslambanon oligou melitos kai pepereos*, almond milk with the addition of a little honey and pepper [a digestive to prevent colic]: Alexander of Tralles, *Therapeutics* vol. 2 p. 341.

Amylon, frumenty (cf. *katastaton*): *Peri trophon dynameos* 470; *De alimentis* 20. *amylia*, porridges and the like: Hierophilus, May.

Anatolika, a variety of plum. *damaskena krokata ta legoun Anatolika ta legoun lagenata*, yellow plums that people call 'Anatolian' or 'gourds': *Prodromic Poems* 4.129c–d.

Andrakhne, purslane, *Portulaca oleracea*: *Peri trophon dynameos* 479.

Anethon, dill, *Anethum graveolens*: Simeon Seth p. 23; *De cibis* 10; Hierophilus, April. *selinoanethon*, 'celery dill', dill stem: Pseudo-Galen, *Signs from Urine*. *anethokoudimenta*, dill and parsley: *Prodromic Poems* 2.40.

Angouria, cucumbers, *Cucumis sativus*: *De cibis* 14; *De alimentis* 47. *ta angouria a prin kai sikya elegonto* [classical equivalent]: Simeon Seth p. 21.

Anison, anneson, glykanison, anise, *Pimpinella Anisum*: Simeon Seth p. 23; *Peri trophon dynameos* 470; *De cibis* 10; Pseudo-Galen, *Signs from Urine*. *anison de to glykanison* [equivalents]: *Scholia on Theocritus, Idylls* 7.63. *annesaton, anisaton, oinos anisatos*, anise wine: Oribasius, *Medical Collections* 5.33; Alexander of Tralles, *Therapeutics* vol. 2 p. 341; Hierophilus, April. *anisata kondita*, anise-flavoured spiced wines: Hierophilus, June.

Antakoskylos, a large dogfish? *Opsarologos* 29.

Anthomela, variety of apple: *Prodromic Poems* 2.65e.

Apakia, apakin, fillet steak: *Prodromic Poems* 3.180; *Diegesis ton tetrapodon zoon* 379. *akropaston apakin*, well-salted fillet steak: *Prodromic Poems* 4.166–195.

Apalosarkoi, 'soft-fleshed molluscs' or cephalopods: *De cibis* 15.

Aphratitsin, a kind of bread: see *psomin*.

Aphraton, aphratozeston, afrutum, chicken mousse or soufflé: Isidore, *Etymologies* 20.2.29; Alexander of Tralles, *On Fevers* vol. 1 p. 335, *Therapeutics* vol. 2 p. 125; *Prodromic Poems* 3.317. *de pullo fit et de albumen de ovo ... solemus et de pisce bono admiscere aut de pectinibus quia apud nos abundant*, it is made of [minced] chicken and white of egg; we often add fine fish or scallops because they are common at home: Anthimus 34. *afrutum Graece quod Latine dicitur spumeum* [Greek and Latin equivalents]: Anthimus 34.

Aphyai, whitebait, *Aphya minuta* and other species: *Timarion* 21.

Apia, apidia, pears, *Pyrus communis: Peri trophon dynameos* 468; Hierophilus, January. *apia aora,* unripe pears: *De cibis* 14. *apidia ta agourotera,* not-too-ripe pears: *De alimentis* 30. *apia ta oxizonta,* acid pears: *Peri trophon dynameos* 473. *apiaton,* pear-flavoured wine: Alexander of Tralles, *Therapeutics* vol. 2 p. 341.

Apoktia, cured meat: Constantine Porphyrogennetus, *On Ceremonies* p. 464 Reiske. For a modern recipe see chapter 7.

Apotherma, pulse soups: Hierophilus, May.

Apotyra, small new cheese? *Prodromic Poems* 3.182.

Apozema, liquor from boiling: *De cibis* 12.

Apsinthion, wormwood, *Artemisia absinthium:* Oribasius, *Medical Collections* 5.33; *De cibis* 8. *apsinthaton,* wormwood wine, vermouth: Oribasius, *Medical Collections* 5.33; Alexander of Tralles, *Therapeutics* vol. 2 p. 341. *apsinthiou apobregma,* wormwood infusion: Paul of Aegina, *Medical Epitome* 1.95. *apsinthorosatoi oinoi,* wormwood and rose wines: Hierophilus, September.

Aristo, take lunch. *euthys eparisto,* take lunch straight afterwards: *De cibis* 12.

Arktoi, bears, *Ursus Arctos: Peri trophon dynameos* 477.

Arneia, arnia, arnes, caprines, sheep and goats: *De cibis* 5; Simeon Seth p. 20. *arneia krea,* mutton and goat: *De cibis* 15. *arnes nemomenai,* pastured lambs: Hierophilus, April. *arneion pentamenon,* a five-month lamb: *Timarion* 46. *arnas me karykeuein aneu tou koliandrou kai stakhous kai anisou,* do not spice the lamb except with coriander, spikenard and anise: Hierophilus, June.

Aromata, spices: Psellus, *Letters* 88 Kurtz and Drexl; Tzetzes, *Letters* 51 Leone; Hierophilus, January. Latin *aromata:* Liutprand, *Embassy* 46; William of Tyre, *Historia transmarina* 19.26. *aromata therma,* hot spices: *Peri trophon dynameos* 471.

Artos, bread, loaf: *Peri trophon dynameos* 469. Latin *panes,* loaves: Liutprand, *Embassy* 46. *artos katharos, oi katharoi ton arton,* white loaves: Eustathius, *Commentary on Odyssey* 2.142; *De cibis* 2; *De alimentis* 30. *katharos aleurites artos,* white flour bread: *De cibis* 21. *metaxoutoi artoi, bounizomenoi artoi,* loaves of silk-sifted flour: Nicetas Choniates, *Chronicle* Isaac Angelus 3.6 [Demotic text]. *artos kybaros,* wholemeal bread: *De cibis* 12. *artoi pityrodeis kai kybaroi, artoi pityritai kai ryparoi,* bran loaves and brown loaves: *De cibis*

22; *De alimentis* 20. *artos kakhrydias kai autos pityrias*, bread made of barley, and, what's more, full of bran: Theodoret, *Religious History* 2.2. *kakhrydias artos tois alsin edynomenos*, barley bread made palatable with salt: Theodoret, *Religious History* 2.4. *klibanitai artoi, klibanitai*, crock-baked loaves: Simeon Seth p. 19; *De cibis* 20. *phournitai*, oven-baked loaves: Simeon Seth p. 19. *artoi autozymoi, artos zymites*, leavened bread: *De cibis* 25; Eustathius, *Capture of Thessalonica* 96. *plytoi artoi*, 'washed' loaves: *De alimentis* 20.[1] For other phrases see *dipyros artos, psomin*.

Artymata, artymatika, artysiai, flavourings, spices: *Prodromic Poems* 3.404h; *Peri trophon dynameos* 469; *De cibis* 10. *artymata dia karnabadou Anatoles kai pepereos kai ton aromaton*, mixtures of flavours emphasizing caraway, pepper and aromatic spices: Hierophilus, January.

Asaron, hazelwort, *Asarum europaeum*: Oribasius, *Medical Collections* 5.33.

Askalonion oinou. khilia askalonia oinou, one thousand Ascalonian measures of wine: Leontius of Naples, *Life of St John the Almsgiver* 20.

Asparagoi, asparagus, *Asparagus spp.* and others: Simeon Seth p. 24; *De cibis* 22; *De alimentis* 71. *asparankoi agrioi*, wild asparagus: Hierophilus, January. *asparankoi pantes*, all kinds of asparagus: Hierophilus, September.

Assyria phryganis, 'Assyrian sticks', periphrasis for *xylaloe*, aloeswood, *Aquilaria malaccensis*: Tzetzes, *Letters* 29 Leone.

Atherina, sand-smelt, *Atherina Hepsetus*: *Opsarologos* 20. *diploteganon pakhyn megalon atherinon*, a deep double-sized pan of big sand-smelts: *Prodromic Poems* 3.160.

Athotyra, 'flower of cheese', whey cheeses: *Prodromic Poems* 3.182 (ms. g).

Attagenai, francolins, *Francolinus Francolinus*: Alexander of Tralles, *Therapeutics* vol. 2 p. 193.

Augotarikha, ootarikha, 'pickled egg', botargo: Simeon Seth p. 125; *Prodromic Poems* 3.281 (emended). *melan oon tetarikheumenon*, 'black pickled egg', caviar: Michael Apostoles, *Letters* p. 77 Noiret.

---

[1] 'Those who have decided to make 'washed' bread [*plytos artos*] have found it not a very nourishing food, one that is the least likely of any to cause digestive blockage. This bread has the smallest proportion of thickness and stickiness; it is airy rather than earthy. Its lightness can be judged not only on the scales but also because it does not sink in water but floats like a cork' (Galen, *On the Properties of Foods* 1.5.1).

Aukhos, okhros, species of grass pea, *Lathyrus Ochrus*: *De cibis* 7; Simeon Seth p. 133. *apobrekhousi mekhri tou phyesai rizan kai esthiousin pro tes alles trophes, enapobaptontes garois*, they keep the seeds moist till they sprout and then eat them as a starter, dipped in fish sauce: *De alimentis* 40. *e artysis auton di' elaiou kai kyminou triptou*, they are cooked with olive oil and ground cumin: Hierophilus, January.

Axoungin, oxyngin, fat (of animals): *De alimentis* 20.

Balania, balanoi, acorns, *Quercus spp.*: Simeon Seth p. 30; *De cibis* 20; *Peri trophon dynameos* 474.

Balsamon, barzen, balsam of Mecca, *Commiphora Opobalsamum*: *Book of the Eparch* 10; Simeon Seth p. 28 (perhaps lemon balm, *Melissa officinalis*: *Geoponica* 11.27). French *bauces, basseme*: *Chanson de Girart de Roussillon* 207, 288.

Barbilos, brabilos, seedling peach: *Geoponica* 10.13.4–5, cf. Eustathius, *Commentary on Odyssey* 10.242.

Barniotikon, Varna wine. *emeis to barniotikon to nerokopemenon*, we get Varna wine cut with water: *Prodromic Poems* 3.313.

Basilika, basil, *Ocimum spp.*: Simeon Seth p. 29.

Bathrakoi, angler-fish, *Lophius spp.*: *Prodromic Poems* 3.95, 3.311.

Batoi, 'skates', larger rays, *Raja spp.*: *De cibis* 7, 21; *Peri tes ek ton zoon trophes*; *Opsarologos* 20. *batopoula*, little skates: *Prodromic Poems* 3.404f.

Batzena, batzina, blackberries, *Rubus fruticosus*: *De cibis* 13; *De alimentis* 9; *Porikologos* 8. *ton ton baton karpon onomazousin oi par' emin anthropoi batinon*, my countrymen call the fruit of the bramble *batinon*: Galen, *On the Properties of Foods* 2.13 [6.589 Kühn], cf. *On the Properties of Simples* 12.920 Kühn.

Berikokka, apricots, *Armeniaca vulgaris*: *De cibis* 12, 22. *ta pyrokoukka e berrikoukka* [alternative spellings]: *Peri trophon dynameos* 472. *armeniakon esti to berikokkon* [classical equivalent]: *Geoponica* 10.73, cf. Simeon Seth p. 27.

Bertzitika, berzitika, a fish of the southern Russian rivers, a sturgeon, *Acipenser spp.* or *Huso Huso*: Constantine Porphyrogennetus, *De administrando imperio* 42, *On Ceremonies* p. 464 Reiske; Tzetzes, *Khiliades* 10.93. *apakin berzitikou*, a salted sturgeon steak: *Prodromic Poems* 3.180.

Bikos, bykos, vetch, *Vicia sativa: De cibis* 16; *De alimentis* 12.

Blakhikon tyritsin, Blakhikon, Blakhos tyros, Vlach cheese: *Prodromic Poems* 3.182, 4.52; Michael Italicus, *Letters* 42 Gautier.

Blastos. Ton dendron oi blastoi di' almes kai oxalmes syntithemenoi, young shoots of trees prepared with salt and vinegar dressings: *De cibis* 16.

Blita, bleta, blite, *Amaranthus Blitum: De alimentis* 5; *De cibis* 9; *Peri trophon dynameos* 479.

Blyskounin, bliskouni, glikhonin, glekhon, sphlekoune, pennyroyal, *Mentha Pulegium:* Simeon Seth p. 33; *De cibis* 10; *De alimentis* 26; used for flavouring *phouska* but not wine, Leontius of Naples, *Life of St Simeon Salos* p. 164 Rydén. *phliskounitzin oligon dia ten euodian,* a little bit of pennyroyal for the aroma: *Prodromic Poems* 3.412e. *bleskounin eis ten groutan,* pennyroyal to flavour emmer gruel: *Prodromic Poems* 2.42a.

Boidia, rowan-berries or cranberries *Apophthegmata Patrum, Macarius* 37.

Bolboi, grape-hyacinth bulbs, *Muscari comosum:* Aetius, *Medicine* 11.35; *De cibis* 7. *bolboi (dis) epsethentes en elaio kai garo met' oxous* (or *di' oxous*) *esthiomenoi,* (twice-)boiled bulbs in olive oil and fish sauce, eaten with vinegar: *De cibis* 18; *De alimentis* 16, 72. *bolboi oi omoteroi,* bulbs rather lightly cooked: *De cibis* 19. *bolboi dis epsethentes,* bulbs boiled twice: *De cibis* 21.

Botanai, greens, leaf vegetables. *ton botanon ai edodimoi kai lakhanodeis,* edible green plants: Theodoret, *Religious History* 1.2. *me prosdokas na trephomai botanas oreitrophous,* don't think I live on mountain herbs: *Prodromic Poems* 2.102.

Boubaloi, buffaloes, *Bubalus Bubalis:* Agathias, *History* 1.4. French *buffles:* Geoffroi de Villehardouin 492. *kree ton boubalon,* buffalo meat: *Peri trophon dynameos* 477.

Bouglossa, bouglosson, bugloss, *Anchusa italica:* Simeon Seth p. 30; *Peri trophon dynameos* 479.

Bouglossos, bouglossa, sole, *Solea Solea: De alimentis* 1; *De cibis* 5, 24.

Boukakraton, bread dunked in wine: [Athanasius], *Story of Melchisedek* [*PG* vol. 28 col. 529]; *Life of St Dositheus.*

Boukellaton, boukellos, ring-shaped biscuit, hard tack, army ration: Aetius, *Medicine* 3.101; Photius, *Library* 80 citing Olympiodorus; Maurice,

Stratagems 5.4.5, 7B.17.37 Dennis; Zonaras, *Lexicon. boukellos to krikeloeides psomion kaleitai*, boukellos is the name of a ring-shaped loaf: Constantine Porphyrogennetus, *Themes* Asia 6.

Bous, ox, *Bos Taurus*: *De cibis* 6. French *bués et vaches*, oxen and cows: Geoffroi de Villehardouin 492. *boeia krea*, beef: Simeon Seth p. 26; *Peri trophon dynameos* 476. *notoi boeion kreon*, ox chine, ox ribs [a Crusader favourite]: Nicetas Choniates, *Chronicle* p. 594 van Dieten. *e kephale tou boos epi trisi khrysinois statersin apempoleito*, the price of an ox head was three nomismata: Anna Comnena, *Alexiad* 11.4.3.

Boutyron, butter: *Book of the Eparch* 13; Simeon Seth p. 27; *Peri trophon dynameos* 478.

Bromata, foods: Agathias [*Anthologia Palatina* 9.643]. *Bromatomixapate*, deceitful blending of foods [a joke-word]: Agathias [*Anthologia Palatina* 9.642].

Brome, bromos, oats, *Avena sativa*: Simeon Seth p. 30; *De cibis* 14.

Bryonia, bryony shoots, *Tamus communis, Bryonia dioica* and other species, used like wild asparagus: Hierophilus, January, March.

Damaskena, plums, *Prunus spp.*: *Peri trophon dynameos* 472. *kokkymelon estin o kaloumen damaskenon* [classical equivalent]: *Geoponica* 10.73. *brabela: ta kaloumena damaskena* [approximate equivalent]: *Etymologicum Magnum. damaskena de kat' exokhen dia to en Damasko te polei georgoumena einai euthalestera kai kalliona*, called *damaskena* ('damsons') originally because the ripest and choicest were grown in the city of Damascus: *Etymologicum Magnum. damaskena ta ygra*, fresh plums: *De cibis* 12. *damaskena ta oxizonta*, acid plums: *Peri trophon dynameos* 472. *damaskena ta glykea kai pepemmena*, sweet, ripe plums: *Peri trophon dynameos* 472. *damaskena leuka*, white plums: Simeon Seth p. 34; Hierophilus, August. *damaskena okhra*, yellow plums: Simeon Seth p. 34. *damaskena ta xera*, dried plums or prunes. *damaskenon ton xeron ta eis eukratomeli bebregmena*, dried plums steeped in honey water: *De cibis* 12. *o ton damaskenon zomos*, plum juice: Simeon Seth p. 34.

Daphne, bay, *Laurus nobilis. daphneioi karpoi leukotatoi*, very white bay berries: Psellus, *Chronographia* 6.62.

Daukoi, daukia, carrots, *Daucus Carota*: *De cibis* 7; *De alimentis* 73. *oi erythroi ton okhron kreittones*, red ones are better than yellow ones: Simeon Seth p. 35. *daukos, daukon sperma*, carrot seed: Oribasius, *Medical Collections* 5.33; *De cibis* 24. *daukiou zema oligo meliti kai stakhei artythen*, carrot soup seasoned with a little honey and spikenard: Hierophilus, July. *daukomeli*, carrot honey. *emballetai auto drimea artymata*, bitter flavourings are added to this: Simeon Seth p. 35.

Delphakion, delphax, piglet, sucking pig: *Scholia on Aristophanes, Acharnians* 739. *delphakion galathenon meniaion*, sucking-pig one month old: *Timarion* 46.

Dendrolibanon, rosemary, *Rosmarinus officinalis*: Constantine Porphyro-gennetus, *On Ceremonies* 1.1 [vol. 1 pp. 4 and 18 Vogt]; Tzetzes, *Letters* 100 Leone; *Porikologos* 18; Agapius, *Geoponicon* 55.

Derma, skin: *De cibis* 5, 15.

Diaklysmos, collation of wine and bread often served after communion. *diaklyein*, take collation: *Typikon of Stoudios* B37, cf. *Typikon of Pakourianos* 8.

Dikardin, variety of lettuce. *maroullia diaphora, toutesti dikardin, phygiatikon kai rigitanon*: lettuce of various kinds, i.e. double-heart, Phrygiatic and Regitan: *Geoponica* 12.1.

Dipyros artos, paximadion (q.v.): Procopius, *Secret History* 6. *dipyrites katharos*, white paximadion: Constantine Manasses, *Moral Poem* 901. Latin *biscoctum delicatum*, fancy biscuits: William of Rubruck, *Report* 9.

Dorkades, dorkoi, gazelles, *Gazella spp.*: Theophanes, *Chronicle* AM 6118; *Peri trophon dynameos* 477; Hierophilus, July. *dorkia esthiein khre psakhna kai khlia en oxymeliti*, lean gazelle meat to be eaten hot with honey vinegar: Hierophilus, August.

Drakaina, drakontion, weever, *Trachinus Draco*: *De cibis* 7; *Peri tes ek ton zoon trophes*.

Edyosmon, edyosmos, mint, *Mentha spp.*: *De cibis* 24; Hierophilus, January.

Egrauli, anchovy, *Engraulis Encrasicolus*: *Opsarologos* 28. *aphye: e para ton pollon legomene engraulis* [classical equivalent]: *Suda* s.v. 'aphye'. *engraulopastophagos*, eater-of-salted-anchovies: *Prodromic Poems* 3.94.

Eide, spices, trade goods: Theophanes, *Chronicle* AM 6118. French *especiez*: *Chanson de Girart de Roussillon* 206, 280.

Ekhinos. thalassios ekhinos, sea urchin, *Paracentrotus lividus*: *De cibis* 12.

Ekzeston, baked dish: *Prodromic Poems* 3.147.

Eladin, ladi, elaion, khristelaion, olive oil: *Book of the Eparch* 13; *De cibis* 9; *Prodromic Poems* 2.53, 3.183; Agapius, *Geoponicon. to elaion e' litrai to nomisma*, olive oil at five pounds to the nomisma: Theophanes, *Chronicle* AM 6235. *elaion omphakion, elaion omphakinon*, green olive oil: *Miracles of St Artemius* 40; Hierophilus, March.

Elaiai, olives, *Olea europaea*: *De cibis* 24. *elaai tines smikrotatai*, very small olives of a certain kind: Psellus, *Chronographia* 6.62. *elaiai asprai*, white [green] olives: *De alimentis* 4. *elaiai maurai*, black olives: Hierophilus, August; *De alimentis* 20. *elaiai thlastai*, young olives bruised and cured in salt: *Typikon of Pantokrator*; *Geoponica* 9.32. *elaiai ai met' oxous* (or *di' oxous*) *syntithemenai*, olives conserved in vinegar: *De cibis* 8; *De alimentis* 57. *kolymbades, elaiai kolymbades, ai elaiai asprai aitines ginontai kolymbades*, 'kolymbades', green olives conserved in brine: Paul of Aegina, *Medical Epitome* 1.81.3; Eustathius, *Letters* 31 Tafel; *De cibis* 8; *De alimentis* 57. *ai kolymbades legomenai pro ton trophon syn garo lambanomenai*, the so-called 'kolymbades' taken before the meal with fish sauce: Simeon Seth p. 39. *elaiai oxomelitai, elaiai di' oxymelitos*, green olives in honey vinegar: Hierophilus, March; *Geoponica* 9.29.

Elaiodaphnia, elaiodaphnon asparagoi, shoots of butcher's broom (cf. *khamaidaphnia*): Simeon Seth p. 24; *De cibis* 8; Hierophilus, January.

Elaiogaron, olive oil and fish sauce dressing: Stephanus, *Commentary on Hippocrates' Aphorisms* 2.18 [vol. 1 p. 174 Westerink]; Hierophilus, January.

Elaiosparanka, shoots of asparagus: Hierophilus, January.

Elaphos, red deer, *Cervus Elaphus*: Hierophilus, July. *elapheia krea, kree ton elaphon*, venison: *De cibis* 7; *Peri trophon dynameos* 477. French *venesun de cerfs*: *Voyage de Charlemagne* 410.

Eliakon, wine made from raisins and honey, an Egyptian speciality: Simeon Seth p. 96.

Elyme, elime, elymin, elimen, foxtail millet, *Setaria italica*: *De cibis* 14, 22; *De alimentis* 9, 12.

Embammata, epembammata, dips: Hierophilus, January; Nicetas Choniates, *Chronicle* p. 594 van Dieten.

Enkephalos, brain: *De cibis* 7; *Peri tes ek ton zoon trophes. boon enkephalos*, ox brain: *De cibis* 21.

Enkhelyes, enkhelia, akhelia, eels, *Anguilla Anguilla*: *De cibis* 20; *De alimentis* 18; *Opsarologos* 30.

Enkryphiai, loaves baked under embers. *oi ek pityron enkryphiai*, ember-bread made with bran: Eustathius, *Capture of Thessalonica* 96.

Enodios edode, street food: Nicetas Choniates, *Chronicle* p. 57 van Dieten.

Entera, tripe: *De cibis* 7; *Peri tes ek ton zoon trophes*; *Prodromic Poems* 4.235. *enterokoila*, tripe and intestines: Hierophilus, May.

Epapion, variety of apple (possibly one grafted on pear stock): *De cibis* 13.

Epar, epata, liver: *De cibis* 6 etc.; *Peri trophon dynameos* 478.

Epiroudion, variety of apple: *De cibis* 13.

Epsema, grape syrup: *De cibis* 20.

Epsema, pot of soup or stew: *Apophthegmata Patrum, Macarius* 33.

Erebinthoi, erebintha, chickpeas, *Cicer arietinum*: *Peri trophon dynameos* 469; *De cibis* 2. *erebinthoi khloroi esthiomenoi*, chickpeas eaten fresh: Simeon Seth p. 38; *De alimentis* 37. *ean de phrygosin oi erebinthoi*, if the chickpeas are roasted: *De alimentis* 37. *melanes erebinthoi, mauroi erebinthoi*, black gram, urd, *Vigna Mungo*?: Simeon Seth p. 37; *De cibis* 10; *Lexikon kata alphabeton* 89. *o touton zomos syn amygdelaio*, [black gram] soup seasoned with almond oil: Simeon Seth p. 38.

Eriphos, kid: Simeon Seth p. 36; *De cibis* 5. *eriphoi galakteroi*, suckling kids: Hierophilus, April. Latin *haedus pinguis, allio, cepe, porris suffarcinatus, garo delibutus*, a fat kid, stuffed full of garlic, onion and leeks, drenched in fish sauce: Liutprand, *Embassy* 20.

Eukratomeli, honey water: *De cibis* 11, 12. *eukratomeli kalos epsethen*, honey water well boiled: *De cibis* 21.

Eukraton, cumin-flavoured drink. 'This *eukraton* consists of pepper, cumin, anise and hot water:' *Typikon of Stoudios* AB30, cf. *Typikon of Blemmydes* 11 [see Thomas and Hero 2001 pp. 111, 1204, 1698, 1701].

Euokhia, festivity: Anna Comnena, *Alexiad* 2.6.5.

Euzomon, rocket, *Eruca sativa* (cf. *rouka*): *De cibis* 10 etc.; *De alimentis* 70.

Gala, milk: Theophanes, *Chronicle* AM 6122; Simeon Seth p. 31; *De cibis* 5. *to nearon gala*, fresh milk: *Peri trophon dynameos* 478. *gala euthy melgeton, gala euthymelkton*, freshly milked milk: *De cibis* 5; *De alimentis* 1. *gala to ekhon oligon tyrogala*, milk with only a little cream: *De cibis* 11. *gala psykhron*, cold milk: *De cibis* 19. *gala to epipleon epsethen*, fully boiled milk: *De cibis* 20. *to pagen gala*, curds: *Peri trophon dynameos* 478.

Galia, galeai, smoothhounds, *Mustelus Mustelus*: *De cibis* 5, 14; *Opsarologos* 28.

Ganitikos oinos, wine from Mount Ganos in Thrace: *Prodromic Poems* 3.285.

Garisma, fish brine, cooking liquor. *garisma ydrokopemenon*, watery brine: *Prodromic Poems* 3.215.

Garos, fish sauce: *Geoponica* 20.46; *Prodromic Poems* 3.161–162; *De cibis* 9. Latin *garum*: Liutprand, *Embassy* 20; Belon, *Observations* 1.75. *cena oleo delibuta alioque quodam deterrimo piscium liquore aspersa*, a meal drenched in oil and spattered with some other very unpleasant liquid made from fish: Liutprand, *Embassy* 11. *ydor garou*, fish sauce diluted with water: *De cibis* 10. *dei tous dipsodeis rodostagmati touto mignyein*, those inclined to thirst should mix it with attar of roses: Simeon Seth p. 33.

Gazelia, gazelles, *Gazella spp. dorkades ta koinos legomena gazelia* [alternative terms]: Simeon Seth p. 33.

Gentiane, gentian, *Gentiana spp.*: Oribasius, *Medical Collections* 5.33.

Geranoi, cranes, *Megalornis Grus*: Simeon Seth p. 30; Michael Italicus [Browning in *Byzantinobulgarica* vol. 1 (1962) p. 185]; *De cibis* 5. French *grues*: *Voyage de Charlemagne* 411. *kree ton geranon*, crane meat: *Peri trophon dynameos* 477. *ta akre krasata*, [cranes'] feet cooked in wine: *Poullologos* 182.

Glaukoi, unidentified small fish: *Prodromic Poems* 3.180.

Gleukos, must, juice. *barbarikon ti gleukos*, some barbaric juice: Menander Protector, *History* 10.3 Blockley. *gleukos glyky*, sweet must: *Geoponica* 19.9.6.

Glossa, tongue: *De cibis* 20; *Peri tes ek ton zoon trophes*.

Glykismata, sweets: *Scholia on Aristophanes, Plutus* 660. *glykismata me tas apalareas*, spoon sweets: Prodromic Poems 3.321.

Glykomela, variety of apple: *Prodromic Poems* 2.65e.

Glykonerantza, sweet oranges, *Citrus sinensis*: Agapius, *Geoponicon* 26.

Glyky, sweet wine: Leontius of Naples, *Life of St Simeon Salos* p. 164 Rydén; *Prodromic Poems* 3.185, 4.70.

Gongylia, gonkylia, gongylai, gongyloi, turnips, *Brassica Rapa*: Simeon Seth p. 32; *De cibis* 7; Hierophilus, January; *Prodromic Poems* 2.41.

Gongylosparagon, young turnip shoots: *Geoponica* 12.1.

Gopharia, gompharia, lopharia, bluefish, *Pomatomus Saltator. Prodromic Poems* 3.179a, 3.325c. *amiai: ta gompharia* [incorrect classical equivalent]: *Scholia on Oppian, Halieutica* 1.112. Cf. Turkish *lüfer.*

Granata, pomegranate conserves or candies: *Prodromic Poems* 3.283b.

Grouta, kourkoute, kourkoutin, cracked wheat or barley: *Prodromic Poems* 2.42a; *Typikon of Kosmosoteira* 19. *athara egoun kourkoute, atharan legei ten grouten os oimai* [classical equivalent]: *Scholia on Aristophanes, Plutus* 673; Zonaras, *Lexicon. o legousin oi agroikoi kourkoutin,* what peasants call *kourkoutin*: *De alimentis* 34. *grutarium,* a bit of nourishment: Rufinus, *Historia Monachorum* 2.9. *gryte thalassia, lepte gryte,* sprats, negligible sea fish: *Geoponica* 20.7. *gryte potamia,* minnows, negligible river fish: *Geoponica* 20.12.

Gypson, gypsum: *Book of the Eparch* 13. Latin *gypsum*: Liutprand, *Embassy* 1.

Ia, violets, *Viola odorata*: Hierophilus, April; *Peri trophon dynameos* 474. *ion desmidia,* bunches of violets (a standard quantity). *iaton,* violet wine: Oribasius, *Medical Collections* 5.33.

Iasme, Persian jasmine, *Jasminum officinale,* and its oil: Aetius, *Medicine* 1.120. *to ex iasmion skeuazomenon elaion,* jasmine oil: *Peri trophon dynameos* 475. Cf. Du Cange 1688 *s.v. iasme*; see also *zambax.*

Ikhthyes, fish. *ikhthyes pelagioi,* deep sea fish: *De cibis* 5. *ikhthyes petraioi,* 'rock fish', inshore fish: *De cibis* 5. *ikhthyes petraioi meta skordon edeos prospheresthai,* rock fish to be served nicely with garlic: Alexander of Tralles, *Therapeutics* vol. 2 p. 339. *ikhthyes potamioi,* river fish: *De cibis* 23. *ikhthyes limnaioi,* lake fish: *De cibis* 23. *ikhthyes oi en borboro diaitoumenoi,* fish that feed on mud: *De cibis* 23. *ikhthyes trypherosarkoi,* soft-fleshed fish: Hierophilus, June. *ikhthyes plataioi,* flatfish: Hierophilus, August. *ikhthyes khloroi,* fresh fish: Hierophilus, August. *ikhthyes tetarikheuomenoi,* pickled and salt fish: *Book of the Eparch* 13.

Indikai karykeiai, ta ex Indikes aromata, Eastern spices, E. aromatics: Theophylact Simocatta, *Histories* 7.13.6; Asterius of Amasea, *Homilies* 1.5.3. *ta Indikotata aromata,* the most exotic of aromatics: Psellus, *Chronographia* 6.62.

Indikon phyllon, tejpat leaf (see *phyllon*).

Intyba, intibon, intibion, entybia, endives, *Cichorium Endivia*: *De alimentis* 1, 3; *De cibis* 5, 7, 14; *Prodromic Poems* 2.40 (ms. G). *intibon met' elaiou kai garou esthiomenon*, endive eaten with olive oil and fish sauce: *De alimentis* 67. *entibon en oxei skillitiko baptomenon*, endive dressed with squill vinegar: Hierophilus, June.

Ioularoi, rainbow wrasse, *Coris Julis*: Hierophilus, June.

Iskhades, iskhadai, dried figs: *De alimentis* 6; *De cibis* 19 etc. *iskhades takhy pephtheisai*, figs dried rapidly: *De cibis* 5. *iskhades khronisasai*, figs dried slowly: *De cibis* 5. *iskhades meta karyon esthiomenai, karya met' iskhadon esthiomena*, dried figs with walnuts: *De cibis* 5; *De alimentis* 58. *iskhades meta karyon kai peganou pro ton sition*, dried figs with walnuts and rue before the main meal [as protection against poison]: Simeon Seth p. 49.

Itria, itrin, pasta: *De cibis* 11, 20; *De alimentis* 18.

Kakkabai, partridges, *Perdix Perdix*: Eustathius, *Commentary on Iliad* 23.101.

Kalamaria, squid, *Loligo vulgaris*: *De cibis* 7 etc.; *Peri tes ek ton zoon trophes*.

Kalaminthe, kalaminthos, catmint, *Nepeta spp.*?: Simeon Seth p. 32; *Peri trophon dynameos* 475; *Scholia on Nicander, Theriaca* 60. *to dia kalaminthes*, a digestive with catmint: Aetius, *Medicine* 9.24; Paul of Aegina, *Medical Epitome* 7.11.33, cf. 2.25, 3.37; Leo, *Outline of Medicine* 4.13, 5.2.

Kamelion, camel, *Camelus spp.*. *apo kameliou omon*, raw camel [which only a madman would eat]: Leontius of Naples, *Life of St Simeon Salos* p. 158 Rydén.

Kamphora, kaphoura, camphor, *Dryobalanops aromatica*: Aetius, *Medicine* 16.130; *Peri trophon dynameos* 475; Simeon Seth p. 58.

Kanabokokkon, kanabouri, kannabosperma, cannabis seed, *Cannabis sativa*: *De cibis* 18; *De alimentis* 16; *Prodromic Poems* 2.45 (ms. G); *Porikologos* 14. *kanaben*, cannabis, hemp: *Book of the Eparch* 13. *en tois Arabois touto massatai anti oinou kai ekmethyousi*, among the Arabs it is chewed and they become intoxicated as if from wine: Simeon Seth p. 61.

Kaparis, kapparis, capers, *Capparis spinosa*: Michael Choniates, *Letters* 127; *De cibis* 22, 24. *kapparis di' oxymelitos e oxelaiou emprosthen* (or *pro ton allon sition*) *esthiomene*, capers eaten as a starter with honey vinegar or oil and vinegar: *De cibis* 10; *De alimentis* 63.

Kapnisma, incense. *kapnismatitzin*, tiny bit of incense: Tzetzes, *Letters* 59 Leone. *kapnismata diaphora*, various incenses: Constantine Porphyrogennetus, *On Ceremonies* p. 468 Reiske.

Karabis, crayfish, *Nephrops norvegicus*: *De cibis* 7; *Peri tes ek ton zoon trophes. karabides ekzestai*, stewed crayfish: *Prodromic Poems* 3.276.

Kardama, kardamon, cress, *Lepidum sativum*: *De cibis* 8, 22, 24.

Kardamomon, cardamom, *Elettaria Cardamomum*. Latin *cardamomum*: Justinian, *Digest* 39.4.16.7.

Kardia, heart: *De cibis* 7. *boon kardia*, ox heart: *De cibis* 21.

Kareophylla, karophalon, karyophyllon, xerokaryophyllon, cloves, *Syzygium aromaticum*: Cosmas Indicopleustes 11.15; Aetius, *Medicine* 1.131; *Prodromic Poems* 3.150; *Peri trophon dynameos* 476; Hierophilus, January.

Karidia, karides, shrimps and prawns: *De cibis* 7, 21; *Peri tes ek ton zoon trophes. kariditsai teganou*, pan-fried prawns: *Prodromic Poems* 3.276.

Karkinos, species of crab: *De cibis* 7, 13; *Peri tes ek ton zoon trophes.*

Karnabadin, caraway, *Carum Carvi*: *Prodromic Poems* 3.162; *De alimentis* 26; Pseudo-Galen, *Signs from Urine. karnabadi: karoe* [alternative terms]: *Lexikon ton Sarakenon* 154; Pseudo-Galen, *Lexeis Botanon. to karos touto einai ena khorton os to anithon*, caraway, which is a herb like dill: Agapius, *Geoponicon. karnabadon Anatoles*, Eastern caraway: Hierophilus, January.

Karpos, fruit. *autophyeis karpoi*, wild fruits: Theodoret, *Religious History* 1.2.

Karya, karydia, walnuts, *Juglans regia*: *De cibis* 5, 8; *Peri trophon dynameos* 474. *karyon basilikon to nyn legomenon karyon* [classical equivalent]: *Geoponica* 10.73. *karydokoukounaria*, nuts and pine kernels: *Prodromic Poems* 2.44 (ms. G). *karya ta khlora, karydia khlora*, green walnuts: *De cibis* 12; *De alimentis* 27. *karya ta xera*, dry walnuts: *De cibis* 12. *ton xeron karyon ta apobebregmena en ydati kai apolepisthenta*, dry walnuts, steeped in water and shelled: *De cibis* 12; *De alimentis* 58. *karydaton*, walnut conserve: *Prodromic Poems* 3.283a.

Karya basilika, walnuts: Hierophilus, September. nutmegs, *Myristica fragrans*: *Peri trophon dynameos* 476. *to aromatikon karyon*, nutmeg: Simeon Seth p. 56.

Karykeumata, meat dishes with sauces: Hierophilus 1. *karykeia*, saucing, serving with sauces: Anna Comnena, *Alexiad* 2.6.5.

Kasia, cassia, *Cinnamomum Cassia*: Oribasius, *Medical Collections* 5.33; Theophylact Simocatta, *Histories* 7.13.6. *silíkhan* [i.e. Arabic *sallīkha*]: *kasian*: *Lexikon ton Sarakenon* 303. Latin *cassia turiana*, an unknown grade: Justinian, *Digest* 39.4.16.7. Latin *xylocassia*, a low grade: Justinian, *Digest* 39.4.16.7.

Kastana, chestnuts, *Castanea sativa*: *De cibis* 5; *Peri trophon dynameos* 474; *Prodromic Poems* 2.65d. *Dios balanos esti to kastanon* [classical equivalent]: *Geoponica* 10.73. *kastana optomena*, roast chestnuts: Simeon Seth p. 50.

Kataplasma, dough: *De cibis* 2.

Katastaton, frumenty. *katastaton o kai amylon legetai* [classical equivalent]: *Peri trophon dynameos* 470, cf. *Lexikon kata alphabeton* 5, *Scholia on Aristophanes, Acharnians* 1092. *katastaton epsethen syn amygdalois tetrimmenois kai sakkharei*, frumenty made with ground almonds and sugar: *Peri trophon dynameos* 470.

Kedraia, cedar oil: *Book of the Eparch* 13.

Kedrokokka, juniper berries, *Juniperus spp.*: *De alimentis* 31.

Kenkhris, kenkhros, broomcorn millet, *Panicum miliaceum* (cf. *pistos*): Theophanes, *Chronicle* am 6235; Anna Comnena, *Alexiad* 6.14.1; *De cibis* 2. *kenkhrinos artos*, millet bread: Nicolaus Mesarites, *Journey* p. 42 Heisenberg. *aprosphoros sitesis, phemi de kenkhros*, inadequate food, by which I mean millet: Anna Comnena, *Alexiad* 13.2.4.

Kephale, head. *ai kephalai panton ton zoon*, heads of all kinds of animals: *Peri trophon dynameos* 477.

Kephalos, grey mullet, *Mugil Cephalus*: *De cibis* 5; *Peri tes ek ton zoon trophes*; *Prodromic Poems* 3.325a. *kephalos tripithamos augatos ek to Rygin*, a grey mullet of three hands' breadths, with its roe, from Region harbour: *Prodromic Poems* 3.153.

Kerasia, sweet cherries, *Prunus avium*: *De cibis* 12; *Peri trophon dynameos* 472. *kerasia ek ton Leukaten*, cherries from Leucate near Constantinople: *Prodromic Poems* 2.65b.

Kerykia, horn-shells, *Cerithium vulgatum*: *De cibis* 20, 21.

Kestreus, grey mullet, *Liza Ramada* and other species: Gregory of Cyprus, *Letters* 3.

Ketodes. oi ketodeis ton ikhthyon, ta ketode ton en thalasse zoon, shark-like fish, *Squaliformes*: *De cibis* 20, 23.

Khabiarion, caviar: *Dream Book of Nicephorus* 334; Theodore Ducas, *Letters* 54 Festa [according to Georgacas 1978 p. 202]. French *caviar*: Belon, *Observations* 1.75. *khabiaritzin*, a bit of caviar: *Prodromic Poems* 2.347 Korais, cf. 3.280. *tarterou khabiarin*, cheap caviar from the bottom of the barrel: *Prodromic Poems* 3.83. *khabiaropouloi*, the caviar-sellers: *Prodromic Poems* 3.208.

Khalbane, galbanum, *Ferula galbaniflua*. Latin *ghalbane*: Justinian, *Digest* 39.4.16.7.

Khamaidaphnia, large butcher's broom, *Ruscus hypoglossum* [young shoots treated like asparagus]: Hierophilus, January, June.

Khamaimelon, wild chamomile, *Matricaria Chamomilla*: Hierophilus, April; *Peri trophon dynameos* 475. *khamaimelon kokkia*, chamomile seeds. *khamaimelaton*, chamomile wine: Oribasius, *Medical Collections* 5.33. *khamaimelelaion*, chamomile oil: Pseudo-Galen, *Signs from Urine*.

Khanoi, perch, *Serranus Cabrilla*: Hierophilus, April.

Khebades, clams, *Veneridae*: *De cibis* 20.

Khedropa, legumes: Nicolaus Mesarites, *Journey* p. 42 Heisenberg.

Khenaria, khenes, geese, *Anser Anser*: Constantine Porphyrogennetus, *On Ceremonies* p. 487 Reiske; *De cibis* 5. French *gauntes*, wild geese: *Voyage de Charlemagne* 411. *ta pterygia ton khenon*, goose wings: *De cibis* 21.

Khersaia zoa, land animals. *oma krea khersaion zoon*, raw meat of animals: Anna Comnena, *Alexiad* 10.11.3.

Khion, snow: Simeon Seth p. 122.

Khiotikon, Chian wine: *Prodromic Poems* 3.156, 3.260.

Khoiridia, khoiroi, pigs, *Sus Scrofa*: *De cibis* 5, 18. *ta mikra khoiridia, khoirea mikra*, sucking pigs: *De cibis* 23; Hierophilus, January. *khoiridia eniausia*, pigs one year old: *De cibis* 5. *khoiria siteuthenta dia tyrogalaktos*, pigs fattened on cream (cf. *plymma*): *De cibis* 6. *khoireia krea*, pork: *De cibis* 20, 21. *en optesei ton khoireon kreon aleiphesthosan oinomeliti*, when roasting pork baste with honeyed wine: Hierophilus, January. *ta khoireia esthiomena opta meta pepereos e sinapeos*, pork roasted and eaten with pepper or mustard: *Peri trophon dynameos* 476, cf. *optoutsikon myrodaton*, nicely roasted and spiced: *Diegesis ton tetrapodon zoon* 373. *khoiromeria*, legs of pork: *Diegesis ton tetrapodon zoon* 378.

Khoirobotanon, purslane, *Portulaca oleracea*: *De cibis* 13. *khoirobotanon to kai traulon legomenon*, purslane, also called 'lisper': *De alimentis* 20.

Khoirogryllos, unidentified sea fish: Psellus, *Letters* 274 Kurtz and Drexl.

Kholokokka, kholokouka, castor oil seeds, *Ricinus communis*: *Life of St Theodore of Syceon* 1.77; *Prodromic Poems* 3.202.

Khondros, khondrokhylon, emmer gruel: *De cibis* 5; *Prodromic Poems* 3.318, 3.400gg.

Khordia, khordai, intestines, especially of sheep: Alexander of Tralles, *Therapeutics* vol. 2 p. 403; Arethas, *On Lucian's Lexiphanes* 13; *Scholia on Aristophanes, Acharnians* 1040. *khordokoilitsia*, sausages and offal: *Prodromic Poems* 4.51. *khordokoilistra*, butcher's wife, charcutière: *Prodromic Poems* 4.233.

Khoumele, hops, *Humulus Lupulus*, and an alcoholic drink flavoured with hops. *sikera esti pan to aneu oinou methen empoioun ... os e legomene khoumele kai osa omoios skeuazontai*, 'strong drink' means all intoxicants except wine, such as the so-called *khoumele* and others made similarly: Zonaras, *On the Apostolic Canons* 3 [*PG* vol. 137 col. 40].

Khrysaphia, khrysophrya, daurade, gilt-head bream, *Sparus aurata*: Hierophilus, January.

Khrysolakhanon, orach, *Atriplex hortensis*: *De cibis* 9; *Peri trophon dynameos* 479; *Prodromic Poems* 2.41.

Khylos, cooking liquor: *Peri trophon dynameos* 469; *De cibis* 10.

Kikhlai, mistle thrushes, *Turdus viscivorus*: *De cibis* 5. corkwings or smaller wrasses, *Crenilabrus spp.*: Hierophilus, February.

Kiki, kikinon elaion, castor oil, *Ricinus communis*: *Peri trophon dynameos* 468; *Glossae Jatricae*.

Kinamomon, kinnamomon, cinnamon, *Cinnamomum spp.*: *Book of the Eparch* 10; Simeon Seth p. 55; Constantine Porphyrogennetus, *On Ceremonies* 1.42 [vol. 1 p. 166 Vogt]. Latin *cinnamomum*: Justinian, *Digest* 39.4.16.7. *xylokinnamomon*, cinnamon wood, a low grade: Constantine Porphyrogennetus, *On Ceremonies* p. 468 Reiske. Latin *xylocinnamomum*: Justinian, *Digest*

39.4.16.7. *kinnamomon alethinon proton kai deuteron*, true cinnamon, first and second grades: Constantine Porphyrogennetus, *On Ceremonies* p. 468 Reiske.

Kinara, artichoke, *Cynara Scolymus*: *De cibis* 14, 16.

Kithargos, a flatfish, perhaps flounder, *Platichthys Flesus*? *De alimentis* 1; *De cibis* 5 (emended). *kithargos optoutsikos akeraios me to garos to karnabadin anothen eos kato pepasmenos*, a flounder, nicely grilled on its own, with fish sauce, sprinkled from top to tail with caraway: *Prodromic Poems* 3.161–162.

Kitron, lemon, *Citrus Limonia*: *De cibis* 7; *Peri trophon dynameos* 473. *phloios kitrou*, lemon peel: *De cibis* 7, 8. *kitrou sarx*, lemon flesh: *De cibis* 20. *to dia kitrou*, lemon conserve: *Prodromic Poems* 3.283. *to syn meliti kai artymasi skeuazomenon, dia kitriou onomazomenon*, the conserve made with honey and spices called *dia kitriou*: Simeon Seth p. 53. *kitraton*, lemon-flavoured wine: Alexander of Tralles, *Therapeutics* vol. 2 p. 341.

Kletorion, reception, dinner hosted by the Emperor: Constantine Porphyrogennetus, *On Ceremonies* 1.74 [vol. 2 p. 102 Vogt].

Klibanota, baked meats, e.g. lamb: Eustathius, *Commentary on Iliad* 23.33 (cf. Koukoulès 1948–55 vol. 5 p. 50 notes 9–10).

Knekos, safflower, *Carthamus tinctorius. phyllosperma knekou*, the 'leaf-seed' (fruit) of safflower: Hierophilus, April.

Kobidia, koubidia, kobia, kobioi, gobies, *Gobius spp.*: *De cibis* 5, 7, 14; *Opsarologos* 27.

Kodia, poppy head, *Papaver somniferum* (cf. *mekon*). *to tes kodias blyta sperma*, poppy seed: *De alimentis* 27.

Kodimenta, koudoumenta, aromatics: Hierophilus, January; *Prodromic Poems* 1.13. Probably specifically parsley, *Petroselinum crispum*: Anastasius, *Narrative* 9; *Prodromic Poems* 2.40.

Koiliai, koilia, intestines: *De cibis* 7; *Peri trophon dynameos* 478; *Peri tes ek ton zoon trophes*.

Kokhlioi, kokhliai, snails and winkles: *De cibis* 7, 12; *De alimentis* 3, 12.

Kokkimela, plums, *Prunus spp.*: *De alimentis* 25.

Kokkodaphna, bay berries, *Laurus nobilis*: Paul of Aegina, *Medical Epitome* 3.28; Hierophilus, October, November.

Kokkygia, kokkyges, gurnard, *Trigla spp.*: *Peri tes ek ton zoon trophes*; Hierophilus, April.

Kollikia, ring-shaped loaves: Athenaeus, *Deipnosophists* 112f; Gregory of Corinth, *On the Violet* 549.

Kollyba, boiled wheat pudding: *Life of St Theodore of Syceon* 6; *Typikon of Stoudios* A30.

Kolokasion, taro, *Colocasia esculenta* var. *antiquorum*: Aetius, *Medicine* 1.120.

Kolokyntha, kolokynthe, kolokynthos, gourd, *Lagenaria vulgaris*: *De cibis* 6; *De alimentis* 25; *Diegesis ton tetrapodon zoon* 371. *kolokyntha ekzeste*, boiled gourd: *De cibis* 26. *koptousi kai xerainousi ten kolokynthen kai xeran esthiousin en kheimoni*, they slice and dry the gourd and eat it, dry, in winter: *De alimentis* 44.

Kommatia, slices, steaks. *khontra kommatia*, thick steaks: *Prodromic Poems* 1.267.

Konditon, kondyton, spiced wine: Oribasius, *Medical Collections* 5.33; *Apophthegmata Patrum, Petrus Pionites* 1. French *clarez*: *Voyage de Charlemagne* 412. *konditon ekhon peperi kinamomon stakhos kareophyllon*, spiced wine containing pepper, cinnamon, spikenard and cloves: Hierophilus, March. *euode kai anisata kondita*, aromatic and anise-flavoured spiced wines: Hierophilus, June.

Konkharia, konkhylai, konkhylia, kokhlidia, shellfish: *De cibis* 7, 12; *De alimentis* 18. wedge-shells, *Donax trunculus*: *Peri tes ek ton zoon trophes*.

Kopadin, bit of meat to dip in sauce. *idou touto kalon kopadin esti, phage, abba*, look, here's a nice bit: eat this, Father: *Apophthegmata Patrum, Theophilus* 4.

Koriandron, koliandron, coriander, *Coriandrum sativum*: *De cibis* 24; *Porikologos* 18.

Kossyphoi, blackbirds, *Turdus Merula*: *De cibis* 5.

Kostos, kostarin, putchuk, kushth, *Saussurea Lappa*: Oribasius, *Medical Collections* 5.33; Cosmas Indicopleustes 11.15; Theophylact Simocatta, *Histories* 7.13.6. Latin *costum*: Justinian, *Digest* 39.4.16.7.

Kostos, perhaps costmary, *Tanacetum balsamina*: *Geoponica* 11.27.

Koubebe, cubebs, *Piper Cubeba*. *koubébe* [i.e. Arabic *kabbāba*]: *karpopesion*: *Lexikon ton Sarakenon* 153, 170 [this is intended as a classical equivalent, but it is a false one; cubebs were not familiar in the classical world, while *karpe-*

sion was an Anatolian herb, perhaps *Valeriana Dioscoridis*: see e.g. Oribasius, *Medical Collections* 5.33.8]. *koumpeper*: *to kardamomon*: *Scholia on Nicolaus Myrepsus, Antidotes* 22 [another false equivalent; cubebs are not cardamom].

Koukia, broad beans, *Vicia Faba*. Agapius, *Geoponicon*; Du Cange.

Koukoubai, a variety of grape: Eustathius, *Letters* 3.

Koukounaria, koukonaria, kokonaria, konaria, pine kernels, *Pinus spp.*: *Poriko-logos* 6; Hierophilus, January, September; *Prodromic Poems* 2.44 (ms. G). *konaria etoi oi strobiloi* [classical equivalent]: Simeon Seth p. 51.

Koullouritsi, ring-shaped bread roll: *Prodromic Poems* 2.26h.

Koumara, arbutus fruits, *Arbutus Unedo*: *De cibis* 20.

Kounoupidin, cauliflower: *Prodromic Poems* 2.42 (ms. G).

Kourkoutin see under *grouta*.

Koutzourina, unidentified fish (cf. modern *koutsomoura*, red mullet): *Opsaro-logos* 29.

Koutzoulos, korydallos, korydos, lark, *Galerida cristata*. *ophelei tous kolikous zomo lito epsomenos kai synekhos ama to zomo lambanomenos*, it helps those with colic if cooked in a thin broth and eaten together with the broth: Aetius, *Medicine* 9.31.

Krama, lunch: Constantine Porphyrogennetus, *Book of Ceremonies* 1.9 [p. 61 Vogt].

Krambin, krampin, krambe, cabbage, *Brassica oleracea*: *De cibis* 10. *krambiou o kaulos*, cabbage stalk: *De alimentis* 10. *krambe Phrygia*, Phrygian cabbage: *Timarion* 17. *krambin kardiai tessarai khontrai kai khionatai*, four cabbage hearts, fat and snow-white: *Prodromic Poems* 3.178. *ten kramben epsein met' elaiogarou*, boil cabbage and serve with olive oil and fish sauce: Hierophilus, January.

Krambosparagon, young cabbage shoots: *Geoponica* 12.1 [see Koder 1992].

Krana, krania, cornels, *Cornus mas*: *De cibis* 22; *De alimentis* 20; *Porikologos* 18.

Krasin, wine: *Prodromic Poems* 1.179. *akrasia*, not having any wine: *Prodromic Poems* 3.419f.

Krea, kree, kreas, meat: *De cibis* 5 etc.; *Peri trophon dynameos* 477; *Book of the Eparch* 13. *ei kreas esti ou trogomen*, if it's meat, we don't eat it: *Apophthegmata Patrum, Theophilus* 4. French *viande*: Geoffroi de Villehardouin 130. *oma krea, oma kreata*, raw meat: Anna Comnena, *Alexiad* 10.11.3, 4. *ta rousia kree*, red meat: *Peri trophon dynameos* 478. *kree tryphera kai eusarka*, plump, tender meat: Hierophilus, April. *kree psakhna, psakhnon, kree ta me ekhonta lipos*, lean meat, meat with no fat: Hierophilus, April, November; *Peri trophon dynameos* 478; Agapius, *Geoponicon*. *kree ta ekhonta lipos*, fatty meat: *Peri trophon dynameos* 478. *pasta krea, kree pasta*, salt meat: *De cibis* 16; Hierophilus, October.

Kretikos oinos, Cretan wine: *Prodromic Poems* 3.285. *Kretikon tyritsin, Kretikon tyron*, Cretan cheese: *Prodromic Poems* 3.179; Michael Apostoles, *Letters* p. 92 Noiret.

Krikellos, ring-shaped pasta? *ek semidaleos pyrou tou aristou leptotatoi krikelloi*, the lightest krikelloi of the best durum wheat: Theodore of Cyzicus, *Letters* 1.

Kriaria, krioi, rams: Constantine Porphyrogennetus, *On Ceremonies* p. 487 Reiske; *De cibis* 7. *krion neon kai eunoukhon krea psakhna diephtha*, lean meat of young and castrated rams, twice boiled: Hierophilus, April.

Krina, lilies, *Lilium spp.*: Hierophilus, April; *Peri trophon dynameos* 475.

Krithe, kritharin, barley, barley meal, *Hordeum vulgare*: Constantine Porphyrogennetus, *On Ceremonies* p. 658 Reiske; *De cibis* 10; *De alimentis* 27. *krithai apolepistheisai*, hulled barley: *De cibis* 5. *khylos tes krithes*, barley water: *Peri trophon dynameos* 469. *artos krithinos, psomin krithinon*, barley bread: *Dream Book of Daniel* 480; *De cibis* 18.

Krokos, saffron, *Crocus sativus*: Oribasius, *Medical Collections* 5.33; Constantine Porphyrogennetus, *On Ceremonies* p. 468 Reiske; Simeon Seth p. 58; *De alimentis* 31; *Peri trophon dynameos* 476. *krokatomagereia ekhousa stakhos, sysgouda, karophala, tripsidin, amanitaria, oxos te kai melin ek to akapnin*, a sweet-and-sour saffron dish with spikenard, valerian, cloves, cinnamon, and little mushrooms, and vinegar and unsmoked honey: *Prodromic Poems* 3.149.

Krommya, krommydia, onions, *Allium Cepa*: *De cibis* 10, 14, 22; *Prodromic Poems* 3.412. *mikroutzikon kephalin kromyditzin*, a tiny little onion bulb: *Prodromic Poems* 3.412c.

Krystallinoi, 'frost-grapes', grapes conserved till winter: Eustathius, *Letters* 6.

Ktenia, scallops, *Pectinidae*: *Prodromic Poems* 3.278; *De cibis* 20; *Peri tes ek ton zoon trophes*.

Kyamoi, broad beans, *Vicia Faba*: *Peri trophon dynameos* 469; *De cibis* 5, 19, 21. *kyamoi khloroi*, fresh broad beans: *De cibis* 23. See also *phaba*.

Kydonia, mela kydonia, melokydonia, quinces, *Cydonia vulgaris*: *Peri trophon dynameos* 468; *De cibis* 8; Hierophilus, September. *kydonia ta skeuasthenta ek te melitos kai aromaton*, quinces conserved with honey and spices and eaten with the syrup: *Peri trophon dynameos* 473. *ei tis epsesas ton kydonion ton kylon meta melitos apotithesin*, if one boils the juice of quinces with honey and makes a conserve: *De alimentis* 53. *kydonata*, quince marmalade: Simeon Seth p. 48; *Prodromic Poems* 3.283a; Hierophilus, January.

Kyknoi, swans, *Cygnus Olor*: *De cibis* 5; Critobulus of Imbros 2.12.6.

Kyminon, cumin, *Cuminum Cyminum*: *De cibis* 10. *kyminon tripton*, ground cumin: Hierophilus, January.

Kypeiros Alexandreias, chufa, tigernut, *Cyperus esculentus*: Pseudo-Galen, *Signs from Urine*.

Kyprinaria, carp, *Cyprinus Carpio*. *kyprinariou e mese*, a middle cut of carp: *Prodromic Poems* 3.179.

Labrax, laurax, laurakion, bass, *Dicentrarchus Labrax*: *Miracles of Ss Cyrus and John* 9; *De cibis* 5; *Prodromic Poems* 3.163.

Ladanon, ladanum, exudate of *Cistus spp.*: Simeon Seth p. 63; Pseudo-Galen, *Signs from Urine*.

Lagenata, a variety of plum (see *Anatolika*).

Laginis, a wild fruit tree, possibly azarole, *Crataegus Azarolus?*: *De cibis* 13; *De alimentis* 9; cf. *Porikologos* 59.

Lagos, hare, *Lepus spp.*: *De cibis* 14; Hierophilus, July. *lageia krea*, hare meat: *De cibis* 20. *to lagomageireuma to legousi krasaton*, so-called drunken hare, a dish of hare cooked in wine: Peter Zyphomustus, *Physiologike diegesis* [*Neos Ellenomnemon* vol. 1 p. 447]. Latin *[lepores] sumendi in dulci piper habentem, parum cariofili et gingiber, costo et spica nardi uel folio*, hares to be taken in sweet wine with pepper, a little cloves and ginger, with putchuk and spike-nard or tejpat: Anthimus 13.

Lakerta, salted tunny: *Opsarologos* 29.

Lakhana, vegetables, greens: Nicetas Choniates, *Chronicle* p. 57 van Dieten; *De cibis* 5; Latin *lachana*: Liutprand, *Antapodosis* 5.23. *emera lakhana*, cultivated vegetables: *Peri trophon dynameos* 479. *autophye lakhana*, wild greens: Theodoret, *Religious History* 2.4. *lakhanitzin*, a few greens: *Prodromic Poems* 3.277. *lakhanogoula*, cabbage stalks: *Prodromic Poems* 4.129f. *lakhana syntheta*, pickled greens: *Historia Monachorum in Aegypto* 2. *ton autophyon lakhanon syllegontes eita keramous emphorountes kai tes almes oson apokhre mignyntes eikhon opson*, gathering wild greens and putting them in jars with brine to cover them, they had something to eat with their bread: Theodoret, *Religious History* 2.4.

Laktenta, suckling animals: Hierophilus, November. sucking pigs: *De alimentis* 21. Latin *lactantes*: Anthimus 10.

Lalangia, fritters: *Suda* s.v. 'kollyra'. *lalangia me to meli*, fritters with honey: *Prodromic Poems* 3.319.

Lapara, slice of meat: Palladas [*Anthologia Palatina* 9.486]. *lapara traganodekhtos*, slice of goat meat: *Prodromic Poems* 4.237.

Lapathon, sorrel, *Rumex spp.*: *De cibis* 10.

Lapinai, wrasses, *Labrus spp.* [cf. Turkish *lapina*]: Hierophilus, February.

Lardin, larden, lardoi, bacon: Constantine Porphyrogennetus, *On Ceremonies* p. 464 Reiske; Michael Italicus, *Letters* 42; Zonaras, *Lexicon* s.v. 'tarikheuton opson'. Latin *laredum*: Anthimus 14. *koptein kai trogein omon to lardin*, slicing and eating the bacon raw: Leontius of Naples, *Life of St Simeon Salos* p. 158 Rydén, cf. Anthimus 14. See also *sys*.

Larinon, a kind of fish. *larinon oxodes*, pickled 'larinos': Tzetzes, *Letters* 39 Leone. *larinon to legomenon kylas* [alternative terms]: *Scholia on Oppian, Halieutica* 3.399.

Lathyris, lathyrin, lathyros, grass pea, *Lathyrus sativus*: *De cibis* 7; Simeon Seth p. 133. *e artysis auton di' elaiou kai kyminou triptou*, they can be seasoned with olive oil and ground cumin: Hierophilus, January.

Leiobatoi, rays, *Raja spp.*: *De cibis* 7, 21; *Peri tes ek ton zoon trophes*.

Lemonia, lemons, *Citrus Limonia*: *Porikologos* 2; Agapius, *Geoponicon*.

Leptokarya, hazelnuts, *Corylus spp.*: *De cibis* 6; *Peri trophon dynameos* 474; *De alimentis* 20. *karyon pontikon: to leptokaryon* [classical equivalent] : *Geoponica* 10.73, cf. Simeon Seth p. 62. *leptokarya ta megala*, filberts, *Corylus colurna*: *De alimentis* 20.

Leukoskaros, kind of wrasse, *Labridae*: Psellus, *Letters* 48 Sathas, 263 Kurtz and Drexl.

Libanos, frankincense, *Boswellia* spp.: Constantine Porphyrogennetus, *On Ceremonies* p. 468 Reiske; *Book of the Eparch* 10.

Libystikon, lovage, *Levisticum officinale*: Hierophilus, January; Pseudo-Galen, *Signs from Urine*. *libystikou sperma kai e riza*, seed and root of lovage: *De cibis* 18. *libystikaton*, lovage-flavoured wine: Alexander of Tralles, *Therapeutics* vol. 2 p. 341.

Linokokka, linarion, linseed, *Linum usitatissimum*: *De cibis* 18; *De alimentis* 16 etc.; *Book of the Eparch* 13. *epipattousi d'enioi kai tois artois auto*, some people sprinkle it on loaves: Simeon Seth p. 138.

Linozostis, garden mercury, *Mercurialis annua*: *De cibis* 12.

Lipanabata, shortbread: *Prodromic Poems* 2.26g; Theodore Balsamon, *Commentary on Trullo* 11th canon.

Loboi, lablab beans, *Dolichos Lablab*: *De alimentis* 19.

Loukanika, lokanika, loukanika sausage: *Philogelos* 237; *Diegesis ton tetrapodon zoon* 379.

Loupinaria, loupenaria, loupinos, lupins, *Lupinus alba*: Theophanes, *Chronicle* am 6235; *De cibis* 19–21; *De alimentis* 19; Pseudo-Galen, *Signs from Urine*.

Lykhnos, stargazer, *Uranoscopus scaber*: *Opsarologos* 29.

Mainidia, picarels and mendoles, *Spicara spp.*: *Timarion* 21.

Mainomene, a grape variety: Leontius of Naples, *Life of St John the Almsgiver* 20.

Maioumas, military feast hosted by the Emperor: Constantine Porphyrogennetus, *On Ceremonies* pp. 487, 490 Reiske; Georgius Monachus, *Short Chronicle* [*PG* vol. 110 col. 983]; cf. Joannes Lydus, *On the Months* 4.80.

Maker, mace, *Myristica fragrans. maker: pespés* [i.e. Arabic *basbās* 'mace, fennel']: *Lexikon ton Sarakenon* 272.

Malabathron, tejpat, *Cinnamomum Tamala*. Latin *malabathrum*: Justinian, *Digest* 39.4.16.7.

Malakhe, mallow, *Malva spp.*: *De cibis* 6; *Peri trophon dynameos* 479.

Malakia, soft-bodied seafood: *De cibis* 18; *Peri tes ek ton zoon trophes*.

Malathron, marathron, fennel, *Foeniculum vulgare*: *De cibis* 2, 24. *marathrorriza,* fennel root: Pseudo-Galen, *Signs from Urine. razanon etoi marathrosporon*, fennel seed: Pseudo-Galen, *On Similar Remedies* p. 564.

Manna, manna (exudate on leaves of the manna ash, *Fraxinus Ornus*, and other trees): *Peri trophon dynameos* 474.

Maraon, cornel, *Cornus mas. o de karpos autes kaleitai pittaxis, oi de barbilon phasin, oi de maraon* [*pittaxis* and *maraon* are the classical and Byzantine names, if Eustathius is right; but he seems to be wrong about *barbilos*, q.v.]: Eustathius, *Commentary on Odyssey* 10.242.

Mareotikon oinon, Mareotic wine [from Egypt: its taste is nothing to boast of and its price is low]: *Life of St John the Almsgiver* [ed. Delehaye] 10.

Maroullia, maioulia, lettuces, *Lactuca sativa*: *De cibis* 5; *De alimentis* 66; *Prodromic Poems* 2.40 (ms. G). *ta maroullia a kai thridakinai kalountai* [classical equivalent]: Simeon Seth p. 64. *marouli metrios oxygarizein en oxei skillitiko baptomenon*, lettuce to be dressed moderately with squill vinegar: Hierophilus, April, cf. June. *to tou maroulliou sperma*, lettuce seed: *De alimentis* 27.

Mastarin, udder: *De cibis* 5; *Peri tes ek ton zoon trophes*; *Prodromic Poems* 4.235.

Mastikhe, mastic, *Pistacia Lentiscus* var. *Chia*: Constantine Porphyrogennetus, *On Ceremonies* p. 468 Reiske; Psellus, *Letters* 136 Kurtz and Drexl; *De cibis* 2. *opomastikhe*, 'liquid mastic', fresh mastic: Pseudo-Galen, *Signs from Urine. mastikhinon*, oil of mastic: Nicolaus Myrepsus, *Compounds* 37.43, cf. Simeon Seth p. 21. *mastikhaton*, mastic-flavoured wine: Alexander of Tralles, *Therapeutics* vol. 2 p. 341.

Mastoi, udders: *De cibis* 20.

Matzanai, mazizania, matitania, bazizania, aubergines, *Solanum Melongena*: *Prodromic Poems* 2.41, 4.129f; *De cibis* 22; *De alimentis* 20, 28. *to matitanion para to Galeno strykhnos kepeutos onomazetai*, the aubergine is called 'garden nightshade' in Galen's works [in fact the fruits are related but not identical]: Simeon Seth p. 70. *kolokasion e manzizanion*, taro or aubergine [confusion]: Aetius, *Medicine* 1.120.

Mazos, a fish, perhaps a kind of hake: *Prodromic Poems* 3.148; *Opsarologos* 32.

Mekon, poppy, poppy seed, *Papaver spp. kreitton tes melaines e leuke*, the white is better than the black: Simeon Seth p. 68.

Mela, melitzia, apples, *Malus pumila*: *Prodromic Poems* 3.282; *Peri trophon dynameos* 468; *De cibis* 13. *mela aora, mela agoura, mela ta me orima,* unripe apples: *De cibis* 15; *De alimentis* 11, 18. *mela ta agourotera,* underripe apples: *De alimentis* 30. *mela ta orima,* ripe apples: *De cibis* 20. *mela ta glykea,* sweet apples: *De cibis* 13, 25; *Peri trophon dynameos* 473. *mela ta glykytera e drimytera,* apples that are rather sweet than sharp: *De cibis* 13. *mela ta styphonta,* astringent apples: *De cibis* 13. *mela ta oxyna,* acid apples: *Peri trophon dynameos* 473.

Melanouroi, oblade, *Oblada melanura:* Hierophilus, April.

Meli, honey: Oribasius, *Medical Collections* 5.33; *De cibis* 10; *Book of the Eparch* 13. *meli proteion,* the best honey: Leontius of Naples, *Life of St John the Almsgiver* 12; *De cibis* 12. *akapnin, meli akapniston,* unsmoked honey: Leontius of Naples, *Life of St John the Almsgiver* 12; *Prodromic Poems* 3.151. *meli pikron,* bitter honey: Mai in *Nova Patrum Bibliotheca* vol. 6 p. 407. *meli epsethen,* boiled honey: *De cibis* 19. *oinos o skeuastheis ek tou melitos,* mead: *De cibis* 11; *Peri trophon dynameos* 471. *ta dia melitos skeuazomena,* conserves made with honey: Simeon Seth p. 69.

Melipekton, a honey cake. *melipekton psathyron,* a crumbly melipekton: Tzetzes, *Letters* 68 Leone.

Melissophyllon, lemon balm, *Melissa officinalis. skeuazetai di' autou zoulapion,* a julep is made with it: Simeon Seth p. 66.

Melopepones, watermelons, *Citrullus vulgaris: De cibis* 10, 26; *De alimentis* 46.

Melorodakina, nectarines, *Prunus persica* var. *nectarina:* Hierophilus, September.

Meon, spignel, *Meum athamanticum:* Oribasius, *Medical Collections* 5.33.

Mespila, mouspoula, medlars, *Mespilus germanica:* Paul of Aegina, *Medical Epitome* 7.3.12; *De alimentis* 55; *Porikologos* 7. *nespole,* medlar tree: Agapius, *Geoponicon* 79. *ta pepeira mespila,* ripe medlars: Simeon Seth p. 71.

Metra, womb: *De cibis* 7 etc.; *Peri tes ek ton zoon trophes.*

Minsa, collation, buffet: Constantine Porphyrogennetus, *On Ceremonies* 1.74 [vol. 2 p. 102 Vogt].

Mitylenaios oinos glykys, sweet Lesbian wine: *Prodromic Poems* 2.355 Korais, cf. 3.285.

Molokhe, mallow, *Malva spp.*: Hierophilus, March.

Monembasios, malmsey grape. French *malvoisie:* Belon, *Observations* 1.19.

Monokythron, fish stew, bouillabaisse: Eustathius, *Commentary on Iliad* 4.243. *monokythritsin yperakhlizon oligon kai pempon euodian*, a nice *monokythron* slightly blackened on the top and preceded by its aroma: *Prodromic Poems* 3.175–186.

Mora, moura, mulberries, *Morus nigra. moura egoun sykamina* [alternative terms]: Agapius, *Geoponicon. mora ta glykea*, sweet mulberries: *Peri trophon dynameos* 473. *mora ta drimea*, sharp mulberries: *Peri trophon dynameos* 473.

Moria. ton zoon ta moria, offal: *De cibis* 7, 18; *Peri tes ek ton zoon trophes.*

Moskhatos, muscat wine. Latin *vinum muscatos*: William of Rubruck, *Report* 9. French *muscat*: Belon, *Observations* 1.19. *ampelin moskhatelin*, muscatel grape: *Glossae Jatricae.*

Moskhioi, calves: *De cibis* 6. *moskhion, moskheia kree*, veal: *Apophthegmata Patrum, Theophilus* 4; *Peri trophon dynameos* 476.

Moskhitai, curled octopuses, *Eledone spp.*: *De cibis* 7; *Peri tes ek ton zoon trophes.*

Moskhokarphi, cloves, *Syzygium aromaticum*: Agapius, *Geoponica.*

Moskhokarydon, moskhokaryon, nutmeg, *Myristica fragrans*: Simeon Seth p. 56 ms. B; Pseudo-Galen, *Signs from Urine*; Nicolaus Myrepsus, *Compounds*; cf. *Porikologos* 7.

Moskhos, musk (secretion of *Moschus moschiferus*): Cosmas Indicopleustes 11.15; Constantine Porphyrogennetus, *On Ceremonies* p. 468 Reiske; *Book of the Eparch* 10; Hierophilus, April; Pseudo-Galen, *On Similar Remedies* p. 547; *Prodromic Poems* 2.42g. *o kreitton ginetai en polei tou Khorase anatolikotera legomene Toupat*, the best comes from a city east of Khwarezm called Tibet: Simeon Seth p. 66. *moskhomyrizo*, add a musky flavour: *Prodromic Poems* 4.132.

Moskhositaron, fenugreek, *Trigonella Foenum-graecum*: *Glossae Jatricae.*

Mourouna, beluga sturgeon, *Huso Huso*. Cf. *mourzoulin*, a fish of the Russian river Kouphis: Theophanes, *Chronicle* am 6171. *mourounas mesoypokoilon*, a middle belly steak of sturgeon: *Prodromic Poems* 3.178a. French *mouronne*: Belon, *Observations* 1.27.

Moustopitai, must cakes: *De cibis* 20; *De alimentis* 18.

Moustos, moustarin, moustarion, must, grape juice: *De cibis* 20; *De alimentis* 8, 18.

Mydia, midia, omidia, omydia, mussels, *Mytilus galloprovincialis: De cibis* 13; *De alimentis* 18; *Peri tes ek ton zoon trophes;* Hierophilus, February; *Opsarologos* 12.

Myelos, marrow. *ton oston myelos, o en tois ostois myelos,* bone marrow: *De cibis* 9; *Peri tes ek ton zoon trophes. myelos tes rakheos, myelos tes rakhes,* spinal marrow: *De cibis* 15, 21, 23; *De alimentis* 18.

Myelos tes kephales, brain: *De cibis* 23. *enkephalos toutesti myelos o tes kephales* [alternative terms]: *De alimentis* 18. *myelos tes kephales meta pepereos e sinapeos,* brain with pepper or mustard: *Peri trophon dynameos* 477.

Myes, muscles. *oi myes ton kreon,* muscle meat: *Peri trophon dynameos* 478.

Myrismata, aromatics: Constantine Porphyrogennetus, *On Ceremonies* p. 468 Reiske.

Myrsiokokka, myrsinokokka, myrtiokokka, myrtle berries, *Myrtus communis: De cibis* 13; Simeon Seth p. 70. *myrta,* myrtles: *Peri trophon dynameos* 474. *myrsinokokka ta agria,* bilberries, *Vaccinium Myrtillus: De alimentis* 9.

Mytia, snout: *De cibis* 18; *De alimentis* 14; *Peri tes ek ton zoon trophes.*

Myxaria, sebestens or gundas, *Cordia Myxa:* Simeon Seth p. 126. *zepistania* [i.e. Arabic *sabastān*] *etoi myxia:* Pseudo-Galen, *On Similar Remedies* p. 563.

Myzethra, kind of cheese: Peter Zyphomustus, *Physiologike diegesis* [*Neos Elleno-mnemon* vol. 1 p. 442]; Agapius, *Geoponicon.*

Nanakhoua, ajowan, *Trachyspermum Ammi:* Pseudo-Galen, *On Similar Remedies* p. 547. *ami: e nanoukhá* [classical equivalent]: *Lexikon ton Sarakenon* 8. *anoukha: to karnabadin* [i.e. caraway: an imprecision]: *Glossae Jatricae.* Cf. Arabic *nūnakha, nānakhwa, nakhwa* 'ajowan'.

Nardostakhys, nardostakhyn, nardon, spikenard, *Nardostachys Jatamansi:* Oribasius, *Medical Collections* 5.33; Cosmas Indicopleustes 11.15; Constantine Porphyrogennetus, *On Ceremonies* 1.1 [vol. 1 p. 28 Vogt]. *nardostakhys etoi stakhos* [alternative terms]: *Lexikon ton Sarakenon* 234. Latin *nardi stachys:* Justinian, *Digest* 39.4.16.7.

Narkai, electric rays, *Torpedo spp.: De cibis* 21, 24; *Peri tes ek ton zoon trophes.*

Nephroi, nephrika, kidneys: *De cibis* 7, 20; Hierophilus, May.

Ner, species of plum, *Prunus Mahaleb. Ner: makhleb* [Arabic equivalent]: *Lexikon ton Sarakenon* 229.

Nerantzia, oranges, *Citrus Aurantium*: *Porikologos* 4; Agapius, *Geoponicon*. *to medikon melon ho esti to nerantzion* [false classical equivalent]: *Scholia on Nicander, Alexipharmaca* 533.

Nero, water: *Prodromic Poems* 2.56. *neroutzikon oligon*, a tiny drop of water: *Prodromic Poems* 3.413.

Nessai, nessaria, mallards, *Anas platyrhynchos*: Hierophilus 1.2 Ideler; *De cibis* 5, 7. *kree ton nessarion*, duck meat: *Peri trophon dynameos* 477.

Neuron, gristle; offal? Constantine Porphyrogennetus, *On Ceremonies* p. 464 Reiske. *ton zoon ta neurode moria*, gristle: *De cibis* 14.

Nymphaiai, water-lilies, *Nuphar luteum, Nymphaea alba*: *Peri trophon dynameos* 475. *nymphaiozoulapon*, water-lily julep: Simeon Seth p. 73.

Oa, eggs: *De cibis* 5. *oa ropheta*, runny egg: *De cibis* 5; Latin *ova sorbilia*: Anthimus 35. *oa trometa*, soft-boiled eggs: Simeon Seth p. 124; *De cibis* 5. *oa ekzesta*, hard-boiled eggs: Alexander of Tralles, *Therapeutics* vol. 2 p. 7; *De cibis* 7. *oa opta*, baked eggs, oeufs en cocotte: *De cibis* 7. *oa optoropheta*, lightly-baked eggs: *Life of St Dositheus* p. 114 Brun. *oa opta sklera genomena*, eggs baked till they are hard: *De cibis* 20. *oa pnikta*, poached eggs: Paul of Aegina, *Medical Epitome* 1.83; Simeon Seth p. 125. *oa tagenista, oa tyganista, oa ta teganou*, fried eggs: *De cibis* 7; *De alimentis* 9, 18. *oa ton ornithon*, hens' eggs: *De cibis* 5; *Peri trophon dynameos* 478. *oa ton khenon*, goose eggs: *De alimentis* 1. *oa ton perdikon*, partridge eggs: *Peri trophon dynameos* 478. *oa ton nessarion*, duck eggs: *Peri trophon dynameos* 478. *oa ton taonon*, peahens' eggs: *Peri trophon dynameos* 478. *oa ton mikron strouthion*, eggs of small birds: *Peri trophon dynameos* 478. Latin *fasiana oua*, pheasant eggs: Anthimus 38. *ta leuka ton oon*, white of egg: *Peri trophon dynameos* 468, 478. *ta kokkina ton oon etoi oi krokoi*, yolk or yellow of egg: *Peri trophon dynameos* 478. *pyrra oa*, brown eggs: Alexander of Tralles, *Therapeutics* vol. 2 p. 7.

Oinogaron, wine and fish sauce: Hierophilus, January.

Oinomeli, honeyed wine: Hierophilus, January.

Oinos, wine: *Peri trophon dynameos* 471; *De cibis* 5 etc. Latin *vinum*: Liutprand, *Embassy* 46. French *vin*: *Voyage de Charlemagne* 412. *o xestes tou oinou semisiou*, a pint of wine for a semissis [during a famine]: Theophanes, *Chronicle* AM 6235. *oinos kalos*, fine wine: *De cibis* 10. *oinos protios, oinos aristos*, top quality wine: Oribasius, *Medical Collections* 5.33; Leontius of Naples, *Life of St Simeon Salos* p. 159 Rydén. *oinaria diaphora*, various fancy wines: Leontius of Naples, *Life of St Simeon Salos* p. 164 Rydén. *oinos melas*, black wine: *Peri trophon dynameos* 471; *De cibis* 9. *erythros oinos*, red wine: *Peri trophon dynameos* 471. *oinoi rousioi*, rosé wines: *De cibis* 21. *khrysoeides oinos*, golden wine: *Peri trophon dynameos* 471. *oinos xanthos*, yellow wine: *De cibis* 13; *De alimentis* 31. *oinoi elaiokhrooi*, wines of the colour of olive oil: Hierophilus, September. *leukos oinos*, white wine: *Peri trophon dynameos* 471; *De cibis* 10, 24. *oinos pakhys*, thick wine: *De cibis* 9 etc. *oinos leptos*, thin wine: *De cibis* 10, 24. *neos oinos*, new wine: *Peri trophon dynameos* 471; *De cibis* 7. *palaioi oinoi*, old wines: *Peri trophon dynameos* 471; *De cibis* 25. *oinos palaios, leukos, euodes, anisatos*, an old, white, aromatic, anise-flavoured wine: Hierophilus, June [ed. Ideler]. *oinos propalaios*, very old wine: Oribasius, *Medical Collections* 5.33. *euodeis oinoi*, aromatic wines: *De alimentis* 31. *oinou kalou euodestatou rophemata tria mikra*, three small doses of fine and very aromatic wine: Hierophilus, January. *ydatodes oinos*, watery wine (without strong flavour or aroma): *De cibis* 10; *De alimentis* 25, 31. *oinos glykys*, sweet wine: *De cibis* 6. *oinoi styphontes, oinos stryphnos*, astringent wine: *De cibis* 21; *De alimentis* 30. *oinos austerizon, oinos austeros*, austere wine: *Peri trophon dynameos* 471; *De cibis* 14; *De alimentis* 31. *oinos o skeuazomenos apo ton astaphidon*, raisin wine: *Peri trophon dynameos* 471. *oinos enkhorios*, local wine: Constantine Porphyrogennetus, *On Ceremonies* p. 464 Reiske.

Oinouttai, must cakes: Eustathius, *Letters* 15 Tafel.

Okima, basil, *Ocimum spp.*: Simeon Seth p. 29 (some mss. substitute *basilika*). *okima panta*, all kinds of basil: *Peri trophon dynameos* 474.

Oktapodia, oktapodes, ktapodes, octopuses, *Octopus spp.*: Paul of Aegina, *Medical Epitome* 7.1; *De cibis* 7; *Peri tes ek ton zoon trophes*.

Olyra, emmer, *Triticum dicoccum*. *artos olyrites*, emmer bread: Nicetas Choniates, *Chronicle* p. 305 van Dieten.

Omphake, omphakion, verjuice (cf. *agouris*): *Lexikon ton Sarakenon* 245. Latin *umfacium*: Anthimus 94.

Onagroi, wild asses, *Equus Asinus*: Theophanes, *Chronicle* AM 6118. Latin *quos ipsi dicunt onagros*, what they claim to be wild asses: Liutprand, *Embassy* 38.

Ootarikha see *augotarikha*.

Opion, opium: Alexander of Tralles, *Therapeutics* vol. 2 p. 431.

Opobalsamon, pure balsam of Mecca, *Commiphora Opobalsamum*: Anna Comnena, *Alexiad* 3.10.7. a compound drug including *xylobalsamon* and oil of mastic: Nicolaus Myrepsus, *Compounds* 37.43.

Oporai, fruits: *De cibis* 5, 24. *panta ta oporode*, everything of the nature of fruit: *De cibis* 14. Latin *poma*: Liutprand, *Embassy* 46.

Opson, relish accompanying bread. *opson de oi ales*, his only relish was salt: Theodoret, *Religious History* 2.2. *opsaria, opsa*, seafood, fish dishes: *De cibis* 18; Anna Comnena, *Alexiad* 10.11.3. *opsaria zesta teganou*, pan-fried fish: Leontius of Naples, *Life of St Simeon Salos* p. 159 Rydén. *opsaria pasta*, salt fish: Constantine Porphyrogennetus, *On Ceremonies* p. 464 Reiske. *tous opsarion zomous karykeuein dia stakhous kai anisou kai koliandrou*, fish soups should be spiced with spikenard, anise and coriander: Hierophilus, June.

Optoutsikon, grilled or roasted dish: *Prodromic Poems* 3.158.

Origanon, ariganen, oregano, *Origanum vulgare*: *De cibis* 10; Agapius, *Geoponicon*.

Orizin, oryzin, oryza, rice, *Oryza sativa*: Constantine Porphyrogennetus, *On Ceremonies* p. 463 Reiske; *De cibis* 2. *oryza epsetheisa meta artymatos*, rice boiled with seasoning: *Peri trophon dynameos* 469. *orizin me to melin*, rice with honey: *Prodromic Poems* 3.279. *oryza meta galaktos skeuazomene kai syn sakkharo metalambanomene*, rice cooked with milk and taken with sugar: Simeon Seth p. 75.

Orkheis, testicles: *De cibis* 5 etc.; *Peri tes ek ton zoon trophes. boon orkheis*, bull's testicles: *De cibis* 21.

Orminon, clary, *Salvia Sclarea*: Aetius, *Medicine* 11.35.

Ornea, ornithes, birds. *pan genos ornithon*, all kinds of birds: *De cibis* 22. *ton orneon ta mikra*, smaller birds: *De cibis* 24. *ta en tais limnais boskomena ornea*, birds that feed in lakes, water birds: *De cibis* 23. *ton ornithon oi en xerois topois diaitomenoi*, birds that feed on dry land: *De cibis* 24. *ton orneon ta en tois oresi diaitomena*, birds that feed in the mountains: *De cibis* 24.

Ornithes, ornithes oikidiai, ornithes katoikidioi, domestic hens, *Gallus gallinaceus*: Hierophilus, January; *De cibis* 5. *kree ton ornithon*, chicken: *Peri trophon dynameos* 477. *ornithes gegymnasmenai*, free range hens: *De cibis* 5. *ta pterygia ton ornithon*, chicken wings: *De cibis* 21. *o zomos ton ornithon*, chicken soup: *Peri trophon dynameos* 477. *ekheto o zomos anison e kyminon e prason e selinon kathepsethen e peperi*, this soup should contain anise, cumin, leek, boiled celery or pepper: Alexander of Tralles, *Therapeutics* vol. 2 p. 339.

Oroboi, bitter vetch, *Vicia Ervilia*. *oroboi dis epsethentes kai apoglykanthentes pollakis di' ydatos*, bitter vetch twice boiled and thoroughly sweetened in water: *De alimentis* 26. *oroboaleuron*, bitter vetch flour: Pseudo-Galen, *Signs from Urine*.

Orphoi, groupers, *Epinephelus Guaza*: *De cibis* 7; *Peri tes ek ton zoon trophes*; *Geoponica* 20.20.

Orros tou galaktos, whey: *Peri trophon dynameos* 478.

Ortyges, quails: Hierophilus, January.

Osmarides, picarels, *Spicara Smaris*: *Opsarologos* 30.

Ospria, ospreon, pulses, legumes: Cyril, *Life of St Sabas* p. 131; *Book of the Eparch* 13; *De cibis* 5. *ospreoutsikon*, bit of pease pudding: *Prodromic Poems* 2.30a.

Osta, bones: *De cibis* 18.

Ostrakode, ostrakodermoi, hard-shelled seafood, shellfish: Hierophilus, February; *De cibis* 12. *ton ostrakodermon ta sklerotera, ta sklera*, hard-shelled seafood or shellfish with relatively coarse flesh: *De cibis* 21; *Peri tes ek ton zoon trophes*. *ton ostrakodermon ta malakosarka*, hard-shelled seafood or shellfish with soft flesh: *De cibis* 22; *Peri tes ek ton zoon trophes*.

Ostridomyditzia, fruits de mer: *Prodromic Poems* 3.277.

Ostroudia, ostrydia, ostrea, ostreia, oysters, *Ostrea edulis*: *De cibis* 13, 20, 22; *De alimentis* 20; *Peri tes ek ton zoon trophes*.

Otia, ota, ears: *De cibis* 5 etc.; *Peri tes ek ton zoon trophes*.

Otis, bustard, *Otis tarda*: *De cibis* 5; Simeon Seth p. 125.

Oura, tail: *De cibis* 7, 22.

Oxalme, salt and vinegar: *De cibis* 16.

Oxelaion, oil vinegar dressing: *De cibis* 10; *De alimentis* 63 (emended).

Oxidin, xydi, oxos, vinegar: Leontius of Naples, *Life of St Simeon Salos* p. 165 Rydén; *De cibis* 9, 10; Agapius, *Geoponicon*.

Oxota, pickles: Eustathius, *Letters* 31 Tafel.

Oxygala, xygala, xygalon, buttermilk, yoghourt (cf. modern *xinogalo*): *De cibis* 18; *Prodromic Poems* 4.109; Belon, *Observations* 3.27. *oxygalatas*, buttermilk-seller: *Prodromic Poems* 4.109. *eparete droubaniston oxygala, gynaikes*, buy your buttermilk from the churn, ladies! *Prodromic Poems* 4.112. *tyroi oxygalaktinoi*, cheeses made from buttermilk: *Peri trophon dynameos* 479.

Oxygarita, conserves in vinegar and fish sauce: Hierophilus, July.

Oxykraton, krasion oxous, vinegar and water: John Moschus, *Spiritual Meadow* 113; the basis of a medicinal *phouska*: Aetius, *Medicine* 3.45.2; Paul of Aegina, *Medical Epitome* 7.5.10.

Oxylapathon, curled dock, *Rumex crispus*: *De cibis* 22.

Oxymeli, honey vinegar: *De cibis* 10; *De alimentis* 63; Nicolaus Myrepsus, *Compounds* 37. *apaphristhen oxymeli*, skimmed honey vinegar: *De cibis* 18. *ta oxymelita*, conserves in honey vinegar: Hierophilus, July.

Oxynoglykos, 'sweet and sour' or sweet and savoury dish: *Prodromic Poems* 3.149.

Oxyporion, digestive drink or medicine: Aetius, *Medicine* 3.91–92; Photius, *Library* 221.177b.

Oxyrrynkhoi, sturgeons, especially beluga sturgeon, *Huso Huso*.

Pagone, pagonion, paonion, e ek Paionon ornis, peafowl, *Pavo cristatus*: Tzetzes, *On Lucia* p. 83 Papadopoulos-Kerameus.

Pagouria, pagouroi, species of crab: *Prodromic Poems* 3.275; *De cibis* 7. *pagouroi potamioi kai thalassioi*, river and sea *pagouroi*: *Peri tes ek ton zoon trophes*.

Palamidin, bonito, *Sarda Sarda*: *Prodromic Poems* 3.205.

Pandaisia, feasting, festive meal: Anna Comnena, *Alexiad* 2.6.5.

Paphlagonikos tyros, Paphlagonian cheese: Psellus, *Letters* 206 Kurtz and Drexl.

Paskha, the Easter lamb. *e pempte e megale kath' en to mystikon paskha thyomen ama kai estiometha*, Great Thursday, on which we both sacrifice and partake of the mystical Paschal lamb: Anna Comnena, *Alexiad* 2.10.4.

Pastellon, pasteli, honey and sesame sweet: *Miracles of Ss Cyrus and John* 68.

Paston, salt fish: Hierophilus, September; *Prodromic Poems* 1.265, 2.42a. *ta pasta osa eisi malaka*, soft-fleshed salt fish: *De cibis* 24. *pastomageiria*, dish based on salt fish: *Prodromic Poems* 2.104 (ms. G).

Pastos, banquet: Leo Grammaticus p. 558 [Du Cange]; Constantine Porphyrogennetus, *On Ceremonies* vol. 2 pp. 20–23 Vogt.

Paxamas, paxametes, paxamadion, paxamation, paximadi, barley biscuit (see also *dipyros artos*): *Apophthegmata Patrum, Macarius* 33, *Serinos* 1; John Moschus, *Spiritual Meadow* 184; *Miracles of Ss Cyrus and John* 6; Leo, *Tactics* 6.28, 13.11; Constantine Porphyrogennetus, *On Ceremonies* p. 658 Reiske. Latin *paximacium*: Liutprand, *Embassy* 63. *paximadion toutesti maza* [approximate classical equivalent]: Constantine Porphyrogennetus, *Tactics* p. 45 Meursius. *dipyros artos o para Romaiois legomenos paxamas, kakhrydias o ek krithes artos on paxaman legomen* [further equivalents]: Zonaras, *Lexicon.*

Peganon, rue, *Ruta graveolens*: *De cibis* 24; Hierophilus, January. *Peganon agrion,* Syrian rue, *Peganum Harmala. agrion peganon: kharmel* [Arabic equivalent], *Lexikon ton Sarakenon* 397.

Pelamydes, bonitoes, *Sarda Sarda*: *Timarion* 21.

Pentartyma, 'five-spice', an aromatic herb or mixture: *De cibis* 10; *De alimentis* 26.

Peperi, piper, piperia, pepper, *Piper nigrum*: Cosmas Indicopleustes 11.15; *Book of the Eparch* 10; *De cibis* 10; *Prodromic Poems* 2.38; a spice that northern peoples bought from Byzantium: Theophylact Simocatta, *Histories* 7.13.6; Constantine Porphyrogennetus, *De administrando imperio* 6. *piperin phoukhta mia,* one handful of pepper: *Prodromic Poems* 3.183. *piperogaron,* peppered garum, pepper sauce: Alexander of Tralles, *Therapeutics* vol. 1 p. 543. *to dia trion pepereon,* digestive medicine incorporating the 'three peppers': Aetius, *Medicine* 9.24; Leo, *Outline of Medicine* 5.2. *piperotriptes,* pepper-mill: *Prodromic Poems* 4.121. Latin *piper album,* white pepper: Justinian, *Digest* 39.4.16.7. Latin *piper longum,* long pepper, *Piper longum*: Justinian, *Digest* 39.4.16.7.

Peponia, pepones, melons, *Cucumis Melo*: *De cibis* 9, 20; *De alimentis* 45. *pepones oi glykeis,* sweet melons: *Peri trophon dynameos* 473. *peponia ek tas Plakas,* melons from Plaka: *Prodromic Poems* 2.65c. *o legomenos sarakenikos pepon,* the so-called Saracen melon: Simeon Seth p. 84.

Perdikia, perdikes, rock partridges, *Alectoris graeca*: Tzetzes, *Letters* 93 Leone; *De cibis* 5.

Perikhyma, dish served with sauce: *Prodromic Poems* 3.148.

Peristerai, peristeropoulla, pigeons, *Columba Livia*: Simeon Seth p. 86; *De cibis*

5. *kree ton peristeron*, pigeon meat: *Peri trophon dynameos* 477. *peristerai ai kat' agron diaitomenai*, pigeons that feed in the wild: *De alimentis* 1. *ai peristerai ai diaitomenai en tois pyrgois*, pigeons kept in towers: *De cibis* 24. *peristeropoula leuka kai brakata, tauta gar eisi ta kreittona*, white and 'breeched' pigeons which are the best kinds: Hierophilus, January. *peristeropoula brakata khlia te kai opta*, young 'breeched' pigeons, roasted and served hot: Hierophilus, June.

Persika, mela persika, peaches, *Prunus persica* (cf. *rodakina*): Eustathius, *Letters* 1–2, 17, 28; *Peri trophon dynameos* 473. downy peaches (as opposed to nectarines): Hierophilus, September. See also *rodakina*.

Peteina, petomata, birds: *De alimentis* 1; *De cibis* 21.

Petroselinon, parsley, *Petroselinum sativum*: Oribasius, *Medical Collections* 5.33; *De cibis* 10, 24.

Peza zoa, quadrupeds: *De cibis* 5; *Peri tes ek ton zoon trophes*.

Phaba, phabata, broad beans, *Vicia Faba*: Leontius of Naples, *Life of St Simeon Salos* p. 146 Rydén; *De cibis* 7; *Prodromic Poems* 3.76. Latin *fabae*: Liutprand, *Antapodosis* 5.23. *kyamos to legomenon phaba, kyamos toutestin phaba* [alternative terms]: Hierophilus, March; *De alimentis* 36. *phaba exeston*, boiled beans: Theodore Studites, *Constitutions* 30 [*PG* vol. 99 col. 1716]. *phaba phrykton*, roasted beans: *De cibis* 18; *De alimentis* 37. *phaba khloron*, fresh broad beans: *De cibis* 22; *De alimentis* 36. *phabatitzin aleston*, nice bean soup: *Prodromic Poems* 3.279. *brekhe kai ekzei kala kai alati kai elaio kalo omphakino epiballe*, soak them, boil them well and toss them in salt and the best green olive oil: Hierophilus, March (emended).

Phagria, phagroi, pagre, Couch's sea bream, *Sparus Pagrus*: *De cibis* 7; Hierophilus, June.

Phake, phakos, lentils, *Lens culinaris*: Leontius of Naples, *Life of St Simeon Salos* p. 146 Rydén; Constantine Porphyrogennetus, *On Ceremonies* p. 463 Reiske; *De cibis* 2. *To lepos phakes*, husk of lentils: *De alimentis* 35. *phake tou lepous apheremene*, husked lentils: *De alimentis* 30.

Phasianoi, pheasants, *Phasianus colchicus*: Agathias [*Anthologia Palatina* 9.642]; Theophanes, *Chronicle* AM 6118; *De cibis* 5.

Phasioulia, phasoulia, phaseloi, cowpeas, black-eyed peas, *Vigna sinensis*:

Constantine Porphyrogennetus, *On Ceremonies* p. 463 Reiske; *Peri trophon dynameos* 469; Simeon Seth p. 133. *loboi ton phasoulion*, black-eyed pea pods: *De cibis* 7. *phasoulia apobrekhousi mekhri tou phyesai rizan kai esthiousin pro tes alles trophes, enapobaptontes garois*, they steep black-eyed peas till they sprout and eat them as a starter, dipped in fish sauce: *De alimentis* 40. *phasolia exophthalmista*, 'blinded' (i.e. sprouted) black-eyed peas: *Prodromic Poems* 3.280. *phasioulos ekzestos diephthos en oxymeliti*, black-eyed peas, well boiled, with honey vinegar: Hierophilus, March. *ta brases me peperi e sinapi e ariganen e me to karos kai bales kai ladi kai xydi*, if you boil it with pepper or mustard or oregano or caraway and add olive oil and vinegar: Agapius, *Geoponicon*. *to ek ton phasilon etnos glykytaton tynkhanei panton*, black-eyed pea soup is the sweetest of all the legume soups: Oribasius, *Medical Collections* 4.8.16.

Phassai, phattai, wood pigeons, *Columba Palumbus*: *De cibis* 5.

Philomele, philomela, philomelitsa, gurnard, *Trigla* spp.: Simeon Seth p. 118; *Prodromic Poems* 3.404g; *Opsarologos* 19.

Phoinikes, phoinikia, dates, *Phoenix dactylifera*: *Prodromic Poems* 3.282; *De cibis* 7; *Peri trophon dynameos* 472; *De alimentis* 31. *khloroi phoinikes*, fresh dates: *De cibis* 11, 18, 19. *liparoi phoinikes*, semi-dried dates: *De cibis* 18, 21. *glykeis phoinikes*, sweet dates: *De cibis* 21, 25.

Phouska, phoukas, weakly alcoholic drink, vinegar and water, perhaps also beer, often flavoured with herbs: Aetius, *Medicine* 3.81–82; Paul of Aegina, *Medical Epitome* 7.11.48; Alexander of Tralles, *Treatment* vol. 2 p. 199; *De alimentis* 31. *syn artymasi kataskeuazomenos thermos ginetai kai xeros*, made with spices it becomes hot and dry: Simeon Seth p. 118. *phouskarion*, drinking shop: Leontius of Naples, *Life of St Simeon Salos* p. 165 Rydén. *phouskarios*, keeper of drinking shop: Leontius of Naples, *Life of St Simeon Salos* p. 146 Rydén. (See pp. 84-5.)

Phyllon, phyllon indikon, tejpat, *Cinnamomum Tamala*: Oribasius, *Medical Collections* 5.33; Theophylact Simocatta, *Histories* 7.13.4.

Physalis, Chinese lantern, winter cherry, *Physalis Alkekengi*: Aetius, *Medicine* 11.35.

Pikrides, bitter leaves (chicory, dandelion etc.): *De cibis* 14; Psellus, *Poems* 57.68–71 Westerink. *pikridion*, endive, *Cichorium Endivia*: *Glosses on Dioscorides*

2.132; *Geoponica* 12.1. *Pikralis*, dandelion, *Taraxacum officinale*: [Athanasius], *On Unleavened Bread* [*PG* vol. 26 col. 1328].

Pimele, fat (of meat): *De cibis* 22. *khytra kreon yeion tarikhon pleres kai krambes Phrygias pimeles ta panta mesta*, a pot full of salt pork and Phrygian cabbage, all mixed with fat: *Timarion* 17.

Pinnai, pinnes, fan-mussels, *Pinna nobilis*: *De cibis* 20; *De alimentis* 18.

Pisarion, peas, *Pisum sativum. phaba to par' emin pisarion legomenon*, the dried legumes called peas: Cyril, *Life of St Sabas* p. 130. *to xeron pisarion*, dried peas: Cyril, *Life of St Sabas* p. 131. *to pisinon etnos aphysoteron tou kyaminou*, pea soup causes less wind than bean soup: Oribasius, *Medical Collections* 4.8.14.

Pissa, pitch: *Book of the Eparch* 13. Latin *pix*: Liutprand, *Embassy* 1.

Pistakia, pistachios, *Pistacia vera*: Constantine Porphyrogennetus, *On Ceremonies* p. 463 Reiske; *De cibis* 5; *Peri trophon dynameos* 474; *Prodromic Poems* 2.44. *pistakelaion*, pistachio oil: Simeon Seth p. 39.

Pistos, broomcorn millet, *Panicum miliaceum*: Leo, *Tactics* 6.28, 13.11. *Pistos e kenkhros* [classical equivalent]: *De alimentis* 32; Simeon Seth p. 87. *pistos toutesti kenkhros eklelepismenos elaphros*, pistos i.e. light husked millet: Constantine Porphyrogennetus, *Tactics* p. 45 Meursius.

Pitta, pitta bread: *Prodromic Poems* 2.26g; *Life of St Maximus of Athos*.

Pityra, pityria, bran: *De cibis* 12, 16. *piteraton, pityrias*, bran bread: Theodoret, *Religious History* 2.2; *Prodromic Poems* 3.316. For phrases see *artos*.

Plakiste, kind of cake? Leontius of Naples, *Life of St Simeon Salos* p. 164 Rydén.

Plakounta, plakountaria, plakountes, cakes: Leontius of Naples, *Life of St Simeon Salos* p. 146 Rydén; *De cibis* 20; *De alimentis* 18.

Platones, fallow deer, *Dama Dama*: Hierophilus, September.

Pleures pakhylardates, sides of bacon with thick fat: *Diegesis ton tetrapodon zoon* 379.

Pneumones, lungs: *De cibis* 15.

Podes, podaria, trotters, feet: *De cibis* 5, 15; *De alimentis* 10; *Peri tes ek ton zoon trophes*.

Podokephala ton khoiron pekta kai oxista, pigs' trotters and head, jellied, with vinegar: Hierophilus, January (emended).

Poton, drink: *De cibis* 5.

Prasa, leeks, *Allium Porrum*: *De cibis* 10; *De alimentis* 75. Latin *recentes porri*, fresh leeks: Liutprand, *Antapodosis* 5.23. *prasozema*, leek soup: Hierophilus, February. *prasozemata karykeuta*, spiced leek soups: Hierophilus, October. *dis ydati epsomenon, kai oxei kai garo kai elaio kai kymino artyomenon*, twice boiled in water and seasoned with vinegar, fish sauce, olive oil and cumin: Simeon Seth p. 88. *ton prason ephthon ai kephalai*, boiled 'heads' of leek: Alexander of Tralles, *Therapeutics* vol. 2 p. 339.[1]

Prasomolokha, leek and mallow (classified elsewhere as *gliskhra lakhana* 'glutinous vegetables'): Hierophilus, November.

Probata, sheep, *Ovis Aries*: *De cibis* 23. *probeia kree*, mutton, lamb: *Peri trophon dynameos* 476. *liparon probatikon apo to mesonephrin*, fat loin of mutton: *Prodromic Poems* 2.106 (ms. G). *probata yparna*, suckling lambs: Constantine Porphyrogennetus, *On Ceremonies* p. 464 Reiske. *krea probea khlia kai opta*, roast lamb, served hot: Hierophilus, January.

Progeuma, appetizer: *Prodromic Poems* 3.54.

Prophaia, snack between meals. *prophaia kokkoelaia*, olives as a snack: *Typikon of Stoudios* A30.

Prophournia, prophrounia, first bread (bits of dough put in the oven to test its temperature): *Prodromic Poems* 2.26g, 4.226.

Prosphagin, prosphan, prosphagion, relish accompanying bread: Eustathius, *Commentary on Iliad* 11.638. cheese: Michael Choniates, *Letters* [vol. 2 p. 194 Lampros].

Prosphatos, fresh cheese kept in brine: *Poem on Medicine* 1.209.

Protogala, cream. *protogala meta melitos kai stakhous kai kinamomou leiothentos*, cream blended with honey and spikenard and cinnamon: Hierophilus, January.

Prouna, proumna, bullaces and sloes, *Prunus domestica* var. *insititia, P. spinosa*: *De cibis* 13, 22; *De alimentis* 20.

Psaroi, starlings, *Sturnus spp.*: *De cibis* 24.

Psathyria, a kind of patisserie: Leontius of Naples, *Life of St Simeon Salos* p. 164 Rydén. Cf. *melipekton*.

Psenasis souglitarea, roast meat on a spit (souvlaki): *Prodromic Poems* 4.231.

[1] The Near Eastern variety with distinct 'head' or bulb is *A. Porrum* var. *Kurrat*.

Psikhai, psikhia, bits of bread: Hesychius, *Lexicon; Timarion* 19; *Prodromic Poems* 1.17 (ms. g). *psikhitzai mikrai*, little bits of bread: *Prodromic Poems* 3.412b.

Psissia, psisia, brill, *Scophthalmus Rhombus: De cibis* 5; *De alimentis* 23. *psessopoula*, smaller flatfish, modern *pisi, fausse limande, Bodus Podas* and others. *psessopoulon mpourdaton*, dish of stewed *pisi: Prodromic Poems* 3.147.

Psomin, psomitzin, bread, loaf: *Prodromic Poems* 3.412, 4.17. *psomion katharon*, white loaf: *Dream Book of Daniel* 479. *me na khortaso to psomin to legoun aphratitsin, alla to mesokatharon to legoun kibariten*, I won't eat the bread they call 'foam', but the not-so-white bread they call wholemeal: *Prodromic Poems* 4.80. *epithymo to psomin kai kytalon kai psikhan*, I love bread, both crust and crumb: *Prodromic Poems* 4.17 (ms. g). *oude to kalon psomin to semidaleuraton isazei me to kibaron e meta to krithinon*, fine bread made with durum-wheat flour is not to be compared with wholemeal or barley bread: *Diegesis ton tetrapodon zoon* 366–367. *ton zomon ekkheei ton epano ton psomion*, he pours the soup over the chunks of bread: *Prodromic Poems* 3.300.

Psyllion, fleaseed, *Plantago Psyllium: Peri trophon dynameos* 468.

Ptena, birds: *De cibis* 6. *ptena edodima limnais endiaitomena kai potamois*, birds good to eat, feeding in the lakes and rivers [near Aenus]: Critobulus of Imbros 2.12.6. *oma krea ptenon zoon*, raw meat of birds: Anna Comnena, *Alexiad* 10.11.3.

Pterygia, wings: *De cibis* 6, 21.

Ptisane, barley water: *Geoponica* 3.9; *Peri trophon dynameos* 469.

Ptokes, hares, *Lepus spp. kree ton ptokon*, hare meat: *Peri trophon dynameos* 477. *ptokos: lagos* [alternative terms]: *Lexikon ton Sarakenon* 268.

Pyrethron, pellitory, *Anacyclus Pyrethrum: De cibis* 1; *Peri trophon dynameos* 468.

Pyrgitai, sparrows, *Passer spp.* Latin *passeres*: Anthimus 30.

Raphana, rephania, rephanoi, radishes, *Raphanus sativus: De alimentis* 4; *De cibis* 8; Hierophilus, April. *leptai raphanides*, little radishes: Hierophilus, January.

Rengai, herrings.

Renkhe, snouts: *Peri tes ek ton zoon trophes.*

Retine, pine resin, *Pinus spp.*: *Lexikon kata alphabeton* 148. Latin *taeda*: Liutprand, *Embassy* 1.

Rinai, monkfish, *Squatina Squatina: De cibis* 7, 21; *Peri tes ek ton zoon trophes.*

Rines, snouts: *De cibis* 5.

Rizai ton lakhanon, roots: *De cibis* 7, 14.

Roda, roses, *Rosa spp.*: Hierophilus, April; *Peri trophon dynameos* 474. *rodon phylla*, rose petals: Oribasius, *Medical Collections* 5.33. *rodomeli*, rose petal honey: Simeon Seth p. 35. *rodostagma*, attar of roses: Hierophilus, April; *Peri trophon dynameos* 476. *rodelaion, rodinon elaion*, rose-perfumed oil: Hierophilus, January, April.

Rodakina, peaches, *Prunus persica*: *De cibis* 12; *Porikologos* 2. *rodakina a kai persika legetai* [classical equivalent]: Simeon Seth p. 89.

Rodomelon, rose-flavoured apple wine: Aetius, *Medicine* 16.139.

Rogdia, roidia, rodia, roiai, pomegranates, *Punicum granatum*: Theodore Daphnopates, *Letters* 24; *De cibis* 22; *Porikologos* 2; Agapius, *Geoponicon. roidia ta glykea*, sweet pomegranates: *Peri trophon dynameos* 473. *roidia ta oxizonta, roidia oxyna*, acid pomegranates: *Peri trophon dynameos* 473; *De alimentis* 25.

Roka, rouka, rocket, *Eruca sativa* (cf. *euzomon*): Agapius, *Geoponicon* 67. *tzartzíre* [i.e. Arabic *jirjīr*]: *e roka*: *Lexikon ton Sarakenon* 344.

Rosaton, rose wine: Oribasius, *Medical Collections* 5.33; Hierophilus, July.

Rou mageirikon, rous Syriakos, sumach, *Rhus coriaria*: *Geoponica* 16.8; *Lexikon ton Sarakenon* 278.

Sakkhar, sakhar, cane sugar, *Saccharum officinarum*: Paul of Aegina, *Medical Epitome* 7.3.12; Theophanes, *Chronicle* AM 6118; Constantine Porphyrogennetus, *On Ceremonies* p. 468 Reiske; *Peri trophon dynameos* 468; *De cibis* 2; *Prodromic Poems* 3.340b. *sakharata*, sugar sweets: *Prodromic Poems* 3.283b. *sakkhar kantion*, sugar candy: Pseudo-Galen, *On Similar Remedies* p. 547. *sakharothermon*, hot syrup: *Prodromic Poems* 3.404i.

Salsikia, sausages. *lambanein seiran salsikion kai kratein en te aristera autou kheiri sinepin kai outos baptein kai trogein*, taking a string of sausages, and holding mustard in his left hand, and so dipping them and eating them: Leontius of Naples, *Life of St Simeon Salos* p. 160 Rydén.

Saltsa, sauce: Nicetas Choniates, *Chronicle* Urbs Capta 1.5 [Demotic text].

Sampsykhon, marjoram, *Majorana hortensis*: Constantine Porphyrogennetus, *On Ceremonies* 1.40 [vol. 1 p. 158 Vogt]; *Peri trophon dynameos* 475; Simeon Seth p. 103.

Santalon, sandana, tzandana, sandalwood, *Santalum album*: Cosmas Indico-pleustes 11.15; Aetius, *Medicine* 16.142 (text uncertain); *Peri trophon dynameos* 476.

Sarakenoi. tyros apo ta khoria ton Sarakenon, Turkish cheese: *Assizes of Cyprus* A-B 296, 298.

Sargoi, sars, *Diplodus Sargus*: Hierophilus, January.

Sarx, meat: *De cibis* 5.

Sarxiphagon, burnet saxifrage, *Pimpinella Saxifraga*?: Oribasius, *Medical Collections* 5.33.

Satyrion, salep: Aetius, *Medicine* 11.35. *satyriake*, aphrodisiac: Aetius, *Medicine* 11.35.

Sauroi, sauridia, scad, *Trachurus spp.*: *De cibis* 18; *Prodromic Poems* 3.200; Hierophilus, April; *Opsarologos* 30.

Selakhia, cartilaginous fish: *De cibis* 5; *Peri tes ek ton zoon trophes*.

Selinon, celery, *Apium graveolens*: *De cibis* 10. *selina oma esthiomena*, celery eaten raw: *De alimentis* 69. *selina aspra en oxei skillitiko baptomena*, white celery dressed with squill vinegar: Hierophilus, June. *selinorrizon*, celery root: Pseudo-Galen, *Signs from Urine*. *ton selinon ephthon ai kephalai*, boiled 'heads' of celery: Alexander of Tralles, *Therapeutics* vol. 2 p. 339. *selino-prasorepana*, celery-leek-radishes, vegetables: *Prodromic Poems* 2.40.

Semidalis, semidalis pyros, durum wheat, *Triticum turgidum* ssp. *durum*: Theo-dore of Cyzicus, *Letters* 1; *De cibis* 11, 18, 21. *semidalitai artoi, psomin semidaleuraton, semidalina*, durum wheat loaves: Simeon Seth p. 20; *Prodromic Poems* 3.316; *De cibis* 18, 21; *Diegesis ton tetrapodon zoon* 366. *aspron semidalaton*, white pasta: *Prodromic Poems* 4.101. *khylos semidaleos*, durum wheat gruel: Hierophilus, January.

Sepiai, cuttlefish, *Sepia officinalis*: *De cibis* 7; *Peri tes ek ton zoon trophes*.

Sesamon, sesamos, sisamen, sesame, *Sesamum indicum*: *De cibis* 2; *Peri trophon dynameos* 474. *sesamion*, sesame sweetmeat? *Prodromic Poems* 3.317.

Seutlon, beet, *Beta vulgaris*: *De cibis* 9. *seutloriza, seuklogoulia*, beetroots: Siemon Seth p. 99; *Prodromic Poems* 4.129k. *seutlou khylos*, beet liquor: *De cibis* 10. *seutlon meta sinepeos e oxous*, beet with mustard or vinegar: *De cibis* 10; *De alimentis* 68.

Silignion, bread wheat, *Triticum aestivum*. *Silignion, silignias, silignites artos*, bread-wheat loaf: Leontius of Naples, *Life of St John the Almsgiver* 22. *silignia kathara*, white bread-wheat loaves: Leontius of Naples, *Life of St Simeon Salos* p. 159 Rydén. French *froment*: Geoffroi de Villehardouin 492.

Silphion, asafoetida, *Ferula Assa-foetida*: Simeon Seth p. 24. Latin *laser*: Justinian, *Digest* 39.4.16.7.

Sinepi, sinapi, mustard, *Sinapis alba, Brassica nigra*: *De cibis* 8. mustard sauce: Leontius of Naples, *Life of St Simeon Salos* p. 161 Rydén; *De cibis* 10; *De alimentis* 68. *embamma dia sinepi*, mustard dip or sauce: Hierophilus, August.

Sinon, stone parsley, *Sison Amomum*: Oribasius, *Medical Collections* 5.33.

Sition, food: *De cibis* 5.

Sitos, sitaren, wheat, *Triticum spp.*: *Timarion* 21; *Peri trophon dynameos* 469; *De cibis* 25. *sitinos adromeros alelesmenos*, [gruel] of roughly pounded wheat: *De alimentis* 1. *sitos ephthos, sitos epsetos, sitaren epseton*, boiled wheat: *De cibis* 7, 21, 25; *De alimentis* 19. French *blez*: Geoffroi de Villehardouin 131, 492.

Skarika, skaroi, parrot wrasses, *Scarus cretensis*: Hierophilus, February; J. Darrouzès, *Epistoliers byzantins du Xe siècle* (Paris, 1960) 33.

Skelidia, cloves of garlic: *Scholia on Nicander, Alexipharmaca* 432.

Skelos, foot, trotter: *De cibis* 7.

Skhoinanthos, ginger-grass, *Cymbopogon Schoenanthus*: Oribasius, *Medical Collections* 5.33.

Sklerosarka, coarse-fleshed seafood, crustacea: *Peri tes ek ton zoon trophes*.

Skolymon, skolimon, golden thistle, Spanish salsify, *Scolymus hispanicus*: *De cibis* 24; *De alimentis* 23.

Skombroi, mackerels, *Scomber Scombrus*: *Timarion* 21.

Skorda, skoroda, garlic, *Allium sativum*: *Peri trophon dynameos* 468; *De cibis* 10; *De alimentis* 75. *epeidan aisthontai tinos odynes oi polloi peri ten gastera, mede erotontes iatrous euthys tauta prospherontai*, when ordinary people feel some pain in the stomach they don't ask a doctor, they just eat garlic at once: Alexander of Tralles, *Therapeutics* vol. 2 p. 339. *skorda kephalia dodeka*, twelve little heads of garlic: *Prodromic Poems* 3.184. *skoroda ephtha syn elaio kai alati*, boiled garlic cloves with olive oil and salt: Hierophilus, April. *to ek skorodon epembamma*, garlic dip [a Crusader favourite]: Nicetas Choniates, *Chronicle*

p. 594 van Dieten. *skordaton*, garlic sauce: *Prodromic Poems* 4.64. *skorodozema*, garlic soup: Hierophilus, February. *skoroda karykeuta meta aromaton*, garlic in a spicy sauce: Hierophilus, September. Latin *cena allio et cepa bene olens, oleo et garo sordida*, a meal smelling strongly of garlic and onion, filthy with oil and fish sauce: Liutprand, *Embassy* 32.

Skorpidia, skorpioi, rascasse, *Scorpaena spp.*: *De cibis* 7, 14; *Peri tes ek ton zoon trophes*; *Opsarologos* 29.

Skoumbrin, Atlantic mackerel, *Scomber Scombrus*: *Prodromic Poems* 3.205.

Skylla, squill, *Urginea maritima. to legoun eis ten sterean skyllokrommydon kai eis ta nesia askellan e skellitouran* [dialect terms]: Agapius, *Geoponicon. skyllikon oxos, skillitikon oxos*, squill vinegar: Hierophilus, April; Agapius, *Geoponicon*. See text 4 section iv and note 69.

Smyrna, myrrh, *Commiphora Myrrha*: *Book of the Eparch* 10. Latin *smurna*: Justinian, *Digest* 39.4.16.7.

Soulenes, solenes, razor-shells, *Solen Vagina*: *Prodromic Poems* 3.278; *De cibis* 20.

Soumakin, sumach, *Rhus coriaria*: *Lexikon kata alphabeton* 147. *rou mageirikon: to soumaki* [alternative terms]: *Lexikon ton Sarakenon* 278.

Sourba, sourouba, sorbs or serviceberries, *Sorbus domestica. augarais egoun sourba* [alternative terms]: *Porikologos* 8; Agapius, *Geoponicon. sourba aora*, unripe sorbs: *De cibis* 7. *sourbomesphila*, sorbs and medlars: *Prodromic Poems* 2.65d.

Spanakin, spinach, *Spinacia oleracea*: *Prodromic Poems* 2.41; Agapius, *Geoponicon*.

Sparoi, sparaillon, annular bream, *Diplodus annularis*: Hierophilus, February.

Spetsies, chilli, *Capsicum annuum. spetsiais, kokkines piperiais* [alternative terms]: Agapius, *Geoponicon*.

Sphairia, kind of doughnut (classical Latin *globus, globulus*): Leontius of Naples, *Life of St Simeon Salos* p. 164 Rydén. *sfera niuea*, 'snowball': *de ipsis puris pectinibus fiunt sferae niueae*, 'snowballs' are made just from scallops [the minced meat, presumably]: Anthimus 34.

Sphakta, butchered meat, especially goat: Constantine Porphyrogennetus, *On Ceremonies* pp. 451, 464 Reiske.

Sphoungaton, omelette: *Prodromic Poems* 4.62 (ms. g). *dipla sphoungata*, omelettes folded over: *Prodromic Poems* 3.54. *einai auga syntrimmena kai teganismena me kromidia kai alia myrodika*, it is eggs beaten and pan-fried with onions and other aromatics: Damascenus Studites, *Sermons* 14.

Splankhna, vital organs: *De cibis* 7 etc.; *Peri tes ek ton zoon trophes*.

Splen, spleen: *De cibis* 22.

Stakhos, spikenard, *Nardostachys Jatamansi*: *Book of the Eparch* 10; *Prodromic Poems* 3.150.

Stakoi, astakoi, lobsters and langoustes, *Homarus Gammarus, Palinurus Elèphas*: *Prodromic Poems* 3.275; *De cibis* 7; *Opsarologos* 18.

Staphides, astaphides, astapides, raisins, *Vitis vinifera*: *Peri trophon dynameos* 471; *De cibis* 10. *staphides glykeiai*, sweet raisins: *De cibis* 10, 12, 21. *staphides liparai*, 'oily' raisins: *De cibis* 21, 22. *staphides styphousai*, astringent raisins: *De cibis* 8 etc. *staphiditsas khiotikas*, nice raisins from Chios: *Prodromic Poems* 3.283.

Staphyle, staphylai, grapes, *Vitis vinifera*: *De cibis* 5 etc; *Peri trophon dynameos* 472. *staphylai glykeiai*, sweet grapes: *De cibis* 25. *oxynai staphylai*, acid grapes: *De cibis* 26. *ai oinodeis ton staphylon*, wine-flavoured grapes: *De alimentis* 25. *melaina staphyle, maurai staphylai*, black grapes: *Peri trophon dynameos* 471; Hierophilus, July. *e leuke staphyle*, white grapes: *Peri trophon dynameos* 472. *staphylai kremastousai ep' oligo*, bunches of grapes hung for a short time: *De cibis* 5. *staphyle e en tois traphois* [?] *apotithemene*, bunches of grapes put up in jars: *De cibis* 8.

Stragalia, roasted chickpeas. *stragalostaphides*, nibbles such as roasted chickpeas and raisins: *Prodromic Poems* 2.44 (ms. G).

Strobiloi, pine kernels, *Pinus spp.*: *Peri trophon dynameos* 474.

Stromataioi, a kind of fish: Hierophilus, February.

Stroutheones, ostriches, *Struthio Camelus*: Theophanes, *Chronicle* AM 6118.

Strouthia. mikra strouthia, small birds: *De cibis* 5. *ta krea ton mikron strouthion*, meat of small birds: *Peri trophon dynameos* 477. *ta en tois ampelois eurisko-mena strouthia*, small birds caught in vineyards: *De cibis* 24.

Strouthomela, strouthomelitsia, ancient variety of quince: *De alimentis* 53; *Prodromic Poems* 2.65e. See p.132 note 45.

Styphos, styphon, astringent (often of fruit): *De cibis* 13 etc.

Styrax, storax, *Styrax officinalis*: Hierophilus, January. *styrakaton*, storax wine: Oribasius, *Medical Collections* 5.33. Russian *styuryaka*: Daniel, *Pilgrimage* 3.

Syakia, syakes, a kind of fish: Hierophilus, April; Nicetas Choniates, *Chronicle* p. 56 van Dieten. *eoiken e toutou sarx te ton alektoridon,* its flesh is like chicken: Simeon Seth p. 100. *syaina eos yska e syakion e khoirilla* [guessed equivalents]: *Scholia on Oppian, Halieutica* 1.129.

Syka, figs, *Ficus carica*: *De cibis* 5; *Prodromic Poems* 2.65d. *ta khlora syka,* fresh figs: *Peri trophon dynameos* 472. *ta xera syka* [cf. *iskhades*], dried figs: *Peri trophon dynameos* 472. *syka ta orimotera,* rather ripe figs: *De cibis* 20. *syka ta agourotera,* slightly unripe figs: *De alimentis* 18. *leuka syka meta alatos esthiein,* eat white [i.e. green] figs with salt; Hierophilus, July.

Sykamina, mulberries, *Morus spp.*: *De cibis* 12 etc.

Sykomora, sycomore figs, *Ficus Sycomorus*: *De alimentis* 25, 27.

Sykotia, foie gras: *De alimentis* 30. *sykotokyla ornithon* 'foies gras de volailles', *sykotophlengouna, sykotophlegmona* [expanded expressions]: Eustathius, *Life of St Eutychius.*

Synagrida, denté, *Dentex Dentex*: *Opsarologos* 11.

Synkeraston, spiced water: *Apophthegmata Patrum, Petrus Pionites* 1.

Syntheton, conserve with honey or sugar, spoon sweet: Oribasius, *Medical Collections* 5.33; Hierophilus, March.

Sys, pig, *Sus scrofa. syon temakhe tarikhera kyamois aletois synepsomena,* slices of salt pork cooked with beans, cassoulet [a Crusader favourite]: Nicetas Choniates, *Chronicle* p. 594 van Dieten.

Sysgoudon, valerian: *Prodromic Poems* 3.150. *nardos keltike: to sisgourdon* [classical equivalent]: *Glossae Jatricae.*

Tagenaria, traginaria, francolins, *Francolinus Francolinus*: *De alimentis* 1; *De cibis* 5, 6; *Peri tes ek ton zoon trophes. ton attagan e synetheia tagenarion kalei* [classical equivalent]: *Suda* s.v. 'attagas'.

Taones, peafowl, *Pavo cristatus*: Theophanes, *Chronicle* am 6118; *De cibis* 5. *ta krea ton taonon,* peacock meat: *Peri trophon dynameos* 477. French *pouns enpeverez,* peppered peacocks: *Voyage de Charlemagne* 411.

Tarkhon, tarragon, *Artemisia Dracunculus*: Simeon Seth p. 107; *De alimentis* 31.

Tauros, bull: *De cibis* 7, 16.

Teganou (to), pan-fried dish: *Prodromic Poems* 3.158.

Tele, telis, fenugreek, *Trigonella Foenum-graecum: De cibis* 10. *ou monon telen alla kai boukeras oi d' aigikeras onomazousi* [classical synonyms]: Simeon Seth p. 132. *telis apobrakheisa kai apoglykantheisa kai phytrotheisa, dia garou proesthiomenos, o karpos delonoti, e di' oxous kai garou, e di' oinou kai garou kai elaiou,* fenugreek (the seed, that is) steeped, sweetened, and sprouted, eaten as a starter with fish sauce, or with vinegar and fish sauce, or with wine and fish sauce and olive oil: *De alimentis* 39. *tes teles to sperma apothermon diephthon artythen dia melitos stakhous kai kinamomou,* fenugreek seed well boiled, cold, flavoured with honey, spikenard and cinnamon: Hierophilus, February. *apozema tes teleos,* fenugreek soup: Hierophilus, November, December. See also page 74 note 104.

Terebinthos, terebinth fruit, *Pistacia atlantica. terminthos estin en kaloumen terebinthon* [classical equivalent]: *Geoponica* 10.73.

Tetrangoura, chate melons, *Cucumis Melo* var. *Chate: De cibis* 26; *De alimentis* 18. *sikyia: ta tetrangoura* [classical equivalent]: *Suda* s.v. 'tetrangoura'. *tetrangoura Pegatika,* chate melons from Pegai: *Prodromic Poems* 2.65c.

Tetrapoda, quadrupeds: *De cibis* 16, 22; *Peri tes ek ton zoon trophes.*

Thermia, therma, lupin, *Lupinus albus:* Leontius of Naples, *Life of St Simeon Salos* p. 146 Rydén; *Peri trophon dynameos* 469; *De cibis* 7.

Thridakine, thridax, lettuce, *Lactuca sativa:* Theodore of Cyzicus, *Letters* 11; *Peri trophon dynameos* 479.

Thrymbon, thrimpon, thymbra, savory, Roman hyssop, *Satureja Thymbra: De cibis* 10; *Porikologos* 14. *thymbra khlora prospheromene,* savory served fresh: *De cibis* 24. *agiothroumpon eis ta pasta,* holy savory to flavour the salt fish: *Prodromic Poems* 2.42a. *ballei thrymboxyla tina pros myrodian,* he tosses in some twigs of savory for flavouring: *Prodromic Poems* 3.299.

Thrymmata, leftovers: *Prodromic Poems* 1.265.

Thymon, thyme, especially Cretan thyme, *Coridothymus capitatus: De cibis* 24; *Prodromic Poems* 3.229.

Thynnai, tunnies, *Thunnus Thynnus: Timarion* 21; *De cibis* 16; *Prodromic Poems* 3.259. *thynnas tarikheuontas egoun passontas dei esthiein,* tuna is to be eaten pickled or salted: *Peri tes ek ton zoon trophes. thynnokomman damakin apaston axyston sakhnon aplyton kapnismenon,* a tiny slice of tuna, unsalted, unscaled, tough, unwashed, smoky: *Prodromic Poems* 3.206.

Tourna, barracuda, *Sphyraena Sphyraena*: *Opsarologos* 19.

Tourpainai, electric rays, *Torpedo spp.*: Paul of Aegina, *Medical Epitome* 3.78, 7.17, cf. Alexander of Tralles, *Therapeutics* vol. 2 p. 575.

Tragana, traganos, tragos, trakhanas: *Geoponica* 3.8; *De cibis* 18; *De alimentis* 14. *khondros: traganos* [classical equivalent]: Hesychius, *Lexicon*. French *trachanas*: Belon, *Observations* 1.27, 1.59.

Tragos, billy-goat: *De cibis* 16. *trageia krea*, billy-goat meat: *De cibis* 7. *kree ton agrion tragon*, wild goat meat: *Peri trophon dynameos* 477.

Triglai, red mullets, *Mullus* spp., *M. barbatus*: *De cibis* 7 etc. *triglai ai tas karkinadas esthiousai*, red mullets that eat small crabs: *De cibis* 14. *triglia moustakata*, red mullets complete with moustaches: *Prodromic Poems* 3.159.

Triglai megalai, large red mullets, *Mullus Surmuletus*: *De cibis* 5; *Peri tes ek ton zoon trophes*.

Tripsidin, tripsedin, tripsies, ground spices, especially cinnamon, *Cinnamomum spp.*: Agathias [*Anthologia Palatina* 9.642]; Constantine Porphyrogennetus, *On Ceremonies* 1.1 [vol. 1 p. 28 Vogt]; *Prodromic Poems* 2.38, 3.150; *Glossae Jatricae. tripsidogaropiperon*, flavourings: *Prodromic Poems* 2.38 (ms. G).

Troglitai, trogletai, troglodytai, wrens, *Troglodytes Troglodytes*: Paul of Aegina, *Medical Epitome* 3.45.2; *De alimentis* 1; *De cibis* 5. *trogliton ton agrion genomenon psakhna khlia diephtha*, the meat of wrens taken from the wild is tough and should be well boiled and served hot: Hierophilus, January.

Trophe, food. *trophe e automatos blastanousa*, food that grows wild: Theodoret, *Religious History* 1.2.

Troximos, endive, *Cichorium Endivia*: *Peri trophon dynameos* 479. *seris toutesti troxima* [classical equivalent]: *Geoponica* 12.28.

Trygokrambin ek to goulin, brussels sprouts (or something similar): *Prodromic Poems* 2.42.

Trygon, sting-ray, *Dasyatis Pastinaca*: *De cibis* 21; *Peri tes ek ton zoon trophes*; *Opsarologos* 20.

Trygon, turtle dove, *Streptopelia Turtur*: *De cibis* 5, 7.

Tsiros, tzeros, chub mackerel, *Scomber Colias*: *Prodromic Poems* 3.184; *Opsarologos* 8.

Typhe, tiphe, einkorn, *Triticum monococcum: De cibis* 14, 16.

Tyrin, tyros, cheese: *Book of the Eparch* 13; Constantine Porphyrogennetus, *On Ceremonies* p. 464 Reiske; *De cibis* 20. *xeros tyros,* dry cheese: *Dream Book of Germanos* 152, 229. *tyros palaios,* old cheese: *De cibis* 7, 14, 18. *apalos tyros,* fresh cheese: *Dream Book of Germanos* 228; *Dream Book of Daniel* 449. *nearos tyros,* young cheese: *De cibis* 12. *tyros nearos aneu alon,* young cheese without salt: *Peri trophon dynameos* 478. *tyroi oxygalaktinoi,* cheeses made from buttermilk: *Peri trophon dynameos* 479.

Tyrogala, cream: *De cibis* 6.

Xerophagein, to eat 'dry', to fast: *Prodromic Poems* 3.273.

Xerozema, 'dry soup'. *xerozema dia pepereos kai stakhous kai kinamomou kai kareophyllon kai styrakos kalou oligou kai melitos tou arkountos,* a dry soup with pepper, spikenard, cinnamon, cloves, a little of the best storax and just sufficient honey: Hierophilus, January. See also page 39 and note 37.

Xiphia, swordfish, *Xiphias Gladius: De cibis* 18. *xiphiotrakhelon paston,* a salted neck of swordfish: *Prodromic Poems* 3.179.

Xylaloe, aloeswood, *Aquilaria malaccensis:* Tzetzes, *Letters* 29 Leone; *Peri trophon dynameos* 476; *Book of the Eparch* 10; Pseudo-Galen, *On Similar Remedies* p. 547. *aloe,* aloeswood: Cosmas Indicopleustes 11.15 (text uncertain). *xyla megala aloes,* big pieces of aloeswood: Theophanes, *Chronicle* AM 6118. *xylaloe ygra kai xera,* wet and dry aloeswood: Constantine Porphyrogennetus, *On Ceremonies* p. 468 Reiske, cf. Simeon Seth p. 74.

Xylobalsamon, balsam of Mecca wood (cf. *balsamon*): Nicolaus Myrepsus, *Compounds* 37.43.

Xylokerata, carobs, *Ceratonia Siliqua:* Alexander of Tralles, *Therapeutics* vol. 2 p. 431; *De cibis* 7; *Peri trophon dynameos* 474. *xylokerata a kai keratia legontai* [classical equivalent]: Simeon Seth p. 73.

Xylokaryophyllon, 'clove wood', an unknown spice: Cosmas Indicopleustes 11.15.

Xylon, wood. *ton eti ten physiken libada me apoliponton xylon,* aromatic woods that had not yet lost their natural juice: Psellus, *Chronographia* 6.62.

Xyston, 'spear', a river fish of the Don, perhaps a sturgeon. *entha to xyston agreuetai, Boulgarikon opsarion,* there the *xyston,* a Bulgarian fish, is caught: Theophanes, *Chronicle* AM 6171.

Ydna, truffles, *Tuber spp.*: Psellus, *Letters* 233 Kurtz and Drexl; *De cibis* 20, 26; *De alimentis* 74.

Ydor, water: *Peri trophon dynameos* 470; *De cibis* 7. *glyky ydor*, fresh, sweet water: *Peri trophon dynameos* 470. *ydor kalliston*, best, purest water: *De alimentis* 29. *ydor ombrion*, rainwater: *Peri trophon dynameos* 470. *ydor pegaion*, spring water: Oribasius, *Medical Collections* 5.33; *Peri trophon dynameos* 470. *almyron ydor*, salt water: *Peri trophon dynameos* 470. *khalkanthion ydor*, vitriolic water: *Peri trophon dynameos* 470. Latin *aqua decocta*, boiled water: Liutprand, *Antapodosis* 5.23.

Ydrogaros, ydor garou, watered fish sauce: *De alimentis* 1; *De cibis* 10; Anthimus 34 [text uncertain].

Ydromeli, honey water. *ydromeli meta zingibareos pinomenon*, a drink of honey water spiced with ginger: *Peri trophon dynameos* 473.

Ydrorosaton, ydrosaton, drosaton, rose cordial: Simeon Seth p. 111; *Prodromic Poems* 3.404i; Nicolaus Myrepsus, *Compounds*.

Yeion, pork. *krea yeia tarikha*, salt pork: *Timarion* 17.

Ypogastrion, udder. *syos theleias galathenon ypogastrion*, the milky udder of a sow: *Timarion* 46.

Yska, iskha, potamios ys, a catfish? (see Karpozelos 1984 p. 23; Robert 1961–2; Thompson 1947 p. 253; Korais 1814 pp. 47–48): Simeon Seth p. 111; Psellus, *Letters* 46, 58, 59 Sathas, 208 Kurtz and Drexl; Theodore Daphnopates, *Letters* 26; *Prodromic Poems* 3.95, 3.325c; *Peri tes ek ton zoon trophes*; *Opsarologos* 19.

Yssopos, yssopon, hyssop, *Hyssopus officinalis*: *De cibis* 11, 23; Simeon Seth p. 46. *zouphan* [i.e. Arabic *zūfā*] *etoi yssopon*: Pseudo-Galen, *On Similar Remedies* p. 564.

Zambax Arabian jasmine, *Jasminum Sambac*: *Appendices to Hippiatrica Berolinensia* 7. *ta leukoia a sarakenisti legontai zampakiasmin*, the white violets that are called 'sambac jasmine' in Arabic: *Peri trophon dynameos* 475. *zampakelaion*, jasmine oil: Simeon Seth p. 30. Cf. Du Cange 1688 *s.vv. zabakon, zambax*.

Zargana, garfish, *Belone Belone*: *Opsarologos* 28.

Zea, zeia, emmer, *Triticum dicoccum*: Simeon Seth p. 40.

Zema, water from boiling vegetables: Hierophilus, February.

Zingiberi, zingibari, zingiber, ginger, *Zingiber officinale*: Simeon Seth p. 40; Theophanes, *Chronicle* AM 6118; *Peri trophon dynameos* 473. *xylozingiberi,* 'wood ginger' [dry or ground ginger]: Pseudo-Galen, *Signs from Urine.*

Zinzipha, zizypha, tzintzipha, jujubes, *Zizyphus Jujuba*: *De alimentis* 20; *Prodromic Poems* 2.65d; *Porikologos* 8. *ounapia* [i.e. Arabic *'unnāb'*] *etoi xyntzipha*: Pseudo-Galen, *On Similar Remedies* p. 563. *kreittona ta meizona: toiauta eisi ta edessena,* the bigger ones are better, such as those from Edessa: Simeon Seth p. 40. *zoulapion apo zizyphon,* jujube syrup: Pseudo-Galen, *Signs from Urine* line 141.

Zoa, animals. *agria zoa,* wild animals: *De cibis* 5; *Peri tes ek ton zoon trophes. emera zoa,* farm animals: *De cibis* 5; *Peri tes ek ton zoon trophes. zoa ta argos biounta,* animals pastured in wild country: *De cibis* 23. *teleia zoa,* uncastrated animals: *De cibis* 7. *eunoukhisthenta zoa,* castrated animals: *De cibis* 14. *pany nea zoa,* very young animals: *De cibis* 12. *zoa eti auxanomena,* animals still at the growing stage: *De cibis* 5, 22. *zoa gegerakota, zoa palaia,* old animals: *De cibis* 5, 22. *zoa tryphera,* plump or fattened animals: *De alimentis* 1.

Zokhia, sow-thistle, *Sonchus spp.*: *De cibis* 14.

Zoulapi, zoulapion, sugar syrup, julep: Simeon Seth p. 41; Maximus Planudes [Ideler 1841–2 vol. 2 p. 321]. *zoulapion apo zizyphon,* jujube syrup: Pseudo-Galen, *Signs from Urine* line 141.

Zoumin, zomos, cooking liquor, gravy, soup: *Prodromic Poems* 3.155; *De cibis* 12; *Peri trophon dynameos* 477. *zomidion,* drink of soup, portion of soup: Nicetas Choniates, *Chronicle* p. 57 van Dieten. *pimelodes zomos,* greasy soup: *Timarion* 19. *zomoi karykeutoi di pepereos stakhous kai kinamomou,* gravies spiced with pepper, spikenard and cinnamon: Hierophilus, January. *mystilasthai: to ekrophesai ton zomon tois psomiois,* [classical term] to sup one's soup using bits of bread: Hesychius, *Lexicon.*

Zygaia, storax, *Liquidambar orientalis* or *Styrax officinalis*: *Book of the Eparch* 10. Russian *zygia*: Daniel, *Pilgrimage* 4.

Zyme, bread yeast: *De cibis* 2. *zymosis,* kneading: *De cibis* 6.

Bibliography

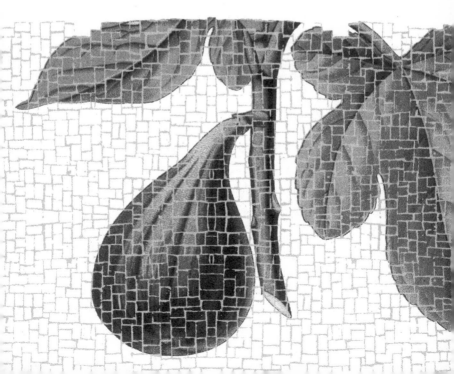

Sources for the phrase-book: Greek

Aetius, *Medicine*. Books 1–8, ed. A. Olivieri, Leipzig, Berlin, 1935–50; Book 9, ed. S. Zervos in *Athena*, vol. 23 (1911), pp. 273–390; Book 11, ed. C. Daremberg and C.E. Ruelle in *Oeuvres de Rufus d'Ephèse*, Paris: Imprimerie Nationale, 1879; Book 12, ed. G.A. Kostomiris, Paris: Klincksieck, 1892; Book 16: *Gynaekologie des Aëtios*, ed. S. Zervos, Leipzig: Fock, 1901.

Agapius, *Geoponicon*, Venice, 1647.

Agathias, *History*, ed. R. Keydell, Berlin: De Gruyter, 1967.

Alexander of Tralles, *On Fevers, Therapeutics*, ed. T. Puschmann, Vienna: Braumüller, 1878–9. French translation: *Oeuvres médicales d'Alexandre de Tralles*, tr. F. Brunet, Paris, 1933–7.

Anastasius, *Narrative*, cited from Magoulias 1971, 1976.

Anna Comnena, *Alexiad*, ed. and tr. B. Leib, Paris: Les Belles Lettres, 1937–45. English translation: *The Alexiad of Anna Comnena*, tr. E.R.A. Sewter, Harmondsworth: Penguin, 1969.

Anthimus, *Letter on Diet. Anthimi De observatione ciborum ad Theodoricum regem Francorum epistula*, ed. E. Liechtenhan, Berlin: Akademie-Verlag, 1963. English translation: Anthimus, *De observatione ciborum = On the observance of foods*, tr. Mark Grant, Totnes: Prospect Books, 1996.

Apophthegmata Patrum [alphabetical collection], Migne, *Patrologia Graecolatina*, vol. 65. English translation: *The sayings of the Desert Fathers: the alphabetical collection*, tr. Benedicta Ward, London: Mowbray, 1975.

Arethas, *On Lucian's Lexiphanes*, cited from Koukoulès 1948–55.

Asterius of Amasea, *Homilies*, ed. C. Datema, Leiden: Brill, 1970.

[Athanasius], *On Unleavened Bread*, Migne, *Patrologia Graecolatina*, vol. 26.

[Athanasius], *Story of Melchisedek*, Migne, *Patrologia Graecolatina*, vol. 28.

Book of the Eparch. To eparkhikon vivlion = *The Book of the Eparch* = *Le livre du préfet,* ed. I. Dujcev [including English translation by E.H. Freshfield], London: Variorum Reprints, 1970.

Constantine Manasses, *Moral Poem,* cited from Koukoulès 1948–55.

Constantine Porphyrogennetus, *De administrando imperio,* ed. G. Moravcsik, Washington: Dumbarton Oaks, 1967.

Constantine Porphyrogennetus, *On Ceremonies.* Book 1 chapters 1–92 cited from the unfinished edition by A. Vogt, Paris: Les Belles Lettres, 1935–9; remainder cited from the edition by J.J. Reiske, Bonn: Weber, 1829.

Constantine Porphyrogennetus, *Tactics,* cited from Du Cange 1688.

Constantine Porphyrogennetus, *Themes,* ed. A. Pertusi, Vatican City: Biblioteca Apostolica Vaticana, 1952.

Cosmas Indicopleustes, *Christian Topography,* ed. and French tr. Wanda Wolska-Conus, Paris, 1968–73.

Critobulus of Imbros, *History of Mehmed II. Fragmenta historicorum graecorum,* ed. Carolus Müller, Vol. 5, Paris: Didot, 1883. English translation: Kritovoulos, *History of Mehmed the Conqueror,* tr. Charles T. Riggs, Princeton: Princeton University Press, 1954.

Cyril of Scythopolis, *Life of St Sabas,* ed. E. Schwartz, Leipzig: Hinrichs, 1939.

Damascenus Studites, *Sermons,* cited from Jeanselme and Oeconomos 1923.

De alimentis, ed. Ideler 1841–2. For translation see chapter 6.

De cibis, ed. Ideler 1841–2. For translation see chapter 6.

Diegesis ton tetrapodon zoon, ed. Wagner 1874.

Dream Book of Daniel. Fr. Drexl, 'Das Traumbuch der Propheten Daniel' in *Byzantinische Zeitschrift,* vol. 26 (1926), p. 290 ff. German translation: Brackertz 1993.

Dream Book of Germanos. Fr. Drexl, 'Das Traumbuch des Patriarchen Germanos' in *Laographika,* vol. 7 (1923), p. 428 ff. German translation: Brackertz 1993.

Dream Book of Nicephorus. F. Drexl, 'Das Traumbuch des Patriarchen Nikephoros' in *Festgabe für A. Erhard* (Bonn, 1922), p. 94 ff. German translation: Brackertz 1993.

Eustathius, *Capture of Thessalonica,* ed. S. Kyriakidis, Palermo: Istituto Siciliano di Studi Bizantini e Neoellenici, 1961. German translation: *Die Normannen in Thessalonike,* tr. Herbert Hunger, Graz: Styria, 1955.

Eustathius, *Commentary on Iliad,* ed. M. van der Valk, Leiden: Brill, 1971–87.

Eustathius, *Commentary on Odyssey,* ed. G. Stallbaum, Leipzig: Weigel, 1825–6.

Eustathius, *Letters,* cited from Karpozelos 1984.

Eustathius, *Life of St Eutychius,* cited from Koukoulès 1948–55.

[Attributed to Galen:] *On Similar Remedies. Galeni opera omnia,* ed. C.G. Kühn, Leipzig, 1821–33, Vol. 14.

[Attributed to Galen:] *Signs from Urine.* P. Moraux, 'Anecdota Graeca minora, 6: Pseudo-Galen de signis ex urinis' in *Zeitschrift für Papyrologie und Epigraphik,* vol. 60 (1985), pp. 68–74.

[Attributed to Galen:] *Lexeis Botanon,* ed. Delatte 1939.

Geoponica, ed. H. Beckh, Leipzig: Teubner, 1895.

Glossae Jatricae, cited from Du Cange 1688.

Gregory of Corinth, cited from Koukoulès 1948–55.

Gregory of Cyprus, *Letters,* cited from Karpozelos 1984.

Hierophilus, *Dietary Calendar,* ed. Delatte 1939; another version ed. Ideler 1841–2. For English translation see chapter 6.

Historia Monachorum in Aegypto, ed. A.-J. Festugière, Brussels: Société des Bollandistes, 1961. English translation: *The lives of the Desert Fathers,* tr. Norman Russell, Oxford: Mowbray, 1981.

John Moschus, *Spiritual Meadow,* cited from Magoulias 1971, 1976.

Justinian, *Digest,* ed. T. Mommsen, P. Krueger, Berlin: Weidmann, 1928.

Leontius of Naples, *Life of St John the Almsgiver. Leontios' von Neapolis Leben des heiligen Iohannes des Barmherziger, Erzbischofs von Alexandrien,* ed. Heinrich Gelzer, Freiburg: Mohr, 1893. English translation: Dawes and Baynes 1948.

Leontius of Naples, *Life of St Simeon Salos,* ed. L. Rydén. Uppsala: Almqvist & Wiksell, 1963. English translation: Derek Krueger, *Symeon the holy fool: Leontius's Life and the late antique city,* Berkeley: University of California Press, 1996.

Lexikon kata alphabeton, ed. Thomson 1955.

Lexikon ton Sarakenon, ed. Thomson 1955.

Life of St Athanasius of Athos, cited from Koukoulès 1948–55.

Life of St Dositheus. Pierre-Marie Brun, 'La vie de l'Abbé Dosithée' in *De Oriente* (Rome: Pontificium Institutum Orientalium Studiorum, 1932, *Orientalia christiana,* 78), pp. 85–267.

Life of St John the Almsgiver. Hippolyte Delehaye, 'Une vie inédite de Saint Jean l'Aumonier' in *Analecta Bollandiana,* vol. 45 (1927), pp. 5–74.

Life of St Maximus of Athos, cited from Koukoulès 1948–55.

Life of St Theodore of Syceon. Vie de Théodore de Sykéôn, ed. and tr. A.-J. Festugière, Brussels, 1970. English translation: Dawes and Baynes 1948.

Maurice, *Stratagems,* ed. G.T. Dennis, E. Gamillscheg, Vienna, 1981. English translation by G.T. Dennis, Philadelphia, 1984.

Maximus Planudes, *On Diet,* cited from Koukoulès 1948–55.

Menander Protector, *History. The History of Menander the Guardsman,* ed. and tr. R.C. Blockley, Liverpool: Francis Cairns, 1985.

Michael Apostoles, *Letters,* ed. H. Noiret, Paris, 1899.

Michael Choniates, *Letters,* ed. S.P. Lampros, Athens, 1879–80.

Michael Italicus, *Letters,* cited from Karpozelos 1984.

Miracles of Ss Cyrus and John, cited from Magoulias 1971, 1976.

Miracles of St Artemius, cited from Magoulias 1971, 1976.

Nicetas Choniates, *Chronicle,* ed. J.-L. van Dieten, Berlin, 1975. English translation: *O city of Byzantium: annals of Niketas Choniates,* tr. Harry J. Magoulias, Detroit: Wayne State University Press, 1984. Demotic text cited from Du Cange 1688 and Koukoulès 1948–55.

Nicolaus Mesarites, *Journey,* cited from Karpozelos 1984.

Nicolaus Myrepsus, *Compounds.* Text and scholia cited from Du Cange 1688. Latin translation by Leonhard Fuchs: Frankfurt am Main, 1626.

Opsarologos. K. Krumbacher, 'Das mittelgriechische Fischbuch' in *Sitzungsberichte der philosophisch-historische Klasse der Bayerischen Akademie der Wissenschaften* (1903 no. 3), pp. 345–380.

Oribasius, *Medical Collections,* ed. I. Raeder, Leipzig, 1928–33. Partial English translation: Mark Grant, *Dieting for an emperor: a translation of books 1 and 4 of Oribasius' Medical Compilations,* Leiden: Brill, 1997.

Paul of Aegina, *Medical Epitome*, ed. J.L. Heiberg, Leipzig, 1921–4. English translation: *The seven books of Paulus Aegineta*, tr. Francis Adams, London: Sydenham Society, 1846.

Peri tes ek ton zoon trophes, ed. Ideler 1841–2. For English translation see chapter 6.

Peri trophon dynameos, ed. Delatte 1939. For English translation see chapter 6.

Peter Zyphomustus, *Physiologike diegesis*, cited from Koukoulès 1948–55.

Philogelos, ed. and tr. A. Thierfelder, Munich: Heimeran, 1968.

Photius, *Library*, ed. and tr. R. Henry, Paris: Les Belles Lettres, 1959–77.

Poem on Medicine, ed. Ideler 1841–2.

Porikologos, ed. Wagner 1874.

Poullologos, ed. Wagner 1874.

Procopius, *Secret History*, ed. J. Haury, G. Wirth, Leipzig: Teubner, 1963. English translation by G.A. Williamson, Harmondsworth: Penguin, 1966.

Prodromic Poems. Unless otherwise stated citations are from *Poèmes prodromiques en grec vulgaire*, ed. D.C. Hesseling and H. Pernot, Amsterdam, 1910. Occasionally cited from A. Korais, *Atakta*, vol. 1 (Paris, 1828).

Psellus, *Chronographia*, ed. E. Renauld, Paris: Les Belles Lettres, 1926–8. English translation: *Fourteen Byzantine rulers: the Chronographia of Michael Psellus*, tr. E.R.A. Sewter, Harmondsworth: Penguin, 1966.

Psellus, *Letters*, cited from Karpozelos 1984.

Scholia on Aristophanes, Acharnians, ed. N.G. Wilson, Groningen: Bouma, 1975.

Scholia on Aristophanes, Plutus, ed. F. Dübner, Paris: Didot, 1877.

Scholia on Nicander, Oppian, Theocritus. Scholia in Theocritum, ed. F. Dübner; *Scholia et paraphrases in Nicandrum et Oppianum*, ed. U.C. Bussemaker, Paris: Didot, 1847.

Simeon Seth, *On the Properties of Foods*, ed. B. Langkavel, Leipzig: Teubner, 1868. French translation by M. Brunet, Bordeaux: Delmas, 1939.

Stephanus, *Commentary on Hippocrates' Aphorisms*, ed. L.G. Westerink, Berlin, 1985.

Suda, ed. A. Adler, Leipzig: Teubner, 1928–35.

Theodore Daphnopates, *Letters*, cited from Karpozelos 1984.

Theodore Ducas, *Letters*, cited from Georgacas 1978.

Theodore of Cyzicus, *Letters*, cited from Karpozelos 1984.

Theodore Studites, cited from Koukoulès 1948–55 and from Jeanselme and Oeconomos 1923.

Theodoret, *Religious History*. Théodoret de Cyr, *L'histoire des moines de Syrie*, ed. P. Canivet and A. Leroy-Molinghen, Paris: Cerf, 1977–9.

Theophanes, *Chronicle*, ed. C. de Boor, Leipzig: Teubner, 1883–5. Partial English translation by H. Turtledove, Philadelphia: University of Pennsylvania Press, 1982.

Theophylact Simocatta, *History*, ed. C. de Boor, P. Wirth, Stuttgart, 1972. English translation by M. and M. Whitby, Oxford: Clarendon Press, 1986.

Timarion. Luciani opera, vol. 4, ed. M.D. Macleod, Oxford: Clarendon Press, 1987. English translation: *Timarion*, tr. Barry Baldwin, Detroit: Wayne State University Press, 1984.

Typika, cited from Thomas and Hero 2001; *Typikon of Kosmosoteira* also from Hesseling and Pernot 1910; *Typikon of Pantokrator* also from Koukoulès 1948–55.

Tzetzes, *Khiliades*, cited from Hesseling and Pernot 1910.

Tzetzes, *Letters*, cited from Karpozelos 1984.

Tzetzes, *On Lucia*, cited from Koukoulès 1948–55.

Zonaras, *Lexicon*, ed. J.A.H. Tittmann, Leipzig: Crusius, 1808.

Zonaras, *On the Apostolic Canons*, Migne, *Patrologia Graecolatina*, vol. 137.

Zonaras, *Commentary on Gangra and Trullo*, cited from Koukoulès 1948–55.

Sources for the phrase-book: other languages

Pierre Belon, *Les observations de plusieurs singularitez et choses memorables trouvées en Grèce, Asie, Judée, Egypte, Arabie et autres pays étrangèrs*, Paris, 1555, 2nd ed.

Brocardus (Wilhelmus Adam), *Guide to the Voyage Overseas*, C.R. Beazley, 'Directorium ad faciendum passagium transmarinum' in *American historical review*, vols 12–13 (1906/8).

Daniel, *Pilgrimage, Zhit'e i khozhen'e Danila Rus'skyya zemli igumena*, ed.

M.A. Venevitinov, St Petersburg, 1885.

Geoffroi de Villehardouin, *Conquest of Constantinople*, ed. and tr. E. Faral, Paris: Les Belles Lettres, 1961. English translation: *Joinville and Villehardouin: Chronicles of the Crusades*, tr. M.R.B. Shaw, Harmondsworth: Penguin, 1963.

Liutprand, *Antapodosis, Embassy*, ed. J. Becker, Hanover: Hahn, 1915. English translation by F.A. Wright, London: Routledge, 1930.

Odo of Deuil, *Expedition of Louis VII*. English translation by V.G. Berry, New York: Columbia University Press, 1948.

Rufinus of Aquileia, *Historia Monachorum*, Migne, *Patrologia Latina*, vol. 21. [This is a version of the Greek *Historia Monachorum in Aegypto*, see above.]

William of Rubruck, *Report. Sinica franciscana, 1. Itinera et relationes fratrum minorum saeculi xiii et xiv*, ed. Anastasius van den Wyngaert, Florence: Quaracchi, 1929. English translation: *The mission of Friar William of Rubruck*, tr. P. Jackson, London, 1990.

General bibliography

Adler 1907: Benjamin of Tudela, *Itinerary*, tr. Marcus N. Adler, London, 1907.

Akerström-Hougen 1974: G. Akerström-Hougen, *The calendar and hunting mosaics of the Villa of the Falconer in Argos*, Stockholm, 1974.

Angelidhis 1989: *I kathimerini zoi sto Vizandio*, ed. Khristina G. Angelidhis, Athens, 1989.

Ashtor 1968: E. Ashtor, 'Essai sur l'alimentation des diverses classes sociales dans l'Orient médiéval' in *Annales: économies, sociétés, civilisations*, vol. 23 (1968), pp. 1017–1053.

Boissonade 1827: 'Traîté alimentaire du médecin Hiérophile', ed. J.-F. Boissonade in *Notices et extraits des manuscrits de la Bibliothèque du Roi*, vol. II part 2 (1827), pp. 178–273.

Bozi 1994: Soula Bozi, *Politiki kouzina*, Athens: Asterismos, 1994.

Brackertz 1993: *Die Volks-Traumbücher des byzantinischen Mittelalters*, tr.

Karl Brackertz, München: Deutscher Taschenbuch Verlag, 1993.

Browning 1989: R. Browning, 'Theodore Balsamon's commentary on the canons of the Council in Trullo as a source on everyday life in twelfth-century Byzantium' in *I kathimerini zoi sto Vizandio*, ed. Kh. G. Angelidhis (Athens, 1989), pp. 421–7.

Burckhardt 1918: J. Burckhardt, 'Über die Kochkunst der spätern Griechen' in his *Vorträge 1844–1887*, ed. E. Dürr (Basle, 1918), pp. 103–115.

Bury 1907: J.B. Bury, 'The Ceremonial Book of Constantine Porphyrogennetos' in *English historical review*, vol. 22 (1907), pp. 209–227, 417–439.

Cekalova 1989: A. Cekalova, *Vizantija: byt i nravy*. Sverdlovsk, 1989.

Clusius 1605: *Caroli Clusii Exoticorum libri decem, quibus animalium, plantarum, aromatum, aliorumque peregrinorum fructuum historiae describuntur*. Leiden: ex Officina Plantiniana, 1605.

Dalby 1997: Andrew Dalby, 'Christmas dinner in Byzantium' in *Food on the move: proceedings of the Oxford Symposium on Food and Cookery 1996*, ed. Harlan Walker (Totnes: Prospect Books, 1997), pp. 75–83.

Dalby 1999: Andrew Dalby, 'Byzantine cookery' in Alan Davidson, *The Oxford companion to food* (Oxford, 1999), pp. 118–119.

Dalby 1996: Andrew Dalby, *Siren feasts: a history of food and gastronomy in Greece*, London: Routledge, 1996.

Dalby 2000: Andrew Dalby, *Dangerous tastes: the story of spices*, London: British Museum Press, 2000.

Dalby 2000 b: Andrew Dalby, 'Mastic for beginners' in *Petits propos culinaires* no. 65 (2000), pp. 38–45.

Davidson 1999: Alan Davidson, *The Oxford companion to food*, Oxford: Oxford University Press, 1999.

Dawes and Baynes 1948: *Three Byzantine saints,* tr. E. Dawes, N.H. Baynes, London, 1948. – Corrected reprint: Crestwood, N.Y.: St Vladimir's Seminary Press, 1977.

De Ligt 1993: L. de Ligt, *Fairs and markets in the Roman Empire: economic and social aspects of periodic trade in a pre-industrial society*. Amsterdam: Gieben, 1993.

Delatte 1939: *Anecdota Atheniensia et alia,* ed. A. Delatte. Vol. 2, Paris: Droz, 1939.

Dembinska 1986: M. Dembinska, 'Diet: a comparison of food consumption between some Eastern and Western monasteries in the 4th–12th c.' in *Byzantion,* vol. 55 (1985/6), pp. 431–62.

Diethart and Kislinger 1992: J. Diethart, E. Kislinger, 'Aprikosen und Pflaumen' in *Jahrbuch der österreichischer Byzantinistik,* vol. 42 (1992), pp. 75–8.

du Cange 1688: C. du Fresne sieur du Cange, *Glossarium ad scriptores mediae et infimae Graecitatis.* Lyon, 1688.

Ehrhard 1932: Anthony of Novgorod, *Livre du pèlerin,* tr. M. Ehrhard in *Romania,* vol. 58 (1932), pp. 44–65.

Eideneier 1970: H. Eideneier, 'Zu krasin' in *Hellenika,* vol. 23 (1970), pp. 118–122.

Fehrle 1920: E. Fehrle, *Richtlinien zur Textgestaltung der griechischen Geoponica.* Heidelberg, 1920.

Gemoll 1883: W. Gemoll, *Untersuchungen über die Quellen, der Verfasser und die Abfassungszeit der Geoponica.* Berlin, 1883.

Gentili 1959: G. Gentili, 'Il medico bizantino Antimo (VI secolo) e la sua epistola *De observantia ciborum*' in *Atti del XVI Convegno Nazionale della Società Italiana di Storia della Medicina* (Bologna, 1959), pp. 1–19.

Georgacas 1978: D.J. Georgacas, *Ichthyological terms for the sturgeon and etymology of the international terms botargo, caviar and congeners,* Athens, 1978.

Ghedheon 1951: M. Ghedheon, 'Peri ton meghaloprepesteron en Konstadinoupoli teloumenon ierokosmikon panighireon' in *Laografia,* vol. 13 (1951), pp. 237–241.

Greppin 1987: John A.C. Greppin, 'The Armenian and the Greek Geoponica' in *Byzantion,* vol. 57 (1987), pp. 46–55.

Harig 1967: G. Harig, 'Von den arabischen Quellen des Symeon Seth' in *Medizinhistorisches Journal,* vol. 2 (1967), pp. 248–68.

Harlow and Smith 2001: Mary Harlow, Wendy Smith, 'Between feasting and fasting: the literary and archaeobotanical evidence for monastic diet in late antique Egypt' in *Antiquity*, vol. 75 (2001), pp. 758–768.

Helbaek 1961: H. Helbaek, 'Late bronze age and Byzantine crops at Beycesultan in Anatolia' in *Anatolian studies*, vol. 11 (1961), pp. 77–97.

Hesseling and Pernot 1910: *Poèmes prodromiques en grec vulgaire*, ed. D.-C. Hesseling, H. Pernot. Amsterdam: Müller, 1910. – *Verhandelingen der Koninklijke Akademie van Wetenschappen te Amsterdam, afdeling letterkunde*, n. s., vol. 11 no. 1.

Hill and Bryer 1995: S. Hill and A. Bryer, 'Byzantine porridge: tracta, trachanas and tarhana' in *Food in antiquity*, ed. J. Wilkins and others (Exeter: Exeter University Press, 1995), pp. 44–54.

Hirschfeld 1992: Y. Hirschfeld, *The Judean Desert monasteries in the Byzantine period*, New Haven, 1992.

Ideler 1841–1842: *Physici et medici graeci minores*, ed. I.L. Ideler, Berlin: Reimer, 1841–2.

Jeanselme 1922: E. Jeanselme, 'Sels médicamenteux et aromates pris par les byzantins au cours des repas' in *Bulletin de la Société Française d'Histoire Médicale*, vol. 16 (1922), p. 327ff.

Jeanselme 1924: E. Jeanselme, 'Les calendriers de régime à l'usage des Byzantins et la tradition hippocratique' in *Mélanges offerts à G. Schlumberger* (Paris, 1924), pp. 217–233.

Jeanselme 1924 b: E. Jeanselme, 'L'alcoolisme à Byzance' in *Bulletin de la Société Française d'Histoire de la Médecine*, vol. 18 (1924).

Jeanselme 1930: E. Jeanselme, 'Sur un aide-mémoire de thérapeutique byzantin contenu dans un manuscrit de la Bibl. Nat. de Paris (supplément grec 764): traduction, notes et commentaires' in *Mélanges Charles Diehl*, vol. 1 (Paris: Leroux, 1930), pp. 147–170.

Jeanselme and Œconomos 1923: E. Jeanselme and L.Œconomos, 'Aliments et recettes culinaires des byzantins' in *Proceedings of the 3rd International Congress of the History of Medicine* (Antwerp, 1923), pp. 155–168.

Johnson and West 1967: *Byzantine Egypt: economic studies*, ed. Allan Chester Johnson, Louis C. West. 1967.

Kaempfer 1712: Engelbert Kaempfer, *Amoenitatum exoticarum politico-*

physico-medicarum fasciculi V, Lemgoviae: H.W. Meyer, 1712.

Kalleris 1953: I. Kalleris, '«Trofe ke pota» is protovizandinous papirous' in *Epetiris Eterias Vizandinon Spoudhon*, vol. 23 (1953), pp. 689–715.

Kaneva-Johnson 1995: Maria Kaneva-Johnson, *The melting pot: Balkan food and cookery*, Totnes: Prospect Books, 1995.

Karali 1989: L. Karali-Yannakopoulos, 'Les mollusques de Porto-Lagos' in *Byzantinische Forschungen*, vol. 14 (1989), pp. 245–251.

Karpozelos 1984: A. Karpozelos, 'Realia in Byzantine epistolography, X–XII c.' in *Byzantinische Zeitschrift*, vol. 77 (1984), pp. 20–37.

Kazhdan 1991: *The Oxford dictionary of Byzantium*, ed. Alexander P. Kazhdan, Alice-Mary Talbot and others, New York: Oxford University Press, 1991.

Kislinger 1987: E. Kislinger, 'How reliable is early Byzantine hagiography as an indicator of diet?' in *Diptycha*, vol. 4 (1986/7), pp. 5–11.

Kislinger 1984: E. Kislinger, 'Phoûska und glékhon' in *Jahrbuch der österreichischen Byzantinistik*, vol. 34 (1984), pp. 49–53.

Kislinger 1984 b: E. Kislinger, 'Kaiser Julian und die (christlichen) Xenodocheia' in *Byzantios. Festschrift für Herbert Hunger zum 70. Geburtstag*, ed. W. Hörandner and others (Vienna: Ernst Becvar, 1984), pp. 171–184.

Kislinger 1982: E. Kislinger, *Gastgewerbe und Beherbergung in frühbyzantinischer Zeit: eine realienkundliche Studie aufgrund hagiographischer und historischer Quellen*, 1982, – Dissertation: Vienna.

Kochilas 2001: Diane Kochilas, *The glorious foods of Greece*, New York: Morrow, 2001.

Koder 1992: Johannes Koder, *O kipouros ke i kathimerini kouzina sto Vizandio*, Athens: Goulandri-Horn, 1992.

Kolias 1984: T. Kolias, 'Eßgewohnheiten und Verpflegung im byzantinischen Heer' in *Byzantios. Festschrift für Herbert Hunger zum 70. Geburtstag*, ed. W. Hörandner and others (Vienna: Ernst Becvar, 1984), pp. 193–202.

Koukoulis 1947–1955: F. Koukoulès, *Vizandinon vios ke politismos*, Athens, 1947–55.

Kremezi 1997: Aglaia Kremezi, 'Paximadia' in *Food on the move: proceedings of the Oxford Symposium on Food and Cookery 1996*, ed. Harlan Walker (Totnes: Prospect Books, 1997), pp. 208–211.

Kyriakis 1973: M.J. Kyriakis, 'Satire and slapstick in 7th and 12th century Byzantium' in *Byzantina*, vol. 5 (1973), pp. 291–306.

Kyriakis 1974: M.J. Kyriakis, 'Poor poets and starving literati in 12th century Byzantium' in *Byzantion*, vol. 44 (1974), pp. 290–309.

Lambert-Gócs 1990: Miles Lambert-Gócs, *The wines of Greece*, London: Faber, 1990.

Lampropoulou 1989: A. Lampropoulou, 'I panigiris stin Peloponniso kata ti meseoniki epokhi' in *I kathimerini zoi sto Vizandio*, ed. Kh. G. Angelidhis (Athens, 1989), pp. 291–310.

Langkavel 1866: B. Langkavel, *Botanik der späteren Griechen vom dritten bis dreizehnten Jahrhunderte*, Berlin, 1866.

Laurioux 1985: Bruno Laurioux, 'Spices in the medieval diet: a new approach' in *Food and foodways*, vol. 1 (1985–7), pp. 43–75.

Laurioux and Redon 1984: B. Laurioux and O. Redon, 'Emergence d'une cuisine médiévale: le témoignage des livres' in *Matériaux pour l'histoire des cadres de vie dans l'Europe occidentale* (Nice, 1984), pp. 91–101.

Lemerle 1958: R. Lemerle, 'Esquisse pour une histoire agraire de Byzance: les sources et les problèmes' in *Revue historique*, vol. 220 (1958), pp. 43–70.

Liddell and Scott 1925–1940: Henry George Liddell, Robert Scott, *A Greek-English lexicon*, Oxford: Clarendon Press, 1925–40, – 9th ed. by Henry Stuart Jones, Roderick McKenzie.

Loewe 1971: M. Loewe, 'Spices and silks: aspects of world trade in the first seven centuries of the Christian era' in *Journal of the Royal Asiatic Society* (1971), pp. 166–179.

Magoulias 1964: H.J. Magoulias, 'The lives of the saints as sources of data for the history of Byzantine medicine in the 6th and 7th centuries' in *Byzantinische Zeitschrift*, vol. 57 (1964), pp. 127–150.

Magoulias 1971: H.J. Magoulias, 'Bathhouse, inn, tavern, prostitution and the stage as seen in the lives of the saints of the sixth and seventh centuries' in *Epetiris Eterias Vizandinon Spoudhon*, vol. 38 (1971), pp. 233–252.

Magoulias 1976: H.J. Magoulias, 'Trades and crafts in the sixth and seventh centuries as viewed in the Lives of the Saints' in *Byzantinoslavica*, vol. 37 (1976), pp. 11–35.

Majeska 1984: George P. Majeska, *Russian travelers to Constantinople in the fourteenth and fifteenth centuries*, Washington: Dumbarton Oaks, 1984.

Marks 2002: Henry Marks, *Byzantine cuisine*, Marks [1270 Montecello Drive, Eugene, Oregon 97404, USA], 2002.

Mathiesen 1993: Johan Mathiesen, 'The children of lucanica' in *Petits propos culinaires* no. 43 (1993), pp. 62–63.

Mayerson 1985: P. Mayerson, 'The wine and vineyards of Gaza in the Byzantine period' in *Bulletin of the American schools of Oriental research*, vol. 257 (1985), pp. 75–80.

Mayerson 1993: P. Mayerson, 'The use of Ascalon wine in the medical writers of the fourth to the seventh centuries' in *Israel exploration journal*, vol. 43 (1993), pp. 169–173.

Menardos 1908: S. Menardos, 'To oxighala tou Prodhromou' in *I meleti* (1908), p. 255.

Motsias 1998: Khristos Motsias, *Ti etrogani i Vizandini?* Athens: Kaktos, 1998.

Mras 1947: K. Mras, 'Anthimus und andere lateinische Ärzte im Lichte der Sprachforschung' in *Wiener Studien*, vol. 61–2 (1943–7).

Oeconomos 1950: L. Oeconomos, 'Le calendrier de régime d'Hiérophile d'après des manuscrits plus complets que le Parisinus 396' in *Actes du VIe Congrès International d'Etudes Byzantines, Paris, 1948* (1950), vol. 1 pp. 169–179.

Patlagean 1968: E. Patlagean, 'Ancienne hagiographie byzantine et histoire sociale' in *Annales: économies, sociétés, civilisations* (1968 no. 1), pp. 106–126. – Reprinted in her *Structure sociale, famille, chrétienté à Byzance* (London: Variorum, 1981).

Paviot 1991: Jacques Paviot, 'Cuisine grecque et cuisine turque selon l'expérience des voyageurs, XV-XVI siècles' in *Manzikert to Lepanto*, ed. A. Bryer, M. Ursinus (Amsterdam, Hakkert, 1991), pp. 167–77.

Perry 1981: Charles Perry, 'The oldest Mediterranean noodle: a cautionary tale' in *Petits propos culinaires* no. 9 (1981), pp. 42–45.

Perry 1997: Charles Perry, 'Trakhanas revisited' in *Petits propos culinaires* no. 55 (1997), pp. 34–39.

Pertusi 1968: A. Pertusi, 'Civiltà della tavola a Bisanzio e a Venezia' in *Atti del Primo Convegno dell'Accademia Italiana della Cucina* (Milano, 1968).

Polak 1982: Lucie Polak, 'Charlemagne and the marvels of Constantinople' in *The medieval Alexander legend and Romance epic: essays in honour of David J. A. Ross*, ed. Peter Noble, Lucie Polak, Claire Isoz (Millwood, NY: Kraus International, 1982), pp. 159–171.

Protopapa-Vouvoulidhou 1973: G. Protopapa-Vouvoulidhou, 'Epenos is to krasi: peri methisou. Dhimodhi meseonika ke neotera kimena' in *Epeteris Etirias Vizandinon Spoudhon*, vols 39–40 (1972/3), pp. 594–611.

Robert 1961–1962: L. Robert, 'Sur des lettres d'un métropolite de Phrygie: philologie et réalités' in *Journal des savants* (July–December 1961), pp. 97–166 and (January–June 1962), pp. 5–74.

Rouillard 1953: G. Rouillard, *La vie rurale dans l'Empire byzantin*, Paris, 1953.

Salaman 1993: R. Salaman, *Greek food*, London: Harper Collins, 1993. – 2nd ed.

Sauner-Nebioglu 1995: Marie-Hélène Sauner-Nebioglu, *Évolution des pratiques alimentaires en Turquie: analyse comparative*, Berlin: Klaus Schwarz, 1995, – *Islamkundliche Untersuchungen*, 193.

Scarborough 1984: *Symposium on Byzantine medicine*, ed. J. Scarborough, Washington, 1984, – *Dumbarton Oaks papers*, 38.

Sideras 1974: A. Sideras, 'Aetius und Oribasius' in *Byzantinische Zeitschrift*, vol. 67 (1974), pp. 110–130.

Spinthiropoulos 2000: Kharoula Spinthiropoulos, *Inopiisimes pikilies tou ellinikou ampelona*, Corfu: Olive Press [2000].

Stannard 1971: J. Stannard, 'Byzantine botanical lexicography' in *Episteme*, vol. 5 (1971), pp. 168–187.

Stannard 1974: Jerry Stannard, 'Squill in ancient and medieval materia medica, with special reference to its employment for dropsy' in *Bulletin of the New York Academy of Medicine*, vol. 50 (1974), pp. 684–713.

Tapkova-Zaimova 1989: V. Tapkova-Zaimova, 'La vie quotidienne d'après le Typicon du Monastère de Bačkovo, 1083' in *I kathimerini zoi sto Vizandio*, ed. Kh. G. Angelidhis (Athens, 1989), pp. 429–438.

Teall 1959: J.L. Teall, 'The grain supply of the Byzantine Empire, 330–1025' in *Dumbarton Oaks papers* no. 13 (1959), pp. 87–139.

Teall 1971: J.L. Teall, 'The Byzantine agricultural tradition' in *Dumbarton Oaks papers*, vol. 25 (1971), pp. 35–59.

Temkin 1962: O. Temkin, 'Byzantine medicine: tradition and empiricism' in *Dumbarton Oaks papers*, vol. 16 (1962), pp. 95–115.

Thomas and Hero 2001: *Byzantine monastic foundation documents: a complete translation of the surviving founders' typika and testaments,* ed. John Thomas, Angela Constantinides Hero, Washington: Dumbarton Oaks, 2001, – 5 vols. *Dumbarton Oaks studies,* 35.

Thomson 1955: *Textes grecs inédits relatifs aux plantes,* ed. Margaret H. Thomson, Paris: Les Belles Lettres, 1955.

Tsiouni 1971: V. Tsiouni, *A critical edition of the Byzantine poem Perì tôn tetrapódon zóon with a linguistic commentary,* 1971, – Dissertation: Birkbeck College, London.

Volk 1991: R. Volk, 'Einige Beiträge zur mittelgriechischen Nahrungs-terminologie' in *Lexicographica Byzantina* (Vienna, 1991, *Byzantina Vindobonensia,* 20), pp. 293–311.

Vryonis 1980: Speros Vryonis, 'Travelers as a source for the societies of the Middle East, 900–1600' in *Charanis studies: essays in honor of Peter Charanis* (New Brunswick, N.J., 1980), pp. 284–311.

Vryonis 1981: Speros Vryonis, 'The panegyris of the Byzantine saint: a study in the nature of a medieval institution' in *The Byzantine saint,* ed. Sergei Hackel (London: Fellowship of St Alban and St Sergius, 1981), pp. 196–226.

Wagner 1874: *Carmina graeca medii aevi,* ed. Guilelmus Wagner, Leipzig, 1874.

Weber 1980: T. Weber, 'Essen und Trinken im Konstantinopel des 10.

Jahrhunderts nach den Berichten Liutprands von Cremona' in J. Koder and T. Weber, *Liutprand von Cremona in Konstantinopel* (Vienna, 1980), pp. 71–99.

Wirtjes 1994: Hanneke Wirtjes, 'Greece: medieval history' in *The Oxford companion to wine*, ed. Jancis Robinson (Oxford: Oxford University Press, 1994), p. 468.

Witteveen 1985: J. Witteveen, 'Rose sugar and other medieval sweets' in *Petits propos culinaires* no. 20 (1985), pp. 22–8.

Index